PORTRAITS OF EXCESS:
READING CHARACTER IN THE
MODERN SPANISH NOVEL

PUBLICATIONS OF THE SOCIETY OF SPANISH AND SPANISH-AMERICAN STUDIES

Luis T. González-del-Valle, *Director*

JULI HIGHFILL

PORTRAITS OF EXCESS: READING CHARACTER IN THE MODERN SPANISH NOVEL

SOCIETY OF SPANISH AND SPANISH-AMERICAN STUDIES

© Copyright, Society of Spanish and Spanish-American Studies, 1999.

All rights reserved. No portion of this book may be reproduced, by any process or technique, without the express written consent of the publisher. The book may be quoted as part of scholarly studies.

The Society of Spanish and Spanish-American Studies promotes bibliographical, critical and pedagogical research in Spanish and Spanish-American studies by publishing works of particular merit in these areas. On occasion, the Society also publishes creative works. SSSAS is a non-profit educational organization sponsored by the University of Colorado at Boulder. It is located in the Department of Spanish and Portuguese, University of Colorado, Campus Box 278, Boulder, Colorado, 80309-0278. U.S.A.

International Standard Book Number (ISBN): 0-89295-093-5

Library of Congress Catalog Card Number: 98-61090

Printed in the United States of America.
Impreso en los Estados Unidos de América

This text was prepared by Sandy Adler, Foreign Language Desktop Publishing Specialist for the College of Arts and Sciences, University of Colorado at Boulder.

CONTENTS

Introduction. On Terms of Character 1

I. Disciplining Character: Benito Pérez Galdós's *Torquemada en la hoguera* 9

    Trial by Fire 9
    The Realist Examination 12
    Characters under Observation 21
    Characters under Construction 30
    Reading in Counterpoint 42

II. The Impossible Character: Benjamín Jarnés' "Andrómeda" ... 53

    "El cuadro excesivo" 53
    The Discourse on Woman 64
    Allegorical Woman 79
    Addendum 87

III. Character Defects: Miguel Delibes' *Cinco horas con Mario* .. 105

    Reading through Received Knowledge 105
    An Iconic Reading: The Uses of Stereotype 116
    A Symbolic Reading: The Uses of Blame 123
    An Indexical Reading: The Uses of Ventriloquism 127

IV. Lacking Character: Lourdes Ortiz's *Luz de la memoria* 143

    A Failure of Character 143
    A Failure of Reading 148
    Death, Desire, and the Other 154

Conclusion. Beyond Character: Towards a Utopian Reference Point 167

Works Consulted 171

INTRODUCTION.
ON TERMS OF CHARACTER

Perhaps the most powerful appeal of fiction is the intimate access it provides to the inner being of characters. As readers, however, we do not act merely as passive voyeurs. Rather, by mentally staging the fictional text, we actively participate in bringing characters to imaginary "life." In doing so, we venture far beyond the text in hand and draw from a "data base" of cultural beliefs regarding selfhood, gender, and social behavior. We therefore read *allusively*, constantly referring to myriad bits of information as we create images of characters and their worlds. And because these mental portraits are never complete, because the process of referral never ends (so long as we are reading or thinking of a given work), characters remain ever *elusive* and incomplete figures.

The process of characterization is necessarily a collaborative effort on the part of writers and readers.[1] Writers instruct us, directly and indirectly, as to how we should imagine various characters. Reading as they write, authors leave "clues" that direct us along the "proper" connotative paths to the relevant information. Then based upon these rather limited instructions, we as readers also actively characterize, "writing" as we read: inferring, hypothesizing, and filling gaps as we form images of fictional beings. In doing so, we necessarily read intertextually, referring not only to other literary texts, but also to our reservoirs of cultural knowledge, to what Roland Barthes terms an "ideology of the person" (*S/Z* 191). We refer, for example, to the expected traits and behaviors of characters, according to psychological, social, and literary typologies. This process of referral can only be circular, for our encounters with "characters" in fiction and in life mutually inform each other.

Character itself has come to be considered an old-fashioned term, and perhaps an increasingly unviable one. The word derives from a Greek verb *Charassein* which described the act of engraving or marking a surface, inflicting a wound, or stamping an impression upon a coin blank (Anderson xv). Over time the term lost its active meaning and *charaktêr* came to mean the stamp or die making the impression. Later, as employed in the works of Aeschylus, Aristotle, and Theophrastus, *charaktêr* referred to a personality *type*—not an individual—for in coinage the stamp was used for a series of impressions, never for a single coin (Anderson xv).[2] Through the centuries, the meaning of character has continued to designate more or less fixed, imprinted, and classifiable patterns of traits found in both worldly and fictional beings. Trait, like character, originates in a term signifying the marking of a surface. Deriving from the Latin *tractus*—drawing or draught—and later evolving as the obsolete French *traict, tret*—for draught, stroke, touch, and line—trait still designates a line or feature of a character.[3]

Spanish retains the Greek-derived term *carácter* to refer to a person's fixed pattern of traits while employing *personaje* to designate fictional character. But significantly, both the Spanish *persona* and *personaje* derive from the word for masks worn by Etruscan actors. The lexical evolution of this theatrical term seems to acknowledge tacitly the representational function of identity.[4] Whether on the theatrical or social stage, whether in fiction or in life, identities are assumed by players. Moreover, if identities are put on like masks, this presumes a certain freedom to exchange "personas"—a freedom that runs contrary to the notion of character as a fixed pattern of traits imprinted upon a given "person." The term character, however, permits a similar mobility of meaning in its semantic field, for its connotations point to the unique as well as to the general type. As J. Hillis Miller observes, "A character is both peculiar, particular, distinctive, and at the same time it is repeatable, generalizable, able to be used and reused in a variety of circumstances" (58).

It is the migratory habits of traits, in turn, that render character repeatable and generalizable; for a character is no more than a configuration of traits drawn from a corpus of all those attributes named and potentially shared by the members of a given society. Given the numismatic origins of the term character, J. Hillis Miller aptly employs a monetary metaphor to describe its circulatory operations:

> The "known traits of character" are, so to speak, the small change on the basis of which the novelist mints his larger facsimile coins. The common possession of these little coins, their free circulation within society, from readers to novelist to novel and back again to the readers, is the fund or reserve out of which the novel is conceived. (70)

Extending the metaphor further, Miller likens fictional characters to counterfeit coins. As counterfeit, characters "pass current" insofar as "the dies with which they are imprinted are modeled accurately on elements from the conceptions of characters" already in circulation (70). Conversely, within this system of exchange, conceptions of characters in life may be modeled after characters in fiction. And while the "counterfeit makes the real coin seem more real," at the same time, it "subtly raises questions about the distinction between real and counterfeit" (71). Miller further argues that "all coin is counterfeit" in the sense that it involves the stamping of matter with signs of value not intrinsic to that matter itself. The value ascribed to it depends upon "the collective faith of the people for whom it is a medium of transfer, figuration, or exchange" (71).

Character then, whether "real" or "counterfeit," historical or fictional, is likewise an article of faith, dependent upon beliefs shared by a society at large. As a pattern of meaning and value imprinted upon social beings, character works to fix, distinguish, and make permanent. But in doing so, character must simultaneously allow for its own repeatability and for the free circulation of its constituent parts, the traits. So while aiming to immobilize, character remains implicitly mobile, thus defying its founding propositions. And while ostensibly anchored in a body, character resides less in the body's physicality (leaving physiognomy aside), than in its sheer movement—in gesture, speech, and behavior—repeated over time. But of course, repetition is what renders character readable and nameable, as an abstract pattern stamped upon mobile and insubstantial "material." In sum, the concept of character would appear fundamentally unstable—aiming towards fixity while depending absolutely upon mobility. As we shall see, the instability immanent in character produces a broad field of play for the authors, narrators, characters, and readers of the novels examined in this study.

Nowadays character is strangely neglected in literary criticism and theory. Since the character-centered studies of A.C. Bradley and E.M. Forster in the early twentieth-century, few analyses of character and characterization have appeared.[5] Both New Critics and structuralists viewed literary works as autonomous, self-sufficient entities and were reluctant to look beyond the perceived confines of the text.[6] The autonomy-minded critics may have neglected character because they could not contain its operations within the closed system of a text; for given that our interpretations of fictional and worldly beings mutually inform each other, textual boundaries are perhaps most permeable at the site of character.

Although poststructuralist critics and theorists have abandoned the notion of a closed, autonomous text, they also reject the concept of the unitary and knowable subject, so bound up with the meaning of character.[7] Moreover, many modernist and postmodernist novels have (to varying degrees) dispensed with coherent and even nameable fictional beings—instead presenting more diffuse and provisional forms of fictional identity.[8] In light of these developments, poststructuralist, feminist, and postcolonial critics have perhaps justifiably focused attention on the broader concepts of subjectivity, representation, identity, and otherness. But albeit old-fashioned and increasingly untenable, the notion of fixed, unitary character continues to operate. Certainly, it governs the codes and conventions of much of the literature we continue to read, whether classic, canonized texts or popular fiction. Even postmodernist novels that render character unknowable, still often react against models engraved in our minds of unified and intelligible subjects; they must affirm the existence of these cultural models in order to defy them. So before dismissing the relevance of critical attention to character, it seems worthwhile to examine the assumptions, codes, and paradigms that govern our readings of character.

In this study I present four case studies of excessive fictional beings who, by virtue of their exorbitant characterization, illuminate the codes that govern our readings of character. Among these "portraits of excess," I consider highly exaggerated versions of stereotypes—the sly usurer, the enigmatic seductress, the domineering mother, and the social misfit. In addition, I examine characters whose heterogeneous traits fail to cohere, and others whose excessive vagueness renders them unknowable. Although "bigger than life," these characters remain always "life-like," and thus, they demonstrate how our interpretations of characters in life and in literature mutually inform each other.

For these case studies I have selected four modern fictional texts, each reflecting a distinct literary period and style: a realist novel, a vanguardist novella, a post-war "Nueva Novela," and a postmodernist text. Given that our concept of novelistic character became fully developed, indeed institutionalized, in nineteenth-century realism, I begin with a late-realist novel by Galdós, *Torquemada en la hoguera* (1889).[9] Drawing from Michel Foucault, I discuss how realist novels participated in the great disciplinary enterprise of the nineteenth century to define, document, and classify both the natural and social world. In *Torquemada en la hoguera*, as in other realist novels, the disciplinary impulse is particularly evident in the detailed descriptions of characters and their settings. But paradoxically, the compulsion to document fictional beings in meticulous detail both reinforces and threatens the realist enterprise: as the excess meanings accumulate, a character may expand beyond the narrator's disciplinary control, losing coherence and intelligibility.

In this first chapter I artificially exclude the question of gender while presenting my general approach to character. But of course, all characters are gendered—both written and read in terms of a vast assemblage of categorical knowledge relating to the masculine or the feminine. In the second chapter, I consider the representation of the feminine in a vanguardist novella, "Andrómeda" (1926) by Benjamín Jarnés. This text explicitly dramatizes the allusive, intertextual process of reading "woman" (in literature and in life) by invoking an excess of impossibly heterogeneous texts and images. Central to the parodic effect of this novella is its relation to a body of contemporary, nonfictional texts that sought to reveal Woman's "true nature." As women in various Western countries won voting rights and began to enter public life, journals such as the *Revista de Occidente* provided as a forum for a broad cultural dialogue on the "Woman Question." Jarnés' novella humorously stages this dialogue, this quest to discover "the feminine soul," and exposes the impossible heterogeneity of the cultural construct of Woman.

Chapter three focuses on another excessive, indeed monstrous, feminine character through an analysis of Miguel Delibes' *Cinco horas con Mario* (1966). Whereas "Andrómeda" relies upon the cultural construct of the feminine as an "idealized and desired other," Delibes's novel partakes in the cultural practice of constructing Woman as an "abject other," as a repository for all that Man loathes and rejects.[10] Moreover, through an act of ventriloquism—placing an authoritarian discourse in the mouth of an abject, feminine character—this novel aims to invalidate the traditionalist discourse of the Franco regime.

The fourth chapter examines Lourdes Ortiz's *Luz de la memoria* (1976), a postmodernist text that renders character unreadable by creating a diffuse and unknowable fictional being. By thwarting our readerly desire for coherence and intelligibility, the novel points towards a liberatory and expansive conception of desire. The exuberant dialogism of the textual pastiche, the metafictional game-playing, the constant shifting of names and pronouns, the permanent elusiveness of the protagonist— all serve to disable explanatory paradigms and to suggest alternate modes of being, desiring, and performing.

Throughout the discussions of these novels, I emphasize how our allusive readings of character are *governed*—both by the text in hand, and by the cultural codes that channel our thinking and imagining along well-worn paths. I suggest that a more self-conscious understanding of these operations might enable us to loosen the strictures of the codes that bind our interpretations of fictional and living characters, as well as of our own identities. In the speculative conclusion, therefore, I consider the possibilities of moving beyond the notion of fixed, unitary character towards a collective and fluid understanding of subjectivity. Although throughout this study I frequently resort to the readerly "we" and refer to "our readings," I do not aim to manipulate unduly my readers or to discount the possibilities of variant readings. In part, I choose "we" as a less-than-satisfying alternative to the stiffness of "the reader." But I also want to call attention to the *collective* nature of the received knowledge to which we all refer as we interpret both literary and worldly phenomena.

NOTES

1. Thomas Docherty in *Reading (Absent) Character* also considers characterization as a collaborative effort by both writer and reader. Conventionally, the term has referred only to the writer's direct or indirect instructions in the text.
2. According to Warren Anderson, *charaktêr* first entered Greek literature in the Aeschylus's *Suppliants*. Aristotle, in his *Poetics*, provided prescriptions for characters in tragedy and comedy. Theophrastus, a pupil of Aristotle, carried on his teacher's categorizing project, both in his scientific treatises and in his thirty *Character Sketches* of human types, including "Insincere Man," "Boor," "Repulsive Man," "Late Learner," "Lover of Bad Company," and "Basely Covetous Man." See Anderson's introduction to Theophrastus and J.W. Smeed, *The Theophrastan 'Character.'*
3. I am indebted to J. Hillis Miller's discussion of this lexical history in *Ariadne's Thread: Story Lines*.
4. See: Hélène Cixous, "The Character of 'Character' " for a discussion of the semantics of the French *personage* as compared to *character*.
5. In recent decades, most studies of character defend it in the name of mimeticism, humanism, and morality against the "attacks" of "theorists" and postmodernist writers. For such defenses of mimeticism, see: W.J. Harvey, *Character and the Novel*; Anthony Winner, *Characters in the Twilight*; Baruch Hochman, *Characters in Literature*; Martin Price, *Forms of Life*; Richard Freadman, *Eliot, James, and the Fictional Self*; and Thomas Petruso, *Life Made Real*. James Phelan in *Reading People, Reading Plots* offers a more qualified defense of mimeticism. Hochman's study provides a useful historical summary of approaches to characters, as does Seymour Chatman's structuralist study, *Story and Discourse*.
6. The classic New Critical dismissals of character include: G. Wilson Knight, *The Wheel of Fire*; and L.C. Knights, "How Many Children Had Lady Macbeth?" Structuralists have generally privileged narration and temporal structure, viewing characters principally as "nodes in the verbal design," as *actants* and *acteurs* called upon to perform specific functions in the plot. For examples of

structuralist approaches to character see: Tzvetan Todorov, *The Poetics of Prose*; and A.J. Greimas, *On Meaning: Selected Writings in Semiotic Theory*. For modified structuralist approaches that assign more importance to character, refer to: Seymour Chatman, *Story and Discourse*; Ricardo Gullón, *Psicologías del autor y lógicas del personaje*; and Fernando Ferrara, "Theory and Model for the Structural Analysis of Fiction."

7. Considerations of character informed by poststructuralist theory include: Leo Bersani, *A Future for Astyanax*; Stephan Cohan, "Figures Beyond the Text"; Thomas Docherty, *Reading (Absent) Character*; J. Hillis Miller, *Ariadne's Thread: Story Lines*, and Hélène Cixous, "The Character of 'Character.'"

8. Both Bersani and Docherty focus on mobile, incoherent characters in modernist and postmodernist novels. For a study of character in recent Spanish metafiction see David K. Herzberger, "Split Referentiality."

9. At first, I naively sought a "generic," "typical" realist novel, but quickly concluded that no such beast exists. Arguably, no novel of the realist genre fully obeys or displays the supposed precepts of realism. And particularly late realist novels, such as *Torquemada en la hoguera*, respond to the untenability of mimesis by resorting to irony.

10. I rely upon Julia Kristeva's concept of the *abject* in *Powers of Horror*.

I. DISCIPLINING CHARACTER: BENITO PÉREZ GALDÓS'S *TORQUEMADA EN LA HOGUERA*

> [A]fter the age of "inquisitorial" justice, we have entered the age of "examinatory" justice. (Michel Foucault, *Discipline and Punish* 68)

Trial by Fire

Voy a contar cómo fue al quemadero el inhumano que tantas vidas infelices consumió en llamas; que a unos les traspasó los hígados con un hierro candente; a otros les puso en cazuela bien mechados, y a los demás los achicharró por partes, a fuego lento, con rebuscada y metódica saña. Voy a contar cómo vino el fiero sayón a ser víctima; cómo los odios que provocó se le volvieron lástima, y las nubes de maldiciones arrojaron sobre él lluvia de piedad; caso patético, caso muy ejemplar, señores, digno de contarse para enseñanza de todos, aviso de condenados y escarmiento de inquisidores. (7)

The irony and humor in this opening paragraph *Torquemada en la hoguera* (1889) derive from the sheer outrageousness of its metaphorical terms.[1] On the literal level the metaphor imposes a series of extravagant, untenable equivalences between don Francisco Torquemada *el Peor* and his implied "better," the Grand Inquisitor himself. Aside from the shared surname, the latter-day Torquemada, a moneylender in a bourgeois society, bears little resemblance to his notorious predecessor. And neither the "agonía pecuniaria" of his debtors nor the pain that he finally suffers resembles the agony of the Inquisitor's victims as they perished in the *hogueras* (8). Rather, Torquemada's agony stems from the fatal illness of his son, Valentín. And in his grief and confusion, he interprets the illness as punishment for past misdeeds and attempts to redeem Valentín's life with hastily performed good deeds. Torquemada's would-be redeemer, however, is not God but *humanity* itself—figured as the usurer's creditor—and this is perhaps the most dissonant element in an ironically unsound metaphor. Influenced by Bailón, the defrocked priest turned positivist, Torquemada reasons: "He faltado a la Humanidad, y esa muy tal y cual me las cobra ahora con los réditos atrasados" (28). Obviously, the only likeness among terms in this extravagant metaphor resides in the *pain* that the two Torquemadas inflict upon their victims, as well as the pain later endured by *el Peor* himself. All the other metaphorical terms—the offender, the crime, the judge, the executioner, the site and method of punishment—stand in striking contrast. Of course it is this very dissonance among supposedly like terms that produces the irony and humor. The metaphor constructs a collapsable bridge across a great historic gulf: while figuratively imposing a "false" set of equivalences between fifteenth- and nineteenth- century Spain, it reveals instead the glaring differences between two social and economic orders, and finally points to the only "true" equivalence—the pain (however different in nature) that both systems inflict upon their subjects. By hyperbolically applying the language of Inquisitorial penalty to bourgeois Spain, Galdós satirizes an economic system in which usury (or rather finance capitalism) has become essential, an order in which a formerly marginalized usurer—an "avaro de antiguo cuño"—may become an upwardly mobile member of society: "Viviendo el Peor en una época que arranca de la desamortización, sufrió, sin comprenderlo, la metamorfosis que ha desnaturalizado la usura metafísica, convirtiéndolo en positivista" (13).[2]

This novelistic transformation of the character Torquemada thus stands for a historical transformation that is underscored by the ironic dissonance within the metaphor of the *hoguera*. It is the same transformation that Michel Foucault analyzes in his history of penality from the fifteenth century to the present, *Discipline and Punish*. Coincidentally, like *Torquemada en la hoguera*, Foucault's study opens with a graphic description of a torture and execution. He then proceeds to describe the reforms that gradually abolished these public spectacles throughout Europe by the mid-nineteenth century. During that time the branded, tortured, or dismembered body of the malefactor—exposed to public view—gradually disappeared. The *inhumane* mode of punishment, in which the sovereign inflicted his vengeance upon the body of the offender, was replaced by a mode of punishment with "humanity as its measure" (*Discipline* 75). As in the fictional world of *Torquemada*, *humanity* (in both senses of the word) takes the place of God's stand-in, the sovereign, as the measure of crime and punishment, and the body of the offender becomes the general property of society.

But Foucault's concept of the new penality refers not only to the uniform legal codes that more humanely meted out punishment; it also pertains to the countless modes of subtle coercion—the disciplines—that became generalized through all of society during the eighteenth and nineteenth centuries. Foucault defines discipline as a "microphysics of power," as "a policy of coercions that act upon the body, a calculated manipulation of its elements, its gestures, its behavior" (*Discipline* 139, 138). In contrast with sovereign power, held and wielded by monarchs and their representatives, disciplinary power cannot be possessed; rather, it is anonymously exercised throughout the social body.

> Traditionally, power was what was seen, what was shown and what was manifested.... Those on whom it was exercised could remain in the shade; they received light only from that portion of power that was conceded to them, or [its] reflection.... Disciplinary power, on the other hand, is exercised through its invisibility; at the same time it imposes on those whom it subjects a principle of compulsory visibility. In discipline, it is the subjects who have to be seen. Their visibility assures the hold of the power that is exercised over them. It is the fact of being constantly seen, of being able always to be seen, that maintains the disciplined individual in his subjection. (187)

Disciplinary power then is "the reverse of the spectacle" (216). Rather than viewing the sumptuous display of the sovereign, the subjects fall under a generalized, omnipresent surveillance, "a faceless gaze" that transforms "the whole social body into a field of perception: thousands of eyes posted everywhere, mobile attentions ever on the alert, a long hierarchized network" (214). This economical and subtle mode of power operates not only in overtly disciplinary institutions, such as prisons, schools, and factories, but also extends into the petty practices of everyday life. All members of society are continually observed, not only from above by supervisors, but by all those who surround them. And while being observed, every member simultaneously observes others and judges their conformance to various norms of behavior. Finally, all observers/observees reflexively turn the gaze inward, as they judge and normalize themselves, thus wielding disciplinary power upon themselves.

This *examination* of others and of self is precisely what Torquemada undergoes in the fictional disciplinary society. Forced by the circumstance of his son's illness, he realizes that all along "humanity" has been observing him and judging him according to its norms. He then turns that gaze upon himself and examines his dealings with other members of the fictional society. Too late, he comically scrambles to perform enough good deeds to rectify his image in the eyes of humanity and thereby save his son. His *hoguera* thus performs a twofold function in the novel: it serves both as punishment and as examination, producing a negative, punitive effect as well as a positive, knowledge-producing effect.[3] Just as during the Inquisition a victim's behavior under torture presumably revealed his guilt or innocence, Torquemada's trial by fire reveals his character. For Torquemada the *hoguera* not only inflicts pain, but also illuminates, forcing him to examine himself and his conduct in the fictional society (although he does so in bad faith and only temporarily rectifies his behavior). For the readers who witness Torquemada's ordeal, the novel itself serves as an *hoguera*, meant to enlighten by showing us an exemplary case of a nonexemplary character. The narrator (albeit tongue-in-cheek) explicitly declares his didactic intent to show us this "caso patético, caso muy ejemplar, señores, digno de contarse para enseñanza de todos, aviso de condenados y escarmiento de inquisidores" (7). As readers we are placed in the position of spectators in an inquisitorial *auto de fe*, thus producing the final ironic turn in this collapsable metaphor. We watch as the body of an offender is tortured, marked, his crime and sentence made a "legible lesson" for all (Foucault, *Discipline* 111). But then we realize that Torquemada's "crimes" of usury and greed have become acceptable and normal in bourgeois Spain, and the focus of examination and indictment shifts from Torquemada to the disciplinary society itself.

The Realist Examination

Although most nineteenth-century realists may not so openly, or ironically, proclaim their didactic intentions, all harbor a definite project: they dedicate themselves to the examination, in detail and in depth, of characters and their actions within a fictional society. This examination in turn rests upon a prior and presumably objective examination of individuals within a "real" society. So within the logic of realism, novels are fictional examinations built upon empirical examinations. Balzac's formula for producing realist writing was simply "observation—expression"

(Coward 46).[4] In explaining his rationale for *The Human Comedy*, Balzac declared,

> French society would be the real author; I should only be the secretary. By drawing up an inventory of vices and virtues, by collecting the chief facts of the passions, by depicting characters, by choosing the principal incidents of social life, by composing types out of a combination of homogeneous characteristics, I might perhaps succeed in writing the history which so many historians have neglected: that of Manners. (Balzac 5)

Galdós, in his writings on the novel, likewise insisted on the importance of observation. In his essay of 1870, "Observaciones sobre la novela contemporánea en España," he lamented that "los españoles somos poco observadores, y carecemos por lo tanto de la principal virtud para la creación de la novela moderna" (*Ensayos* 106). Like Balzac, Galdós considered society, *el vulgo*, as the "autor supremo" of his work (160). In his speech of 1898 to the Royal Academy, "La sociedad presente como materia novelable," he echoes the words of Balzac:

> Imagen de la vida es la Novela, y el arte de componerla estriba en reproducir los caracteres humanos, las pasiones, las debilidades, lo grande y lo pequeño, las almas y las fisonomías, todo lo espiritual y lo físico que nos constituye y nos rodea, y el lenguaje, que es la marca de raza, y las viviendas, que son el signo de familia, y la vestidura, que diseña los últimos trazos externos de la personalidad: todo esto sin olvidar que debe existir perfecto fiel de balanza entre la exactitud y la belleza de la reproducción. (*Ensayos* 160)

Implicit in this view of the novel as "image of life," is the assumption that language is a transparent medium, capable of accurately transcribing observed reality and creating true-to-life imitations.

In the wake of poststructuralist theory these presumptions of nineteenth-century realism now seem rather naive, and recent studies undercut them on various grounds.[5] Some critics raise the question of *which* reality is to be transcribed and call attention to the elusive nature of any stable, objective "reality." Others emphasize the impossibility of linguistically transcribing any "reality" without transforming it. New Historicists consider the realist novel as one discourse among many in a given time and place, all of which contribute to a society's conception of reality. And most critics would agree that realist texts are as conventional as the modes of writing they replaced, although in the nineteenth century, the artifice became so naturalized that readers forgot its artificiality. Reflecting this view, a recent dictionary of literary terms defines realism as "a system of conventions producing a lifelike illusion of some 'real' world outside the text, by processes of selection, exclusion, description, and manners of addressing the reader" (Baldick 184).

For the moment, however, I am less concerned with realism's naiveté or with its failures than with its grand pretensions. The realist novel undeniably participated in the great empirical, scientific, and industrial projects that, beginning with the Enlightenment, produced a vast corpus of knowledge and transformed social life. At a time when the colonial powers were exploring, describing, mapping, and appropriating geographical space, novelists such as Defoe, Fielding, Balzac, Dickens, and Galdós were plotting fictional space and describing it in hitherto unprecedented detail.[6] As scientists in newly founded scientific observatories set about describing and classifying the natural world, novelists were creating fictions that served as social observatories, in which they minutely described and classified characters within their social settings. This was the period when throughout the social body—in industries, prisons, schools, hospitals, and asylums—

> procedures were being elaborated for distributing individuals, fixing them in space, classifying them, extracting from them the maximum in time and forces, training their bodies, coding their continuous behavior, maintaining them in perfect visibiity, forming around them an apparatus of observation, registration and recording, constituting on them a body of knowledge that is accumulated and centralized. (Foucault, *Discipline* 231)

Not only did the realist novel coincide with the development of these disciplinary institutions, but it also adopted many of their documentary techniques, placing its characters under the surveillance of an omniscient narrator who meticulously detailed their behavior and environment. The novel as a literary genre became defined and disciplined during this period, just as the various fields of knowledge—the "disciplines" —were being defined and separated. Hence, the undisciplined and hybrid ancestors of the novel—*El libro de buen amor, La Celestina, Gargantua and Pantagruel,* the *Quijote,* and *Tristram Shandy*—were supplanted by carefully plotted fictional works that obeyed a more rigid system of conventions. At this same time a substantial middle-class reading public was developing, as the publishing industry made novels readily available and often serialized them in newspapers.[7] So as the novel became generically defined and disciplined, its readers were simultaneously being created and disciplined.[8] Readers became trained in novelistic conventions: gradually, they learned to recognize and follow literary codes, to expect certain outcomes, and to filter the noisy activity of signification, thus limiting the potentially infinite process of connotation.

Clearly, the realist novel belongs to the age of discipline, and of necessity the novel both displayed and participated in the development of the disciplinary society. This is not to suggest that the novel served as a mere propaganda tool, nor that it took part in some grand conspiracy. Rather, the novel was one of many modes of power that helped shape the disciplinary society, and to some degree also resisted and moderated it. The novel serves as one discursive site within the dynamic and complex web of discourse that forms our conception of the world.[9] Never stable or complete, subject to pressures and resistances, this discursive web continually undergoes a process of construction, expansion, and repair.

If we view the realist novel as one textual site within a discursive conception of reality, then Balzac's formula "observation-expression" regains a certain validity. Certainly the realists did observe social reality and attempted to express what they saw. But it would be more accurate to say that these writers "read" and then "quoted" in their novels a multiplicity of "texts" drawn from the social world. Such intertexts may be gleaned from other literary works, or from nonliterary genres such as newspapers, biographies, letters, popular songs.[10] But more commonly they derive not from texts written on paper but from those inscribed in our consciousness: stereotypes, conventional wisdom, ethical maxims, clichés, the scripts that we follow in daily encounters, and the action sequences of everyday life.[11] The realist novel draws upon a vast "intertextual space"; its "realness" is constructed through a

> constant cross-echoing of texts, of writing, a circular recollection. And this is precisely the inter-text: the impossibility of living outside the infinite text.... Each text is suspended in the network of all others, from which it derives its intelligibility. Realism is thus "a copy of a copy" supported by connotation, a "perspective of citations." It is

a silent quotation without inverted commas, with no precise source. (Coward and Ellis 52)[12]

Realism's true-to-life effect then rests, not upon the faithful transcription of an objective reality, but upon its faithful *re-presentation* of the dominant discourses that make up our conception of reality. If we view mimesis intertextually, then, the claims made by Balzac and Galdós retain a certain validity: society was indeed the "real author" of their novels. Moreover, realist novels did indeed mirror their contemporary societies insofar as they re-presented the textual images by which these societies conceived themselves—images conditioned, of course, by bourgeois class dominance.[13] And in doing so, the realist novels simultaneously intervened and participated in the on-going production of knowledge.

I began this section by suggesting that the realist novel constitutes an examination built upon a prior examination. The novelist examines the discourses and codified social practices that constitute his society, and later appropriates and reorganizes these textual elements to create a fictional society. Within the fictional society, an omniscient narrator then re-enacts the author's initial examination by observing and eavesdropping upon characters placed on various rungs on the social ladder. For readers, who in turn share the narrator's vantage point, this examination of fictional beings may lead them reflexively to examine themselves, as well as other worldly beings. Like Torquemada's *hoguera*, the realist novel thus serves an illuminating function as well as a punitive one: it simultaneously enlightens and disciplines its readers. As the novel "reveals" knowledge about characters in the fictional society (under the pretense that they truly exist in "real" society), it simultaneously classifies and normalizes—by displaying the "normal" appearances, gestures, and movements for characters in distinct social positions. The disciplinary effects of the realist novel upon nineteenth-century readers would be impossible to measure precisely, but no doubt its effects were profound. From the described appearances, gestures, and actions of characters, readers may have discerned the boundaries of normality. From reading causally constructed plots, often biographical in their trajectories, readers may have learned ways of imposing order upon chaotic social life and of projecting meaning upon their own lives.

Perhaps some of my readers will object to my argument for realism's complicity in the disciplinary society. Must even the pleasurable activity of reading novels, often motivated by a desire to escape the disciplinary society, now be considered a devious mode of discipline?

Indeed, some critics have objected to Foucault's concept of an omnipresent disciplinary power, arguing that it precludes the possibility of successful resistance.[14] Certainly at the same time as realist novels participated in the disciplinary project, they to some degree moderated its effects and challenged the limits set by social norms. These novels, like *Torquemada en la hoguera*, often criticized and satirized the societies they sought to represent. While Galdós generally followed the precepts of realism, he also frequently challenged them, self-consciously mocking conventions even as he employed them, and often carrying them to their absurd conclusions. Particularly in metafictional works, such as *El amigo Manso* (1882) and *Misericordia* (1897), Galdós overstepped the bounds of conventional realist practice. Literature serves an ambivalent function in society, on the one hand defying norms and conventions, expanding the possibilities of being, and on the other hand preserving and reinforcing those norms and conventions. Undeniably, the realist novels provided sites for social criticism and experimentation, but insofar as they participated in the great empirical, totalizing project to impose sense upon the world, they acted more as disciplinarians than as subversives.[15]

The question may also be raised: What of the individual liberties that came into being during the age of discipline? Were not these new individual liberties reflected in realist novels by the creation of unique, willful characters endowed with greater psychological complexity?[16] As Foucault has acknowledged, it may seem paradoxical that "the 'Enlightenment' which discovered the liberties, also invented the disciplines" (*Discipline* 222). But from the beginning, the juridical system of egalitarian rights was supported by all the nonegalitarian mechanisms of discipline.[17] In Foucault's words, "The real corporal disciplines constituted the foundation of the formal, juridical liberties" (*Discipline* 222). Only the guarantee of the organization and control of individuals by disciplinary modes could enable the Enlightenment to go as far as it did in the direction of individual rights. Discipline imposed clear practical limits upon the *formally* unlimited social mobility and individual freedom. Granted, individuals were no longer born into a station in life without prospects for change; they were presumably free to take positions in other stations. But discipline ensured that the stations themselves were defined according to social utility. In order to fill specified slots, individuals must acquire the appropriate reserve of knowledge; they must normalize their appearances, gestures, movements, and modes of speaking—all defined by discipline and bound by class. So when Torquemada undergoes his transformation from "un avaro de antiguo cuño"—crude in behavior, tattered and dirty in appearance—into a bourgeois financier, more moderate in his behavior and respectable in his appearance, he has undergone a process of disciplinary training (12). And when through the trajectory of the four novellas he climbs through the ranks of society and fills various stations, each one disciplines and trains him according to its specifications.

While discipline requires conformity to norms, while it trains individuals to productively perform specified functions, it does not create uniformity, nor does it erase individual differences; rather, discipline *makes* individuals and *depends* upon differences. Discipline must differentiate individuals in order to compare, classify, and rank them. According to Foucault, "it is not that the beautiful totality of the individual is amputated, repressed, altered by our social order, it is rather that the individual is carefully fabricated in it, according to a whole technique of forces and bodies" (*Discipline* 217). During the age of discipline the individual became for the first time an "effect and object of knowledge"; and it was the examination that stood at the center of the procedures that constitute the individual "by combining hierarchical surveillance and normalizing judgment" (*Discipline* 192). Procedures were developed for analyzing differences, measuring gaps, making comparisons, classifying and distributing individuals along a scale. Such systems of documentation place individuals in a field of comparison that displays the shades of individual difference and defines an *acceptable* distance from the norm, thus marking the frontiers of the abnormal. On an individual level, disciplinary writing seeks to pin down each subject in his own particularity, citing "the measurements, the gaps, the 'marks' that characterize him and make him a 'case' " (*Discipline* 192). And on a societal level, the accumulation, correlation, and averaging of data works to "transform the confused, useless or dangerous multitudes into ordered multiplicities" (*Discipline* 148-49).

In all these quotations, Foucault is referring to techniques of disciplinary writing that were (and are) used to examine and document individuals in hospitals, prisons, schools, and government bureaucracies. But not surprisingly, these quotations could just as well describe the ways in which realist narrators examine (or characterize) characters:

> The examination that places individuals in a field of surveillance also situates them in a network of writing; it engages them in a whole mass of documents that capture

and fix them. The procedures of examination were accompanied at the same time by a system of intense registration and of documentary accumulation. A "power of writing" was constituted as an essential part in the mechanisms of discipline. (*Discipline* 189)

The term "disciplinary writing" aptly describes characterization in the realist novel. It accounts for the minute descriptions of characters and their placement in minutely described stations in a vast social world. It also explains the paradox that while realist characters are endowed with unprecedented individuality, they also fall under unprecedented control by their fictional societies, and frequently conform to social "types."

In comparison with the characters of epic, romance, and the sketches of Theophrastus, Horace, and La Bruyère, realist characters no longer correspond to "stock types" or "ideal types." But from the beginning, the depiction of social types was central to the realist project, even as novelists sought to strike a balance between the typical and the unique.[18] Balzac, in conceiving his role as "secretary" to the "real author" —French society—considered himself "a painter of types of humanity," a quantity he estimated to number two or three thousand (5, 11).[19] And Galdós likewise based his characters upon observed social types. Nearly all his characters are typecast in accordance with their social stations— among them, Fortunata, Jacinta, Juanito, Isidora, Rosalía de Bringas, Ramón Villamil (de Miau), and of course, Torquemada—although at the same time, each is endowed with certain unique features.[20] Within Galdós's characters, as well as those of other realists, the balance between typicality and uniqueness always remained tenuous. On the one hand there was the danger of endowing a character with so many attributes of his social type that he lost his "true-to-life" effect. On the other, there was the exhilarating temptation (to which Galdós sometimes succumbed) to create characters so unique, so excessive and incomprehensible (such as Maxi and Mauricia in *Fortunata y Jacinta*) that they jeopardized the novel's mimetic project.[21]

René Wellek addresses this problematic relationship between the typical and the unique and links it to another contradiction immanent in realism—that of prescription versus description. For Wellek, the realist project contains a fundamental "theoretical difficulty," a "contradictoriness," in that its very definition—" 'the objective representation of contemporary social reality'—conceals or implies a certain didacticism" (242).

[T]he mere change to a depiction of contemporary social reality implied a lesson of human pity, of social reformism and criticism, and often of rejection and revulsion against society. There is a tension between description and prescription, truth and instruction, which cannot be resolved logically but which characterizes the literature of which we are speaking. (242)

According to Wellek, this conflict explains the importance of *type* for the theory and practice of realism: "Without always realizing the conflict between description and prescription, realism tries to reconcile the two in the concept of 'type.'" (253). For "type, in spite of its didactic and prescriptive implications, preserves . . . the all-important association with objective social observation" (246). But immanent in "type" is another contradiction between the unique and the general. As Wellek concedes, realism's attempts to resolve these contradictions—uniqueness versus typicality and description versus prescription—are never wholly successful.

Perhaps, while remaining logically unresolvable, these contradictions work together in a relation of interdependency. Throughout this section I have made the claim for a kinship between the empirical examination and the realist novel. The empirical examination requires, indeed creates, both the unique and the typical. Even as the examination produces individuals by objectifying them under the empirical gaze, it compares, ranks, and classifies them into an array of types. Rather than denying individuals their uniqueness, the examination names their dominant traits and uses them for identification, comparison, and classification. Arguably, the concept of the individual as a definable, analyzable object—an assemblage of traits—could not exist without this simultaneous procedure of comparison and classification by type. And conversely, classification by type could not take place without the differentiation and identification of individuals. Furthermore, both activities—individualizing as well as classifying—require description as well as prescription: both rely upon description in order to differentiate individuals and group them by type; both activities are prescriptive (or disciplinary), for as they produce knowledge, they also impose order, contain, and exclude. Without the individual and without the type, we would be left with infinite, undifferentiated difference.

The realist writer borrows from the empirical sciences the techniques of examination and documentation. Before writing, the novelist has presumably observed a multiplicity of individuals, noted their differences, compared, ranked, and grouped them according to type.[22] On the basis of this anterior examination, the novelist reenacts a fictional examination in which a narrator scrutinizes a gallery of characters, who are at once unique and typical. This fictional examination takes place within a vast intertextual space, as the narrator documents, ranks, and typecasts characters through reference to a multitude of coded, conventional texts—literary, nonliterary, and oral. To describe a usurer, Torquemada for example, the narrator resorts to an array of cultural texts regarding the appearance and behavior of usurers and misers. This organized assemblage of texts that comprises the novel is, as Wellek perceived, double-edged—descriptive as well as prescriptive. While it generates knowledge, while it produces individuals, it simultaneously disciplines by imposing order and containing idiosyncrasy. Like Torquemada's *hoguera*, the novelistic examination illuminates as it castigates.

Characters Under Observation

The novel as a fictionalized examination creates the illusion that the narrator is merely observing already existing characters, not creating them. In the opening to *Torquemada en la hoguera*, Galdós's narrator (again tongue in cheek) self-consciously calls attention to this realist convention by insisting upon the "reality" of his protagonist:

> Mis amigos conocen ya, por lo que de él se me antojó referirles, a don Francisco Torquemada, a quien algunos historiadores inéditos de estos tiempos llaman Torquemada el Peor. ¡Ay de mis buenos lectores si conocen al implacable fogonero de vidas y haciendas por tratos de otra clase, no tan sin malicia, no tan desinteresados como estas inocentes relaciones entre narrador y lector! (7-8)

By raising the woeful possibility that his readers themselves may have dealt with the moneylender, Torquemada, the narrator erases the line between the world of his characters and the world of his readers. He thereby carries to its logical conclusion the realist pretense of displaying already existing characters drawn from observed social reality.

Within this realist pretense these apparently ready-made characters must above all have "readable" personalities; they must appear as coherent beings with logical patterns of behavior.[23] In Hélène Cixous's view, characters become "fetishized"; they are offered up to readers "with the prospect of a traditional reading that seeks its satisfaction at the level of a potential identification with such and such a 'personage' " (385). Of course in the case of Torquemada the readers' satisfaction originates in a "nonidentification" with a most unappealing protagonist. Readers may derive gratification by favorably comparing themselves with Torquemada *el peor*. According to Cixous, readers enter "into commerce with the book" on the condition that they be "paid back, that is, recompensed by another who is sufficiently similar to or different" from them (385).[24] Readers are thereby "upheld, by comparison or in combination with a personage," in the representation that they wish to have of themselves (385). Applying similar economic terms to the reading process, Roland Barthes contends that the classic realist text makes readers into *consumers*, rather than *producers*: "Our literature is characterized by the pitiless divorce which the literary institution maintains between the producer of the text and its user, between its owner and its customer, between its author and its reader. This reader is thereby plunged into a kind of idleness" (*S/Z* 4).[25] For readers then, characters, as well as the fictional worlds they inhabit, appear as ready-made commodities.

When a realist narrator examines these commodified characters, he displays them already spatially distributed throughout the fictional society. His omnisicient gaze is *panoptic*, a kind of super-vision that surveys a multiplicity of characters, already typed and assigned to various slots in society, where they perform their appointed functions.[26] For Foucault, the *Panopticon*—Jeremy Bentham's plan for a prison— serves as the "architectural figure" of the disciplinary gaze, as a metaphor for the dominant mode of organizing power relations in the disciplinary society. In Bentham's Panopticon, the prisoner's cells are arranged in a circle around the central watchtower. Each cell has two windows: one on the inside provides visibility for guards in the tower, while the outside window provides backlighting. It is thereby possible to observe from the tower, "standing out precisely against the light, the small captive shadows in the cells of the periphery. They are like so many cages, so many small theaters, in which each actor is alone, perfectly individualized and constantly visible" (*Discipline* 200). The crowd, the mass of inmates, their "individualities merging together, a collective effect, is abolished and replaced by a collection of separated individualities" (*Discipline* 201). This is precisely how characters appear in the realist novel. "Disciplinary space," according to Foucault, "is always, basically cellular" (*Discipline* 143). Although characters may move from one cell to another and interact, they remain perpetually within the captive gaze of the narrator. In the novelistic cosmogonies of Balzac and Galdós, characters inhabit multi-tiered cells in vast fictional societies and reappear (as does Torquemada) across various novels.[27] Readers are "invited" to share the position of this hegemonic gaze, to observe and come to know all the characters in the fictional society. An invitation to partake in the narrator's gaze is also what Bentham had in mind in his utopian model for an "inspection house": "anyone may come and exercise in the central tower the functions of surveillance" and thereby "gain a clear idea of the way in which the surveillance is practiced" (*Discipline* 207).

> There is no risk, therefore, that the increase of power created by the panoptic machine may degenerate into tyranny; the disciplinary mechanism will be democratically controlled, since it will be constantly accessible to "the great tribunal committee of the world." This Panopticon, subtly arranged so that an observer may observe, at a glance, so many different individuals, also enables everyone to come and observe any of the observers. The seeing machine was once a sort of dark room into which individuals spied; it has become a transparent building in which the exercise of power may be supervised by society as a whole. (*Discipline* 207)

For Bentham, the Panopticon suited the Enlightenment model of a transparent society, in which everyone would automatically regulate everyone else—a system infinitely preferable to the tyranny of despots. Panopticism, as a benevolent, rational form of power, would increase productivity, spread education, and raise the level of public morality. Power relations would thereby be innocent, much like "estas inocentes relaciones entre narrador y lector!"—to which Galdós refers (no doubt ironically) in his opening to *Torquemada en la hoguera* (8).[28] But however "innocent," the realist narrator not only invites but compels readers to situate themselves inside his viewpoint, thereby fixing them in a relation of watching. Presumably, there is no other viewpoint available, and readers, lured by the promise of truth revealed, readily assume this position of transcendence.

Having fixed his readers within his viewpoint, the realist narrator proceeds to examine the various characters within their individual domains, generally in that space most valued by the nineteenth-century novel—domestic space. Along with the narrator we voyeuristically peer into each cell, observing and eavesdropping upon the inhabitants. D.A. Miller has commented that in the realist novel, characters appear to us within meticulously described boxes.[29] And Lennard Davis has discussed the unprecedented "thickness" of space depicted in realist novels. More than simply a backdrop,

> novelistic space must have dimensions and depth, . . . byways and back alleys; there must be open rooms and hidden places, dining rooms and locked drawers; there must be thickness and interiority to the mental constructions that constitute the novel's space. It is almost impossible to imagine the novel as a form divorced from a complex rendering of space. (53).

In *Torquemada en la hoguera*, the narrator offers us a view inside Torquemada's home and focuses on each significant feature: he provides an inventory of the foods placed on the table; he notices the new furnishings—the spring mattresses, a new carpet, new dishes, Rufina's *lavabo* with its basin and pitcher of blue glass. Interestingly, the narrator describes the household within a larger surrounding "box"—the historical setting—within the alternately ruling "houses" of liberals and conservatives. He also minutely describes another type of box that encloses his main character—the clothing worn by Torquemada, and how it differs from the soiled rags he wore in his earlier days as an "avaro de antiguo cuño" (12). All these telling details illustrate how the family "pasito a paso y a codazo limpio, se habían ido metiendo en la clase media, en nuestra bonachona clase media, toda necesidades y pretensiones" (14). The Torquemada family has risen in the social panopticon and placed itself in a superior cell, with all the proper appurtenances.

For readers, the minute description of a character's dwelling place serves to expand our view of him, but it also works to discipline the fictional being, to make him readily comprehensible. Balzac believed that the same relationship existed "between a man and his house as between an oyster and its shell" (Mount 18).[30] A character's appurtenances should match not only his station in life but also his personality. He should appear coherent, as an intelligible whole; so as his home and clothing box him in, so also does his personality. This boxing-in of realist characters aids in their fetishization and thus facilitates their consumption by a passive reader.

In this microscopic describability, in this mastery over minutiae, there resides a tremendous power. Miller observes how the realist novel "dramatizes a power continually able to appropriate the most trivial detail" (28). And according to Foucault, description serves as a means of control and domination: For a long time "ordinary individuality"

> remained below the threshold of description. To be looked at, observed, described in detail, followed from day to day by an uninterrupted writing was a privilege. The chronicle of a man, the account of his life, his historiography, written as he lived out his life formed part of the rituals of his power. The disciplinary methods reversed this relation, lowered the threshold of describable individuality and made of this description a means of control and a method of domination. It is no longer a monument for future memory, but a document for possible use. . . . This turning of real lives into writing is no longer a procedure of heroization; it functions as a procedure of objectification and subjection. (*Discipline* 191-92)

To describe an object, an individual, a space is literally to draw a line around it, to enclose, claim, and control it.[31] "Discipline," in Foucault's words, "is a political anatomy of detail" (*Discipline* 139).

From a macroscopic viewpoint, the presentation of characters in their "boxes" also serves to control novelistic space at large—the entire fictional world projected in readers' minds. And of course, plotting—governed by codes of chronology and causality—works to regulate and make intelligible the narrated chain of events. But the realist novel, with its proliferation of detail, its gaggle of characters, also requires a sophisticated plotting of space. To be understood and remembered, each character must appear in a prescribed spot within a well-mapped fictional world. In *Torquemada en la hoguera*, once having viewed the family members in their home, we spy upon a series of minor characters in the cells of a small panopticon—Torquemada's *casa de corredor*. As the usurer makes the rounds to collect rent from his tenants, we catch a brief glimpse of each apartment and its impoverished inhabitants; we overhear the complaints and excuses of each tenant, followed by Torquemada's unexpectedly charitable responses. Later, along with Torquemada, we peer into the well-appointed house—"amueblado con mucho lujo y elegancia"—of a debtor who lives far above his means (49). We also observe the apartment of Isidora, *la desheredada* herself, a home she shares with an artist, "más tísico que la *Traviatta*" (53). Through the usurer's eyes we view a sterotypical artist's garret, right out of a setting of *La Bohème*:

> Hallóse don Francisco dentro de una estancia cuyo inclinado techo tocaba al piso por la parte contraria a la puerta; arriba, un ventanón con algunos de sus vidrios rotos, tapados con trapos y papeles; el suelo, de baldosín, cubierto a trechos de pedazos de alfombra; a un lado un baúl abierto, dos sillas, un anafre con lumbre. (52)

Each of these settings, while minutely described, still leaves many details to be filled in by readers. And of course, each cubicle—whether inhabited by an impoverished tenant, a bourgeois hanger-on, or a starving artist—fits the conventional image already inscribed in readers' minds as to how and where such social types live. As the author "quotes" these already more-or-less fixed images, he simultaneously directs readers to complete the texts by drawing from their cultural image-repertoires.[32] It follows that each act of quotation at once reinforces and adds to the image-repertoire shared by readers in a given culture.

These quoted textual images that depict minor characters and their box-like domains fulfill the realist imperative to represent observed social life in all its variety. At the same time, of course, these vignettes also serve to characterize Torquemada by giving him the opportunity to "show his stuff": they allow us to see and hear him with a variety of characters as he struggles against his nature to perform acts of charity. All of these speeches, descriptions of a character's appearance, setting, actions—in short this assemblage of incorporated texts—comprise a *character zone*. In Mikhail Bakhtin's view, "a character in a novel always has . . . a zone of his own, his own sphere of influence on the authorial context surrounding him, a sphere that extends—and often quite far—beyond the boundaries of the direct discourse allotted to him" (320). Often such a character zone "encroaches in one way or another upon the author's voice" (Bakhtin 316). The very process of representing the speech, thoughts, and *ambiente* of another "may refract authorial intentions and consequently to a certain degree constitute a second language for the author" (315). In the realist novel, a fictional being may be characterized so completely that he threatens to usurp narrative power. So while evoking a character's presence, a narrator may interrupt, or regulate the evocation, to avoid being upstaged and overwhelmed.[33] Characters encroach not only upon the narrator's voice, but also upon each other. We can find an example of both types of encroachment in a hyperbolic passage introducing Torquemada's son Valentín:

> no he conocido criatura más mona que aquel Valentín, ni preciosidad tan extraordinaria como la suya. ¡Cosa tan rara! No obstante el parecido con su antipático papá, era el chiquillo guapísimo, con tal expresión de inteligencia en aquella cara, que se quedaba uno embobado mirándole; con tales encantos en su persona y carácter, y rasgos de conducta tan superiores a su edad, que verle, hablarle y quererle vivamente era todo uno. ¡Y qué hechicera gravedad la suya, no incompatible con la inquietud propia de la infancia! ¡Qué gracia mezclada de no sé qué aplomo inexplicable a sus años! ¡Qué rayo divino en sus ojos algunas veces, y otras qué misteriosa y dulce tristeza! Espigadillo de cuerpo, tenía las piernas delgadas, pero de buena forma; la cabeza, más grande de lo regular, con alguna deformidad en el cráneo. En cuanto a su aptitud para el estudio llamémosla verdadero prodigio, asombro de la escuela y orgullo y gala de los maestros. De esto hablaré más adelante. Sólo he de afirmar ahora que el *Peor* no merecía tal joya, ¡qué había de merecerla!, y que si fuese hombre capaz de alabar a Dios por los bienes con que le agraciaba, motivos tenía el muy tuno para estarse, como Moisés, tantísimas horas con los brazos levantados al cielo. No los levantaba, porque sabía que del cielo no había de caerle ninguna breva de las que a él le gustaban. (11-12)

We detect throughout this passage a triple presence (at the very least) in which the zones of a narrator and two different characters mutually "infect" each other. Ostensibly, the function of this passage is to evoke the presence of this *monstruo* in all his glory. But the narrator makes himself present throughout, in that by his exaggerated prose, he characterizes himself as *embobado* before this prodigy. As a rule in realism, the narrator's voice merges with that of "public opinion" in the fictional world and here he reinforces this consensus by appropriating colloquial exclamations and epithets: *era todo uno*; ¡Qué gracia!; *no sé que*; and *el muy tuno*. Near the end of the passage, the narrator abruptly cuts short the panegyric with an abrupt "De eso hablaré más adelante," and then launches into a sarcastic diatribe against the prodigy's father—his indignation again implicitly shared by "public opinion." Of course, throughout the passage, Torquemada has also been present in the background, having been established as a point of negative comparison by the remark, "No obstante el parecido con su antipático papá." Within this single descriptive passage, meant to characterize Valentín, we find a complex superimposition of two character zones—father and son—and of two voices—of the narrator and "public opinion." In addition, we detect an ironic undertone created by the outrageous hyperbole and by the dissonance between Valentín's divine and grotesque qualities. By playing the *bobo*, the narrator invites readers to feel superior to all the *embobados* in this fictional world. And beneath it all we detect the droll voice of an author, who writing late in the the realist period, perhaps can only employ the realist conventions tongue-in-cheek, with self-conscious exaggeration.

The presumably hegemonic control of the narrator is continually refracted and threatened by the character images and voices that he assembles.[34] In order to evoke the presence of characters, the narrator must create their images in language; he must bring together a chorus of voices that may never harmoniously blend. Inevitably, this mixture produces dissonance—a cacophony over which the narrator must reassert control, lest the jumble of voices drown out his own. This mixing of various voices also decenters the narrator's position within the watchtower of the panoptic society. In theory the realist novel rests upon empiricism, upon the presumption that a detached observer can arrive at truth by examining an objective reality. But in practice the realist novel can only *recreate* the empiricist examination by seeming to observe *an image made of language*, an image that is actually a pastiche of many incorporated voices and images. In Bakhtin's view, "the novel is the expression of a Galilean perception of language, one that denies the absolutism of a single and unitary language" (366). Conscious of the vast plenitude of "social languages" within a given culture, the novel assumes "a verbal and semantic decentering of the ideological world, a certain linguistic homelessness of literary consciousness, which no longer possesses a sacrosanct and unitary linguistic medium for containing ideological thought" (Bakhtin 367). So while in theory realism assumes the possibility of a unitary voice and vision, in practice it contradicts its founding proposition. The narrator's voice is neither unitary, nor does it truly belong to him; it inheres in a pastiche of texts drawn from the culture he inhabits. Since he too is a part of the very textual pastiche he fabricates, his own vision can never be separated from the fictional world he seems to observe.[35] The narrator is, in a sense, homeless, unable truly to inhabit the panoptic watchtower.[36] And readers, whose vision is controlled by the narrator's gaze, also find their vision constantly shifting, as it is refracted among the various perspectives offered in the novel.[37]

Galdós, it seems, had an intimation of the untenability of his narrator's position, for frequently, at some point in his novels, the narrator slips away from the watchtower and joins his characters in the galleries.[38] In *Torquemada en la hoguera* this occurs when, speaking of Valentín, the narrator testifies: "Un día me hablaron de él dos profesores amigos míos que tienen colegio de primera y segunda enseñanza, lleváronme a verle, y me quedé asombrado. Jamás vi precocidad semejante ni un apuntar de inteligencia tan maravilloso" (16). Up to this point the narrator, although occasionally using the first person, has maintained omniscience. Then suddenly he descends from his high perch and becomes one with the masses. The effect of this shift of position is always a bit jarring, and we never know if it is merely an authorial joke, or if Galdós, disturbed by the logical impossibility of omniscience, wants his narrator to appear an "intimate friend" of all these characters. But this in turn introduces another logical impossibility, that any "friend" could be so intimate as to know the inner thoughts of so many characters. In the end the attempted solution is as untenable as was the problem. Then as suddenly as Galdós's narrator descended to his character's world, he once more ascends to his ostensibly detached viewing box, and maintains omniscience throughout the rest of the novel.

Although the practice of realist writing undermines its very premises, the narrator will steadfastly strive to maintain his pretense of detachment and control.[39] And readers, accustomed to the conventions of realism, tend to identify with the narrator, to merge their gaze with his, and to filter out or ignore the dissonance produced by the melange of voices and images. They tend to accept the narration as the "voice of Truth," measuring against it all the other voices incorporated into the text (Coward and Ellis 49). Placed in the role of consumers, readers generally accept the realist pretense and join the narrator in voyeuristically observing the ready-made fictional beings who parade before them.

Characters Under Construction

 The realist project assumes the anterior production of immanently readable characters, whom the narrator presents to readers in their completed forms. This consumerist view of reading, as Roland Barthes noted, plunges readers into idleness (*S/Z* 4). However, readers may only seem idle, because so much of their work takes place on an unconscious or semiconscious level.[40] In actuality, reading is a constructive labor, for readers must fabricate the fictional worlds that fill their imaginations. Just as readers construct a chronologically ordered *story* based upon the *text* (which may or may not be chronologically organized), they also build mental images of characters founded upon the specific information provided in the text.[41] Based upon a *text character's* described appearance, actions, and speech, readers assign him personality traits and attach them to his proper name; in this manner they construct a mental image, a *story character*, that is constantly in process, changing and developing as more information is obtained.[42] In fact, the textual information provided about a character is quite limited—even in a realist novel that abounds in detailed description—and readers must fill the gaps. According to Wolfgang Iser, these gaps stimulate the process of ideation by compelling readers to fill the blanks with their own projections ("Interaction" 111-12).

 This process of ideation reaches far beyond the text in hand, for as readers construct mental portraits of characters, they draw upon prior experiences with other literary and worldly characters. By necessity, this venture outside the text is *intertextual*, extending into "the vast perspective of the already-written," to *intertexts* inscribed in the mind as well as on the page (Barthes, *S/Z* 21). However, this escape from the text is not an uncontrolled free-for-all. For while the images that individual readers form of a particular character will vary, generally their pathways outside the text are guided and restrained by cultural codes. Barthes defines the code as "a perspective of quotations," the wake of the "already read, seen, done, experienced" (*S/Z* 20). When readers assign traits to a character in a process of "expanding nomination," they obey conventional wisdom about human nature and psychology; they follow long-established conventions of reading (*S/Z* 93). This codified cultural knowledge works to control the expansion outside the text and to guide readers along well-trodden intertextual paths.

Although guided by codes, readers are in a sense writers who, as they read, mentally "write" their versions of a story. Conversely, writers are readers: as they write, they read their own texts as they assume others will read them; and of course, a writer's reading, like those of his subsequent readers, is culturally coded and preconditioned. Let us imagine Galdós working through the voice of his narrator to create the character of Torquemada. As he writes the text character, he mentally constructs a story character based upon his own intertextual references; and through the voice of his narrator, he leaves signals in the text—points of departure—that will direct readers to specific intertexts. In the case of a stereotyped character such as Torquemada, these intertexts are easily identifiable. The text mobilizes a long tradition of stereotypical knowledge regarding misers and usurers, an image-repertoire that most occidental readers will share. And indeed, a number of critics have found in Torquemada's character the resonances of other literary misers and usurers—Moliére's Harpagon, Balzac's Gobseck and Père Grandet, Dickens's Scrooge.[43] However, the literary tradition goes back much further, to the character sketches written by Aristotle's pupil, Theophrastus, to the satires of Horace and Juvenal, to the genre of character writing in seventeenth- and eighteenth-century Europe—in all of which misers or usurers figure prominently.[44] Always, these sketches cite the typical behaviors of the miserly character, and frequently his physical appearance as well. Thin, bald, with sallow, loose skin, a sharp face, a long nose, he is perpetually hunched over a table counting his money.[45] Such a stereotypical image, along with a list of predictable behaviors, would have been deeply engraved in the cultural image-repertoire shared by Galdós's readers.

In their intertextual constructs of characters then, writers and readers venture far beyond the *literary* works that precondition a given text; they make use of myriad cultural texts—including visual images, commonplaces, rules of thumb, social scripts, action sequences, sets of traits and expected behaviors—all drawn from a vast storehouse of codified, conventional knowledge about human beings. Galdós explicitly directs readers to such common knowlege by repeatedly applying stereotypical epithets to describe Torquemada *el peor*: "el sucio," "la feroz hormiga," "el tacaño," "el usurero," "el judío" (8, 9, 42, 47, 48, *et passim*). Of course, the epithets *judío*, *usurero*, and *el peor*—the latter comparing him to the Grand Inquisitor Torquemada, allegedly of *converso* descent—all point readers toward stereotypical images of Jews.[46] By so insistently invoking these stereotypes, the narrator tries to solidify the image of

Torquemada that readers form in their minds. *Steros* in Greek means *solid*. And according to Barthes, the stereotype is an idea that has set, that has assumed the solid state, and is "evaluated in terms of *fatigue*." (*Roland Barthes* 58, 89). By repeatedly soliciting these stereotypical images, the narrator seeks to pin down Torquemada, to discipline and control the mental image that readers form of his character.

However, in various ways the narrator also allows Torquemada to spill out of his stereotypical mold. Certainly he is no longer one of those "avaros de antiguo cuño que afanaban riquezas y vivían como mendigos y se morían como perros en un camastro lleno de pulgas y de billetes de Banco metidos entre la paja, eran los místicos o metafísicos de la usura" (12). In this novel, Torquemada, living in an "época que arranca de la desamortización, sufrió, sin comprenderlo, la metamorfosis que ha desnaturalizado la usura metafísica, convirtiéndolo en positivista" (13). The narrator describes at length Torquemada's metamorphosis from marginalized *usurero metafísico*—dirty, ill-kempt, underfed—to a more respectable bourgeois financier. In one sense, rather than diverging from his typecast, Torquemada merely becomes a modernized usurer; the stereotype is brought up-to-date with nineteenth-century bourgeois society and thereby strengthened and validated. In another sense, however, Torquemada exceeds this up-dated stereotype by adopting a distorted and exaggerated version of nineteenth-century positivism, as expressed in his rantings about *humanidad*. And in still another respect, Torquemada overspills his mold—simply by becoming such an exaggerated version of the stereotype. In the initial outrageous scene the narrator paints him as a "fiero sayón," an "implacable fogonero," methodically dismembering, skewering, and roasting his victims over the fire (7). And throughout the novel, by repeating the epithets—*la hormiga, el tacaño, el judío*—the narrator announces to the world—"indeed, Torquemada is a stereotype!" By means of this mocking repetition, this incessant ridicule, he converts the stereotype into farce.[47] It is as if Torquemada were a character enclosed in quotation marks—a graphic technique that serves to denature the stereotype, to display its wear, by drawing excess attention to itself (*Roland Barthes*, 89).[48] Beneath this ironic exaggeration of Torquemada, readers sense once more the voice of an author, so aware of the conventions of character that he can only characterize ironically and self-consciously. Galdós's use of stereotype is thus double-edged: On the one hand it works to solidify and control the character-image that readers will form; but on the other hand, by virtue of its flagrancy and self-ridicule, it works to undermine its disciplinary function. So as readers form an image of the sterotypical usurer and perform this novel in their minds, they do so farcically and excessively. In realism the balance remains precarious between its disciplinary use of stereotype and its tendency towards excess. Certainly, its mimetic project does not preclude characters from expanding beyond their typecasts. As a fictional re-enactment of an empirical examination, the realist novel will produce both individuals and social types. By precisely documenting a character's unique physical features, a realist narrator will endow him with individuality, while simultaneously classifying him as a type. Torquemada, in his physical description, generally comforms to the stereotypical representation of a miser, but he also bears a few unique features that mark his individuality:

> Tenía ya la perilla amarillenta, el bigote más negro que blanco, ambos adornos de la cara tan recortaditos, que antes parecían pegados que nacidos allí. Fuera de la ropa, mejorada en claridad, si no en la manera de llevarla, era el mismo que conocimos en la casa de doña Lupe *la de los Pavos*; en su cara la propia confusión extraña de lo militar y lo eclesiástico, el color bilioso, los ojos negros y algo soñadores, el gesto y los modales expresando lo mismo afeminación que hipocresía, la calva más despoblada y más limpia, y todo él craso, resbaladizo y repulsivo, muy pronto siempre cuando se le saludaba a dar la mano, por cierto bastante sudada. (15)

While certain features—the beard of an *alabardero*, the strange mixture of "lo militar y lo eclesiástico"—deviate from the cultural stereotype of the miser, most of his features correspond.

Through its reference to "la casa de doña Lupe," this description also directs readers to a prior novel, *Fortunata y Jacinta* (1887), where the narrator had described Torquemada in almost identical terms, and where interestingly, he began with a disclaimer: "La fisonomía de aquel hombre era difícil de entender. Sólo doña Lupe, en virtud de una larga práctica sabía encontrar algunos jeroglíficos en aquella cara ordinaria y enjuta, que tenía ciertos rasgos de tipo militar con visos clericales" (222).[49] Here the narrator alerts readers to a difficulty in interpreting this character, in reading the hieroglyphics inscribed on his face. We do indeed read characters (both in fiction and in social life) by interpreting their physical characteristics, gestures, and clothing as signifiers that indicate social class, profession, and psychological type. But while we apprehend a living (or filmed) "character" all at once, as a whole—or in such rapid sequence that it seems so—we read a fictional character consecutively and discontinuously, piece by piece. In Barthes's words, "the total body must revert to the dust of words, to the listing of details, to a monotonous inventory of parts, to crumbling: language undoes the body, returns it to the fetish" (*S/Z* 113). So when we read this description of Torquemada, we proceed in piecemeal fashion, trying to combine each part and to construct a whole image of his character.[50] But as Barthes emphasizes,

> the sentence can never constitute a *total*; meanings can be listed, not admixed: the total, the sum are for language the promised lands, glimpsed *at the end* of enumeration, but once this enumeration has been completed, no feature can reassemble it—or if this feature is produced, it too can only be *added* to the others. . . . [D]escription is then subject to a kind of enumerative erethism: it accumulates in order to totalize, multiples fetishes in order to obtain a total, defetishized body. (*S/Z* 114)[51]

The realist impulse towards a complete description, towards a true-to-life representation, ultimately tends to undo itself. It would seem that the more detailed and extensive the description, the more fully drawn and substantial the character would become in readers' minds. However, the longer the list, the less the individual features cohere, and the more the character's physical image threatens to decompose. So as more terms are used to describe a character, more signification is produced, and the various connotations spin out centrifugally in what Barthes terms "a metonymic skid" (*S/Z* 92).

As the signs attached to a character accumulate, readers group them around his proper name, which "acts as a magnetic field" (*S/Z* 67). But in realism, with its excessive descriptions, the proper name is often besieged by more signs than it can hold. This threat to the realist impulse becomes evident in the aforementioned contradictory description of Torquemada's son, Valentín, who "no obstante el parecido con su antipático papá, era el chiquillo guapísimo . . . con tales encantos en su persona y carácter" (11). The narrator's continual affirmations of Valentín's *gracia* and *preciosidad* are belied by his physical attributes: "Espigadillo de cuerpo, tenía las piernas delgadas, pero de buena forma; la cabeza, más grande de lo regular, con alguna deformidad en el cráneo" (12). Over a series of pages, the narrator enumerates Valentín's astonishing intellectual gifts, his charming tricks, his serious but luminous demeanor, even while insisting:

> En lo que digo que las inauditas dotes intelectuales de aquella criatura no se crea que hay la más mínima exageración. Afirmo con toda ingenuidad que el chico era de lo más estupendo que se puede ver, y que se presentó en el campo de la enseñanza como esos extraordinarios ingenios que nacen de tarde en tarde destinados a abrir nuevos caminos a la humanidad. Además de la inteligencia, que en edad temprana despuntaba en él como aurora de un día espléndido, poseía todos los encantos de la infancia, dulzura, gracejo y amabilidad. (16)

Of course, this tongue-in-cheek disavowal of "la más mínima exageración," this pretense of "toda ingenuidad," even as he employs the most hyperbolic language, immediately introduces an ironic undertone of doubt.[52] Moreover, the descriptions of Valentín are couched in exaggerated, antithetical terms of the diabolical and the divine: "Ese niño es cosa inexplicable," avers his teacher, "tiene el diablo en el cuerpo o es el pedazo de divinidad más hermoso que ha caído en la tierra"; and the narrator exclaims, "Su inocencia y celestial donosura casi nos permitían conocer a los ángeles como si los hubiéramos tratado" (17, 18). All this piling up of exaggerated and contradictory "facts" threatens to overwhelm readers in their attempt to construct a mental portrait of Valentín. His proper name may no longer contain his expanding image. So in an attempt to contain and limit this expansion, the narrator must resort to a very great name—that of Christ himself. Hence, he concludes his long description of Valentín with a Biblical intertext that depicts this "monstruo de la edad presente" at age twelve, as he is questioned by a group of sabios: "Era en verdad interesante aquel cuadro y digno de figurar en los anales de la ciencia: cuatro varones de más de cincuenta años, calvos y medio ciegos de tanto estudiar, maestros de maestros, congregábanse delante de aquel mocoso" (19). After devoting an entire chapter to the description of the prodigy, the narrator concludes: "Valentín los miraba sin orgullo ni cortedad, inocente dueño de sí, como Cristo niño entre los doctores" (20). By soliciting this powerful icon, after going so far in the direction of centrifugal dispersion, the narrator seeks to rein in the character of Valentín. For such an exorbitant character, he resorts to a colossal intertextual image in an attempt to reassert disciplinary control. Of course, this attempt only partially succeeds, for the exaggerated and untenable comparison with Christ is permeated with irony. But ultimately, like Christ, this excessive, "unrealistic" character is sacrificed, expelled from the fictional society. As Leo Bersani has observed, "an energetic excess of being in realistic fiction is inevitably compromised or punished in its heroes; it is tolerated only in the minor figures of fiction, in the degraded form of amusing eccentricities" (70).

Tía Roma, the rag-picker of Torquemada's household, represents another excessive and discontinuous character in the novel. A physically grotesque figure, Tía Roma is immanently paradoxical, for her outer appearance belies her inner substance:

> [E]ra tan vieja, tan vieja y tan fea, que su cara parecía un puñado de telarañas revueltas con la ceniza; su nariz de corcho ya no tenía forma; su boca redonda y sin dientes menguaba o crecía, según la distensión de las arrugas que la formaban. Más arriba, entre aquel revoltijo de piel polvorosa, lucían los ojos de pescado, dentro de un cerco de pimentón húmedo. Lo demás de la persona desparecía bajo un envoltorio de trapos y dentro de la remendada falda, en la cual había restos de un traje de la madre de doña Silvia cuando era polla. (43)

Based upon this passage, the image that readers form of Tía Roma may come to resemble a cubist collage, for the described features never quite cohere. Her face becomes a chaotic site where divergent metaphors collide: her skin a spiderweb, her nose of cork, her mouth a waning and waxing moon, her fish-like eyes lined with crushed red pepper. For readers, these metaphorical vehicles—web, cork, moon, fish, pepper—clash and compete among themselves for dominance. Each image in turn incites a chain of connotations that spins out centrifugally, producing diverse associations with positive or negative values. To cite only a few possibilities: the spiderweb is traditionally an ominous image, one we might associate with witches; a cork nose brings to mind a grotesque, pockmarked face, as well as the comical faces of puppets or clowns; the moon evokes darkness, sterility, and mysterious feminine power; and the repugnant image of staring fish-eyes with pepper-red mucous linings suggests both clairvoyance and disease. As a conjured image in readers' minds, Tía Roma becomes a swarm of contradictory signs that fail to combine, a figure of disruption. Of course, we can evoke the stereotypical image of the witch in an attempt to encapsulate her disturbing presence. But certainly she is an inverse of the witch, an angel in witch's clothing, a contradiction that trips up Torquemada when, in an inversion of the "Hail Mary," he curses her: "El demonio está contigo, y maldita tú eres entre todas las brujas y esperpentos que hay en el cielo ..., digo, en el infierno" (67).[53]

What most effectively works to discipline this disruptive character is that, at the climactic point in the plot, Tía Roma's voice merges with the narrator's powerful voice, thus acquiring his stamp of approval. When she lashes out at Torquemada in a fury of righteous indignation, she expresses the narrator's (and humanity's) judgment of him. This occurs when Valentín is at death's door, as Torquemada, still hoping to redeem his son's life, performs a last desperate good deed by offering to give Tía Roma his mattress. She responds by expressing her repugnance at the idea of sleeping in a bed contaminated by the usurer's "ruines pensamientos":

> ahí dentro, ahí dentro están todos sus pecados, la guerra que le hace al pobre, su tacañería, los réditos que mama y todos los números que le andan por la sesera para ajuntar dinero.... Si yo me durmiera ahí, a la hora de la muerte me saldrían por un lado y por otro unos sapos con la boca muy grande, unos culebrones asquerosos que se me enroscarían en el cuerpo, unos diablos muy feos con bigotazos y con orejas de murciélago, y me cogerían entre todos para llevarme a rastras a los infiernos. Váyase al rayo a guárdese sus colchones.... (65-66)

When Torquemada continues to insist and even vows, if his son is saved, to sleep on her pallet of rags for the rest of his days, she denounces his hypocrisy:

> A buenas horas y con sol. Usted quiere ahora poner un puño en el cielo ¡Ay, señor, a cada paje su ropaje! A usted le sienta eso como a las burras las arracadas. Todo ello es porque está afligido; pero si se pone bueno el niño, volverá usted a ser más malo que Holofernes. Mire que ya va para viejo; mire que el mejor día se le pone delante la de la cara pelada, y a ésta sí que no le da usted el timo. (66)

Continuing her ravings at length, Tía Roma recalls all the suffering that the *tacaño* has inflicted on his family, finally provoking violent curses from Torquemada. In her furious denunciation, she expresses not only the moral outrage of the narrator, but also of public opinion in the novel. The abundance of colloquial expressions—"a cada paje su ropaje!," "como a las burras las arracadas," "más malo que Holofernes"—all link her voice to that of the fictional public, to Torquemada's many victims. In a sense she speaks for all the spectators who witness Torquemada's *auto de fe* in the *hoguera*. She thereby plays the archetypal role of a *nemesis*, who voices the wrath of the gods, although in this case, it is the wrath of the fictional society, *humanidad*. And in turn, this archetypal function as *nemesis*, as castigator, finally provides readers with a means of containing her disruptive, disjointed presence. Paradoxically, having first appeared as a figure of disruption, ultimately she speaks for moral law and order in the fictional society.

José Bailón exemplifies still another extravagant and disruptive character, a false prophet who ostensibly speaks for *humanidad*.[54] Upon introducing him, the narrator once more ironically calls attention to the realist pretense of observing ready-made characters: "tengo prisa por presentar a cierto sujeto que conozco hace tiempo y que hasta ahora nunca menté para nada: un don José Bailón, . . . cuya intervención en mi cuento es necesaria ya para que se desarrolle con lógica" (20). Interestingly, the logic of the story requires the intervention of a supremely illogical character. Formerly a priest, revolutionary, protestant preacher, pamphleteer—and always a womanizer and free-thinker—at the time of this story, Bailón is proprietor of a dairy and "usurer in training" under Torquemada. Even further back in time, in a former life, Bailón claims to have been an Egyptian priest who was burned alive with his illicit lover, a priestess in his temple. If, as conventional wisdom maintains, a character's (or individual's) identity is largely a composite of past experiences, then Bailón's identity would indeed lack logic and coherence. As a character, he is as much an illogical pastiche as the incomprehensible diatribes he writes:[55]

> Escribía Bailón aquellas necedades en parrafitos cortos, y a veces rompía con una cosa muy santa: verbigracia: «Gloria a Dios en las alturas y paz, etc.,» para salir luego por este registro:
> «Los tiempos se acercan, tiempos de redención, en que el Hijo del Hombre será dueño de la tierra.
> »El Verbo depositó hace dieciocho siglos la semilla divina. En noche tenebrosa fructificó. He aquí las flores.
> »¿Cómo se llaman? Los derechos del pueblo.»

Y a lo mejor, cuando el lector estaba más descuidado, le soltaba ésta:
«He aquí al tirano. ¡Maldito sea!»Aplicad el oído y decidme de dónde viene ese rumor vago, confuso, extraño. . . . » (23)

It is Bailón who infects Torquemada's mind with his pseudo-positivistic theory that humanity examines, judges, and punishes him. In Bailón's cosmo-vision,

> es la Humanidad, la Humanidad, ¿se entera usted?, lo cual no quiere decir que deje de ser personal. . . . ¿Qué cosa es personal? Fíjese bien. Personal es lo que es uno. Y el gran Conjunto, amigo don Francisco, el gran Conjunto . . . es uno, porque no hay más y tiene los atributos de un ser infinitamente infinito. Nosotros en montón, componemos la Humanidad, somos los átomos que forman el gran todo; somos parte mínima de Dios, parte minúscula, y nos renovamos como en nuestro cuerpo se renuevan los átomos de la cochina materia. (25)

The more we read of Bailón's past, of his behavior, speech, and writings, the more gargantuan and uncontrollable his image becomes in our minds. The very extravagance and irrationality of Bailón's "text character" encourages readers to form a wildly expanding "story character," as the various associations spin out in different directions. Upon reading the textual information provided about Bailón, we draw upon a storehouse of knowledge and experience, concerning revolutionaries, defrocked priests, protestant preachers, Egyptian priests, womanizers, pamphleteers, and positivists. Normally in realism, this process of referring intertextually, of following chains of connotation, is "parsimonious"—in Barthes' words—a "limited plural" (S/Z 6, 8). The exits from the immediate text into referential fields are guided and restricted by cultural codes. Within a connotative sequence, one word follows another naturally, of itself, along well-traveled paths. But in the case of an exorbitant character like Bailón, one who does not cohere, the connotations are less coded, less controlled. Readers, trying to make sense of such a nonsensical character, may search their storehouses of memory to invoke relevant prototypes and find none. In characterizing Bailón, the text incites too many departures into intertextual space, an excess that overwhelms readers and jeopardizes the efforts of the author, through his narrator's dominating voice, to control the proliferation of meanings.

In an effort to rein in this supremely unruly character and to solidify his image in readers' minds, the narrator resorts to a much-used ploy in Galdós's novels.[56] He likens Bailón's appearance to a historical or mythological figure in a well-known painting, ostensibly providing readers with a familiar, fixed image, so that they might know *exactly* how Bailón looks:

> no tenía cara de cura, ni de fraile, ni de torero. Era más bien un Dante echado a perder. Dice un amigo mío que por sus pecados ha tenido que vérselas con Bailón, que éste es el vivo retrato de la sibila de Cumas, pintada por Miguel Angel, con las demás señoras sibilas y las profetas, en el maravilloso techo de la Capilla Sixtina. Parece, en efecto, una vieja de raza titánica que lleva en su ceño todas las iras celestiales. El perfil de Bailón y el brazo y pierna, como troncos añosos; el forzudo tórax y las posturas que sabía tomar, alzando una pataza y enarcando el brazo, le asemejaban a esos figurones que andan por los techos de las catedrales despatarrados sobre una nube. Lástima que no fuera modo que anduviéramos en cueros para que luciese en toda su gallardía académica este ángel de cornisa. (22)

To ensure that nearly all readers are able to solicit a familiar image, the narrator cites not one "vivo retrato" of Bailón but three: a "dissolute" Dante, a robust sibyl of the Sistine Chapel paintings, and an angel on a cathedral ceiling.[57] Ostensibly, this device should "harden" the mental image that readers form of this extravagant character and render him manageable; it should function like a mold that descends *deus ex machina* upon this fictional being and suddenly creates a solid image set in relief.

But of course, as soon as the mold has set, the reader's image of Bailón begins to dissolve in the acid of irony. Through a mock-epic tone and outrageous exaggeration, the narrator shows himself in the act of employing this "cheap trick" of characterization. He begins the description with a denial, a list of false likenesses—of *cura, fraile,* and *torero*—to set up the reader for the revelation of "true" likeness. Then, the narrator offers readers the choice of three visual images, all ostensibly (but impossibly) interchangeable, for he at once likens Bailón to a male figure—Dante, a female figure—the sybil, and an androgynous figure—the angel. The ludicrousness of these untenable equivalences is finally carried to its absurd conclusion by the tongue-in-cheek comment: "Lástima que no anduviéramos en cueros para que luciese en toda su gallardía académica este ángel de cornisa." Presumably, the narrator is referring only to the last of the three possible likenesses, that of the angel; but after being forced to visualize Bailón as male, as female, and now as an androgynous cherub, readers may catch themselves in the act of trying to imagine the anatomical features borne by this ambiguous and impossible figure.

So while the device of evoking familiar visual images seemingly serves to discipline an excessive, contradictory character, here it functions only partially; for the use of irony works to sabotage the disciplinary control.[58] Irony, however, may not necessarily revoke discipline, but rather mitigate it, making it more bearable. Whenever literary devices become over-used, hackneyed, the classic remedy is to render them ironic and thereby absorb their "naiveté" (Barthes, S/Z 139). Rather than ceasing to employ those conventional devices, a narrator will use them duplicitously, through ironic double-voicing: on the most immediate level, one voice does its duty, while a more distant, implied (and superior) voice mocks the entire endeavor. I will hypothesize that irony and realism work hand in glove, that for realist writers, irony served as a final resort. The realist project rested on the presumption that language could accurately represent objective reality, that signification could be pinned down and disciplined. But in practice, realist writers inevitably found themselves embroiled in the equivocality and polysemy of language. Irony allowed realists to have it both ways: to keep faith with the realist project, while simultaneously (and only partially) conceding its untenability. Irony allows for a provisional and limited plurality of meaning, a partial deconstruction. The denoted ending to a chain of connotation—Bailón's physical likeness, for example—may ultimately be left open, and the very process of trying to impose a final meaning may be mocked, but the realist enterprise itself is never fundamentally called in question. Given that irony by definition creates a superior overtone, and that it targets a victim, it may actually be quite compatible with the disciplinary strategies of a panoptic narrator.

Reading in Counterpoint

The realist disciplinary project carries within it the seeds of its own undoing. In the attempt to describe and document accurately an objective reality, the realist narrator inevitably incites excessive and ungovernable chains of connotation. This potential loss of narrative control may be less evident in the areas of plot and setting; for on that mental stage where readers reenact the novel, plotting is governed by codes of chronology and causality, while setting is regulated by common knowledge—geographical, historical, and cultural. Readers' visualizations of characters are similarly governed by codified knowledge regarding human psychology and behavior patterns. But perhaps owing to the myriad possibilities for human idiosyncrasy, character, among all the elements of narrative, is least amenable to disciplinary control. Consequently, the character-images formed in readers' minds tend to swell beyond the control of the hegemonic narrator. Through various ploys, however ironized, he may try to reassert his authority, to rein in these expansive swarms of signs, to halt the connotative chains by pointing readers along codified paths and towards a designated ending. Denotation, as "the last of the connotations," as an attempt to "close the reading," occurs whenever readers name a trait, behavior, or fixed image (Barthes, *S/Z* 9). In doing so, they subjugate meaning, censor polysemy, and thereby join in the disciplinary enterprise of the realist novel.

In a sense it is impossible to refrain from participating in this novelistic disciplinary regime. The realist novel posits a complicitous, disciplined reader, one conversant with cultural codes and stereotypes, one who responds predictably to textual signals and who will serve as a site for the convocation of all the solicited intertexts. While the realist narrator may politely invite readers to partake in the panoptic gaze, he provides no alternative positions. To refuse absolutely such a position would be to read nonsensically, randomly, disjunctively—amounting to a failed mental performance of the novel.

I would argue then for a partial acquiesence in the realist project: to accept the realist pretense under false pretenses, to assume a complicitous posture under imposture; in other words, to partake in the narrator's panoptic gaze and to observe the machinations of novelistic discipline, but without falling entirely under disciplinary control. With one foot in the panoptic watchtower, and one foot outside, we might occupy a double-stance and read in counterpoint, duplicitously and irresponsibly. While cognizant of the disciplinary structure, we might allow meaning to circulate and play around its scaffolding. The game would be to catch discipline in the act, to allow ourselves as readers to be partially disciplined while watching with amusement—a somewhat masochistic activity perhaps, but not without its pleasures.

Of course, an ironic reading, like ironic writing, is essentially contrapuntal. Just as Galdós's narrator, even as he employs the conventions of realism, creates a distant, ironic overtone, so readers might undertake a conventional reading alongside a distanced, ironic reading. When reading character, for example, we might accept with tongue in cheek the realist pretense of displaying ready-made characters, while also remaining conscious of our own productive role in the creation of fictional beings. But irony, whether as double-reading or double-writing, constitutes a limited counterpoint; it is generally bisemantic rather than polysemantic.

Criticism, of course, involves a double-reading. Critics, as professional readers, will allow themselves to experience as common readers the effects produced by the text while simultaneously analyzing from a distance the techiques that create those effects. But as traditionally practiced, criticism has often sought to pin down meanings and to arrest polysemy. Barthes has proposed instead a criticism that would "yield to an expanding nomination," for "expansion is the very movement of meaning: the meaning skids, recovers itself, and advances simultaneously, we should rather describe it through its expansions, lexical transcendence, the generic word it continually attempts to join" (S/Z 92-93).

To read expansively would involve going beyond the double perspective of an ironic or critical reading and to explore the possibilities of a multi-level reading. In such a contrapuntal reading various perspectives might interweave and oscillate in three, four, or multi-part inventions, in harmony and in dissonance. We might seek various, shifting stances, gaze through multiple perspectives, and listen for the polyphony rising from the textual pastiche. Simultaneously obedient and disobedient as we follow the connotative chains, we might seek to go beyond the generic ending, or to stray off the coded paths. As we form images of minutely described characters, we might take pleasure both in their piecemeal construction and in their decomposition under the weight of excess minutiae. And as the character-image expands in our minds, we might follow with amusement the narrator's efforts to rein in his unruly fictional being. In the case of Benjamín Jarnés's vanguardist novella, "Andrómeda," to be examined in the following chapter, we will share the amusement of a narrator as he parodically dramatizes this process of expansively reading character.

NOTES

1. A number of critics have analyzed the significance of this initial paragraph. Both Diane Urey and Paula W. Shirley demonstrate how it ironizes the conventions of narrating and reading. For other analyses of this paragraph see: Carmen Blanco Villalba, B.J. Zeidner Bäuml, Jennifer Lowe, Pierre I. Ullman (both articles), and Ricardo Gullón (*Galdós novelista moderno* 245). Throughout the chapter and notes, I will cite only the critical works that bear most directly on my approach. For further sources, see Hensley C. Woodbridge's annotated bibliographies of galdosian criticism through 1980.
2. Refer to José Schraibman for a discussion of how the Inquisition serves as subtext to the *Torquemada* series.
3. According to Foucault, "power and knowledge directly imply one another. . . . [T]here is no power relation without the correlative constitution of a field of knowledge, nor any knowledge that does not presuppose and constitute at the same time power relations" (*Discipline* 27).
4. Some critics consider Balzac a precursor rather than a "true" realist, either because he did not consistently practice the precepts of realism, or because the term itself was not applied to literature until after his death. Refer to A.J. Mount's essay for a discussion of Balzac's status as a realist. Also see René Wellek for a history of the term "realism" as a philosophic and literary concept. I consider Balzac to be both a founder and early practitioner of realism. His introduction to the *Human Comedy* can be read as a manifesto that sought to establish scientific, empirical grounds for a realist art. If critics and literary historians were to insist upon complete conformity to a list of characteristics as a criteria for admission to the fold, we would be hard pressed to find a true realist author.
5. Critics and literary historians, past and present, have generally agreed as to the fundamental characteristics of realism: the profession of objectivity, a commitment to a scientific view of humankind, obedience to a doctrine of natural causality, the serious treatment of everyday life, the representation of middle and lower-class subjects, and the embedding of characters and events in society and in contemporary history. However, critics have long differed as to whether realism should be viewed as a perennial mode or as a period concept. Erich Auerbach and René Wellek offer similar definitions of realism, but the former (with some qualifications) views realism as a perennial mode, one that has reappeared throughout the history of Western literature. Wellek, in contrast, considers realism as a period concept that reached its fullest development in the nineteenth century. See Auerbach's *Mimesis* and J.P Stern's *On Realism* for elaborations of this perennial view of realism. See Stephen Heath, George Becker, and Wallace Martin for summations of both sides of this controversy. Martin also offers a sum-

mary of more recent critical views of realism. Darío Villanueva, in *Teorías del realismo literario*, provides a broad overview of realism, as well as case studies within the Spanish context. For studies that focus on Spanish realism, see: Kay Engler, *The Structure of Realism: The Novelas Contemporáneas of Benito Perez Galdós*; Gustavo Correa, *Realidad, ficción, y símbolo en las novelas de Pérez Galdós*; Germán Gullón, *La novela del XIX: Estudio sobre su evolución formal* and *La novela como acto imaginativo*; Ignacio Javier López, *Realismo y ficción*; William H. Shoemaker, *The Novelistic Art of Galdós* (vol. I); Jeremy T. Medina, *Spanish Realism: The Theory and Practice of a Concept*; and Francisco Ayala, "Sobre el realismo en la literatura." In addition, refer to John Kronik, "La retórica del realismo: Galdós y Clarín," and other essays in Yvan Lisourgues's collection, *Realismo y naturalismo en España en la segunda mitad del siglo XIX*. For examples of varied poststructuralist approaches to realism, see: Roland Barthes, *S/Z*; Leo Bersani, *A Future for Astyanax*; Nicholas Boyle and Martin Swales, *Realism in European Literature*; Rosalind Coward and John Ellis, *Language and Materialism*; Steven Cohan and Linda Shires, *Telling Stories*; and Lilian Furst, *All is True*. For post-structuralist approach to Galdosian realism, see: Akiko Tsuchiya, *Images of the Sign* and Hazel Gold, *The Reframing of Realism*. For Foucauldian approaches to the realist novel, refer to: D.A. Miller *The Novel and the Police*; and Mark Seltzer, *Henry James and the Art of Power*.

6. Lennard Davis in *Resisting Novels* draws a connection between European imperialism and the eighteenth- and nineteenth-century novel: "One has the impression that between 1750 and 1850 the entire world was painted and sketched in detail, mapped accurately, and described, so that the visible world now had its correlate in the pages of books and the surfaces of canvasses. The conquering of the world and the establishment of Empire was reproduced, transcribed, contained and organized—largely through explorers' and novelists' use of description and painters' use of landscape—to become what Roland Barthes called in another context an 'empire of signs' " (75).

7. Ian Watt, in *The Rise of the Novel* discusses the growth of a reading public in England along with the development of publishing houses, newspapers, lending libraries and book stores. For sociological histories of the nineteenth-century Spanish novel and its reading public see the works by Juan Ignacio Ferreras, Leonardo Romero Tobar, Jean-François Botrel.

8. Stephen Gilman in *Galdós and the Art of the European Novel* discusses how the nineteenth-century novel created its readers. After an apprenticeship, the reader acquired "novelistic consciousness": "one understood oneself novelistically; one behaved novelistically; and one was ready to participate fully in . . . the novelistic consciousness of one's age" (186).

9. In *The Pleasure of the Text* Roland Barthes extends this metaphor of the textual web: "*Text* means *Tissue*; but whereas hitherto we have always taken this tissue as a product, a ready-made veil, behind which lies, more or less hidden, meaning (truth), we are now emphasizing, in the tissue, the generative idea that the text is made, is worked out in a perpetual interweaving; lost in this tissue—

this texture—the subject unmakes himself, like a spider dissolving in the constructive secretions of its web. Were we fond of neologisms, we might define the theory of the text as an *hyphology* (*hyphos* is the tissue and the spider's web)" (64).

10. The term *intertext* has variously "been used for a text drawing on other texts, for a text thus drawn upon, and for the relationship between both," according to Baldick's *Concise Oxford Dictionary of Literary Terms* (112). Throughout this study I use *intertext* to refer to the *text drawn upon*.

11. The term *intertextuality* should be understood in this very broad sense, as refering not only to *literary* texts, but also to *cultural* texts—to those texts inscribed not on paper but in our consciousness. The term derives from Julia Kristeva's adaptation of M.M. Bakhtin's concept, *dialogism*. According to Bakhtin, "for the novelist working in prose, the object is always entangled in someone else's discourse about it, it is already present with qualifications, an object of dispute that is conceptualized and evaluated variously, inseparable from the heteroglot social apperception of it. The novelist speaks of this 'already qualified world' in a language that is heteroglot and internally dialogized" (330). Unfortunately, many users of the term intertextuality have limited its meaning by considering only the resonances of other *literary* texts within a given work.

12. Here Coward and Ellis concisely summarize the Roland Barthes' view of intertextuality as expressed in *S/Z*, "From Work to Text," and *The Pleasure of the Text*.

13. David Lodge proposes a similar "working definition of realism": "the representation of experience in a manner which approximates closely to descriptions of similar experience in nonliterary texts of the same culture." He contends that the realist novel "modeled its language on historical writing of various kinds, formal and informal: biography, autobiography, travelogue, letters, diaries, journalism and historiography" (25). While I would concur with Lodge, I would add to his list those texts not written on paper, but said (and thought) every day in homes, marketplaces, workplaces, and streets. As indicated in the previous note, Bakhtin's concept of dialogism, as incorporated into the novel, encompasses all these types of texts.

14. In the interviews published in *Power/Knowledge*, Foucault responds to these criticisms and allows for the possibility of localized resistances to power. I would argue that Foucault's conception of power has never been as monolithic and irresistible as some have claimed. He regards disciplinary power as a "network of relations, constantly in tension, in activity, rather than a privilege that one might possess" (*Discipline* 26). These power relations "are not univocal; they define innumerable points of confrontation, focuses of instablity, each of which has its own risks of conflict, of struggles, and of an at least temporary inversion of the power relations" (*Discipline* 27).

15. In *A Future for Astyanax*, Leo Bersani addresses this dual function of the realist novel in somewhat different terms, starting from the premise that "the realist novelist is intensely aware of writing in a context of social fragmentation"

(60). In Bersani's view "realistic fiction serves nineteenth-century society by providing it with strategies for containing (and repressing) its disorder within significantly structured stories about itself" (63).

16. Traditionally, the rise of the novel in the eighteenth and nineteenth centuries has been associated with the rise of individualism. According to Ian Watt, "The novel's serious concern with the daily lives of ordinary people seems to depend upon two important general conditions: the society must value every individual highly enough to consider him the proper subject of its serious literature: and there must be enough variety of belief and action among ordinary people for a detailed account of them to be of interest to other ordinary people, the readers of novels . . . [T]he concept of individualism . . . posits a whole society mainly governed by the idea of every individual's intrinsic independence" (60). Watt, I believe, somewhat overstates the case for the independence of the individual character in the novel and downplays the control exerted by fictional societies upon characters.

17. Michel de Certeau in an article on Foucault's *Discipline and Punish* explains this paradox in terms of "vampirization." He suggests that the democratic, humanitarian, and reformist projects at the end of the eighteenth century were "'colonized' or 'vampirized' by those disciplinary procedures that have since increasingly organized the social realm" (*Heterologies* 185). Although his metaphor is colorful and interesting, it attributes to discipline an insidiousness which may be inappropriate. I rather see discipline and juridical liberties in an open symbiotic relationship, working hand in hand, each relying on the other.

18. Georg Lukacs has written extensively on the importance of type in the realist novel. For Lukacs, "The central aesthetic problem of realism is the adequate presentation of tne complete human personality" (7). This is only possible "if the writer attempts to create types" and thereby establishes "the organic, indissoluble connection between man as a private individual and man as a social being" (8). Lukacs assumes the possibility of a nonproblematic synthesis of the universal and the particular in the type. According to Wellek, Lukacs merely reformulated Hegel's "concrete universal" or "ideal type" (239).

19. Peter Demetz in "Balzac and the Zoologists" discusses the philosophical evolution of the concept of type. He also considers the implications of Balzac's application of biological types to social types in the novel: "The modern novelist, Balzac implies, follows the methodogical example of the natural scientist by closely observing a multitude of individuals, isolating their common traits, separating them from the individual case, and concentrating them in a new model inclusive of all the individuals of the group, or class" (407). This concept of type would correspond to Foucault's notion of discipline as a technology of identification, classification and ranking.

20. However, by 1897, in his speech to the Royal Academy, Galdós placed more emphasis on the individualization of character. Having observed the leveling effect of the expanding middle class, he noted the disappearance of "los caracteres genéricos que simbolizaban grupos capitales de la familia humana. Hasta los

rostros humanos no son ya lo que eran aunque parezca absurdo decirlo. Ya no encontraréis las fisonomías que, al modo de máscaras moldeadas por el convencionalismo de las costumbres, representaban las pasiones, las ridiculeces, los vicios y virtudes. Lo poco que el pueblo conserva de típico y pintoresco se destiñe, se borra" (*Ensayos* 162). For Galdós this disappearance of identifiable types was an opportunity for literature to depict men in their "castiza verdad": "perdemos los tipos, pero el hombre se nos revela mejor, y el Arte se avalora sólo con dar a los seres imaginarios vida más humana que social" (164).

21. Ricardo Gullón in *Galdós: Novelista moderno* discusses Galdós's tendency to create excessive, extraordinary, and marginalized characters. Sherman Eoff also remarks on the number of nervously unstable characters in Galdós's novels and notes the author's interest in abnormal psychology. For further references, see the first volume of William H. Shoemaker's comprehensive study of Galdós, in which he summarizes a number of critical works written on this topic.

22. Balzac in his introduction to the *Human Comedy* likened this procedure to the work of a zoologist: "social species have always existed, and will always exist, just as there are zoological species. If Buffon could produce a magnificent work by attempting to represent in a book the whole realm of zoology, was there not room for a work of the same kind on society?" (2). See also: Peter Demetz, "Balzac and the Zoologists: A Concept of Type."

23. Leo Bersani discusses the importance of "readable characters" in the realist novel: "[The nineteenth-century novelist] in spite of his troubling heroes and heroines . . . is in fact insisting on the readability of the human personality. The apparent chaos of social life is a relatively harmless illusion, and the writer thus sends his society a comforting message about its fundamental stability and order. There are predictable continuities among different people's desires as well as among the desires of each individual; behavior can be interpreted, structured, 'plotted' " (69).

24. Luisa Elena Delgado discusses how the *Torquemada* series calls attention to this contractual, commercial aspect of narrative.

25. According to Barthes the "readerly text," or "classic text," places the reader in the role of consumer. In contrast, the goal of the "writerly text" is to make the reader a producer. While readerly texts "make up the enormous mass of our literature," writerly texts exist rarely, "by accident, fleetingly, obliquely in certain limit works" (*S/Z* 4-5). Rosalind Coward and John Ellis, in a chapter concerning *S/Z*, also elaborate upon this consumer/producer distinction.

26. D.A. Miller in *The Novel and the Police* discusses panoptic vision in the nineteenth-century British novel.

27. Balzac was aware of this cellular mode of organization. He writes in his intoduction to the *Human Comedy*: "This crowd of actors, of characters, this multitude of lives, needed a setting—if I may be pardoned the expression, a gallery. Hence the very natural division . . . into Scenes of Private Life, of Provincial Life of Parisian, Political, Military and Country Life" (12). Regarding the reappearance of characters in various novels, Galdós borrowed this device from

Balzac. Torquemada, for example, appears in four previous novels: *El doctor Centeno, La de Bringas, Lo prohibido*, and *Fortunata y Jacinta*.

28. Concerning the irony in this quotation, Diane Urey remarks: "The 'inocentes relaciones' are not that at all; all statements even individual words, are potentially misleading, especially the narrator's direct remarks to the reader. The reader may be deceived if he is not continually on guard for this ironic *vraisemblance*" (100).

29. Miller develops his concept of "boxed-in characters" in a chapter on *David Copperfield*. He also discusses the implications of the novel's box-like structure, making it a series of nested boxes *en abime*.

30. For a discussion if the importance of milieu in characterizing Torquemada, refer to: Lisa Pasto-Crosby, "Unconventional Character Introduction in the Torquemada Series."

31. Lennard Davis includes a chapter on novelistic space in *Resisting Novels*. He contends that the detailed description of "deep space" in the realist novel reflects the bourgeoisie's concern with property, with inventories of possessions.

32. Throughout this study I make no fundamental distinction between visual images and verbal texts. I maintain that we perceive images "textually," in art and in life, as codified systems of signs.

33. Regarding the disciplinary role of the intrusive narrator in Galdós's novels, Paula S. Shirley comments: "The narrator, dramatized by his use of 'yo,' functions as the organizer of the story, commenting on or signaling his expositional choices or purposes. In this function it is the power of the narrator as *titiritero* that is clearly demonstrated. He indicates his dominion over the reader by making decisions he alone can make but nods in the reader's direction by including him in the expositional movements. This technique appears to place the reader in a privileged position within the narrative enterprise" (78-79).

34. See Kay Engler for a discussion of how the narrator's voice and vision are refracted by indirect free style, character speech, and interior monologue in Galdós's novels, principally in *Fortunata y Jacinta* and *La desheredada*.

35. N. Katherine Hayles in *The Cosmic Web* discusses twentieth- century developments in science that demonstrate the untenability of the empiricist separation of observer and observed. She also shows how the literary strategies in recent narrative reflect this new world view—"the field concept"—which assumes the interconnectedness of subject and object, the indeterminacy of truth, and the self-referentiality of language.

36. See Jennifer Lowe's discussion of the shifting viewpoint of the narrator in *Torquemada en la hoguera*.

37. Wolfgang Iser describes this phenomenon in similar terms: "As the reader's wandering viewpoint travels between all these segments, its constant switching during the time flow of reading intertwines them, thus bringing forth a network of perspectives, within which each perspective opens a view not only of others, but also of the intended imaginary object. Hence, no single textual perspective can be

equated with this imaginary object, of which it forms only one aspect" ("Interaction" 113).

38. William Sherzer contends that the first-person narrator of *Torquemada en la hoguera* is a character in the novel. In my view, notwithstanding the opening phrase—"Voy a contar"—and the narrator's occasional self-placement in the fictional world, generally, he maintains the position of a detached, omniscient observer. According to Kay Engler, only two of Galdós's *Novelas contemporáneas* have true first-person narrators, and both of those are autobiographical novels, *Lo prohibido* and *El amigo manso* (140). Stephen Gilman, in "Cuando Galdós habla con sus personajes," discusses the author's tendency to occasionally and momentarily commune with his characters.

39. According to J.J. Macklin, Galdós's realism is plural and perspectivistic: by allowing a multiplicity of perspectives (from the viewpoints of various characters), Galdós creates a sense of diversity and complexity in the fictional world. Other critics, notably Gustavo Correa, have commented on Galdós perspectivism, often attributing it to Cervantine influence. I would concur with Kay Engler's view: while Galdós's narrator often temporarily allows readers "to perceive the world directly through the consciousness of another, . . . he always returns to manifest his presence" (68). Moreover, he generally subordinates the perspectives of others to his dominant point of view.

40. Wolfgang Iser differentiates between active and passive synthesis in reading. Active synthesis involves explicit assessment or judgment on the part of the reader. Passive synthesis, including the formation of mental images, is passive in that it is largely an unconcious activity (*Act of Reading* 135-39).

41. I rely here upon Shlomith Rimmon-Kenan's translations of Gérard Genette's terms *histoire* and *récit*, as *story* and *text*: "*Story* designates the narrated events, abstracted from their disposition in the text and reconstructed in their chronological order"; *text* is "what we read," the "spoken or written discourse which undertakes the telling" of events (3). I consider Rimmon-Kenan's corresponding terms, *story character* and *text character*, to be useful, although I recognize that strictly speaking, the two phenomena cannot be separated. Connotation occurs instantaneously: as soon as we begin to read, we are already forming a mental object. It is therefore impossible truly to demarcate a writer's instructions about character and a reader's construction of a character.

42. For a more elaborate discussion of how readers form images of character by attaching semes to a proper name, see: Roland Barthes, *S/Z*, pp. 190-92.

43. Both P. Manuel Suárez and Luis Fernández-Cifuentes consider the parallels between Balzac's Gobseck and Torquemada. J.J. Alfieri discusses the representation of avarice throughout Galdós's novels, with the emphasis on the *Torquemada* series. Jeanne Brownlow also discusses the resonances in Torquemada's character of various literary misers. Dimitri Radulian discusses both the typical and atypical aspects of Torquemada as usurer. For a general comparison of the novelistic art of Galdós, Balzac, and Dickens, see Charles David Ley. Stephen

Gilman in *Galdos and the Art of the European Novel* considers Galdos's novels as a dialogue with other novels by Balzac, Dickens, Zola, and Cervantes.

44. Of Theophrastus's thirty sketches, four of them describe in similar terms the avaricious character type: "Shameless Greedy Man," "Pennypincher," "Stingy Man," and "Basely Covetous Man." Horace includes brief portraits of greedy and miserly men in his satires (1.1, 1.2, 2.2). And Juvenal describes the miser in his fourteenth satire," On Education in Avarice." In seventeenth-century France La Bruyère translated Theophrastus's sketches and authored many of his own in *Characters*. See J.S. Smeed's study, *The Theophrastan 'Character,'* which examines the tradition of character writing in seventeenth- and early eighteenth-century England, France, and Germany.

45. The tradition of European genre-painting also played a role in crystallizing the cultural image of the usurer. P. Manuel Suárez describes one such painting: "Por ejemplo, Marinus van Roejmerswaelen ha fijado sobre el lienzo la fealdad y la ansiedad del usurero bajo las facciones del hombre con toca verde en su cuadro 'Dos usureros en su despacho.' Nada falta en el retrato: los dedos largos están cumpliendo el gesto desesperado por el cual se trae todo hacia sí; la piel de la cara amarillenta; la pupila dilatada por los tormentos del cálculo. Nada, en este cuadro, autoriza el menor indicio de humanidad. La boca, entreabierta, deja ver unos dientes de tiburón en la actitud de acecho. Todo en una palabra indica el dominio completo de la pasión del oro sobre ese desdichado individuo" (376).

46. In *The Jew in the Novels of Benito Pérez Galdós*, Sara Schyfter considers Torquemada as a representation of the *converso*, as an outsider trying to buy his way into Spanish society. According to Schyfter, "Galdós presents Torquemada as a caricature of the fears that foster him: a burlesque farce of the projections of Spain upon the Jew . . . [T]he confrontation with the burlesque and, at times, sub-human Torquemada, allows the novelist to ritually release a latent antisemitism of his culture, to examine it and to place it in its proper perspective" (56-57).

47. According to Barthes, "farce is an ambiguous form, since it permits us to read within it the figure of what it mockingly repeats" (*Roland Barthes* 88).

48. Ideally, in Barthes' view, the effect of this use of quotation marks would "be to erase little by little these external signs, while keeping the frozen word from returning to a state of nature; but to do this, the stereotyped discourse must be caught up in a *mimesis* (novel or theater): it is then the characters themselves who function as quotation marks" (*Roland Barthes* 89).

49. The description of Torquemada in *Fortunata y Jacinta* continues: "'Torquemada había sido alabardero en su mocedad, y conservando el bigote y perilla, que eran ya entrecanos, tenía un no sé qué de eclesiástico, debido sin duda a la mansedumbre afectada y dulzona, y a un cierto subir y bajar de párpados con que adulteraba su grosería innata. La cabeza se le inclinaba siempre al lado derecho. Su estatura era alta, mas no arrogante; su cabeza calva, crasa y escamosa, con un enrejado de pelos mal extendidos para cubrirla" (222).

50. Wolfgang Iser describes the reading of character in similar terms, but he asserts that this process of compilation is not additive; rather, it is a process of

synthesis: "in imagining the character, we do not try to seize upon one particular aspect, but we are made to view him as a synthesis of all aspects. The image produced is therefore always more than the facet given in one particular reading moment" (*Act of Reading* 138). Barthes would probably agree that in the readerly text, conventionally read, readers passively synthesize a character's features and traits, but he argues in *S/Z* for a more active and expansive practice of reading.

51. Here Barthes cites a description of La Zambinella in Balzac's "Sarrasine" and refers to the figure of the *blazon*, which predicates a single subject—in this case, beauty—upon a list of anatomical attributes (*S/Z* 114).

52. See Diane Urey's study, *Galdós and the Irony of Language*, for a discussion of irony and parody in the characterization of Valentín.

53. In his article, "Galdós and the Grotesque," John Kronik argues cogently that the "grotesque representation of Tía Roma prevents any identification with her as a person and therefore makes her role all the more divinatory and her imperial spirit untied to earthly strictures" (47). For F. García Sarriá, Tía Roma "representa un cristianismo primitivo y puro" (109). García Sarriá also points out the connection between Tía Roma and San Jerónimo.

54. For discussions of the excessiveness of Bailón's characterization see: F. García Sarriá and B.S. Zeidner Bäumal.

55. Refer to Hazel Gold's study of intertextuality in Bailón's *folletos*. She considers Bailón's texts to be emblematic of the novel itself, as a "highly overcoded literary edifice built upon intertextual operations" (32).

56. Elsewhere in this novel the narrator resorts to this trick when describes a beggar to whom Torquemada gives his old cape: "Cara más venerable no se podía encontrar sino en las estampas del *Año Cristiano*. Tenía la barba erizada y la frente llena de arrugas, como San Pedro; el cráneo terso y dos rizados mechones blancos en las sienes" (41). In *Fortunata y Jacinta* the narrator describes the child Pitusín by referring to the Christ child painted by Murillo (126). Also in this novel José Izquierdo, blessed with a noble visage, becomes a successful artists' model and appears in various paintings as God the Father, el Rey don Jaime, Nabucodonosor, and Hernán Cortés (576). For citations of the many allusions to visual arts in Galdós's novels, see Peter A. Bly, *Vision and the Visual Arts in Galdós*.

57. In a discussion of the intertextual relationships between the *Torquemada* series and the Divine Comedy, Jeanne Brownlow names Bailón as one of Torquemada's would-be guides or mentors—his "Virgils." She also discusses the congruences between Comte's positivism and Dante, and the influences of both upon Galdós's text.

58. For a comprehensive analysis of irony in several of Galdós's novels, including *Torquemada en la hoguera*, see Diane Urey, *Galdós and the Irony of Language*. In Urey's view, however, irony has a far more subversive effect upon the realist project, than I am willing to concede. For a brief study of the ironic narrative voice in the *Torquemada* series, see Paula Shirley, "The Narrator/Reader Relationship in Torquemada, or How to Read a Galdosian Novel."

II. THE IMPOSSIBLE CHARACTER: BENJAMÍN JARNÉS'S "ANDRÓMEDA"

> Much reading is indeed like girl-watching, a simple expense of spirit. (Geoffrey Hartman, *The Fate of Reading* 248)
>
> [W]hat is man that the itinerary of his desire creates such a text? (Gayatri Chakrovorty Spivak, "Displacement and the Discourse of Reading" 186)

"El cuadro excesivo"

Benjamín Jarnés's vanguardist novel, "Andrómeda" (1926), stages the act of reading, revealing it as a process of infinite allusion through an intertextual field.[1] When we read the opening scenes, we envision a young topographer, Julio, strolling in the countryside late at night. His profession is significant, for even at leisure, Julio is a demarcator of boundaries. As he walks, he listens intently and engages in a curious labor of classification: he divides all the nocturnal sounds into categories, determines their origins, and names them: "Era urgente depurar la noche, tan turbia, corregir aquella indisciplina de masas vibratorias, romper aquella espesa malla de resonancias" (11). By imposing discipline upon the cacaphony, Julio is *reading*. By differentiating, classifying, and naming, he is interpreting signs by referring to other signs. At first his act of reading is overtly intertextual, for he identifies sounds in terms of prior readings of literary texts. As he passes through the tall reeds, they produce "un voluptuoso cuchicheo de amantes verlanianos," and when he steps upon dry twigs they repeat "un crujido de huesos, ya ensayado en el capítulo XXXVII de Ezequiel" (12). Once having classified "los ruidos aprendidos en la literatura," he is left with others "de más difícil clasificación" (12). Among these unclassified sounds is an intermittent cry, a lament, without "exacta filiación zoológica" (13). He traces its origin to a grove of olive trees, but before proceeding, he pauses and contemplates el bosquecillo gris, olvidado ya de la melodía lamentable, que se filtraba por los troncos. Solía hacer lo mismo en los conciertos. En vez de oír el programa, prefería gozar de la opulenta línea de los contrabajos, del vientrecillo rubio de los violines, del voluptuoso descote de la arpista. (13-14)

This passage alerts us, as we read Julio reading, to a shift from the aural to the visual mode of perception. His sensuous comparison of string instruments with women's bodies prepares us for the coming scene, in which he discovers the origin of the mysterious sound: "El lamento salía de una boca despintada de mujer atada al árbol. A Julio no le sorprendió verla completamente desnuda. Siempre la había visto así en los cuadros del Museo y en el tomo quinto de la Enciclopedia Espasa" (16). Just as Julio has read the nocturnal sounds of the countryside in terms of various intertexts, he now reads this naked woman by alluding to a well-known painting by Rubens, "Andrómeda."[2]

Julio, in reading this woman by an overt act of allusion, is comically dramatizing what generally occurs in our reading practices: we read characters by alluding constantly to our repertoires of cultural images of men and women. It goes without saying that our readings of character are always gendered (although what goes without saying often goes unexamined), since the fictional texts we read provide us exclusively with characters labeled male or female. Arguably, androgynous characters exist, but they too bear the marks of gender, for in naming a character androgynous, we must specify the typically masculine or feminine traits combined in that fictional being.[3] And as for the "universal" character of nonfictional discourse—the human subject—he, needless to say, derives from a masculine prototype. In literature, as in social life, genderless characters are impossible creatures.

Julio's predicament, in being born to read, then is our predicament. Whether in our readings of life, or in our readings of books, whenever we perceive and interpret characters, we must read allusively and categorically. Albeit semiconsciously, we continually refer to the categories of gender, each consisting of a vast composite of common knowledge about males and females.[4] Inhabiting these broad categories are various masculine/feminine prototypes with corresponding sets of traits, behaviors, speech patterns, and appearances. Never static and forever strained by internal contradictions, the categories of gender may undergo a constant process of revision and realignment, that may either enhance or undermine their stability. But their categorical imperative works always to govern our readings, to order and constrain our visions of fictional and social beings.

Writers, of course, in composing their texts, must simultaneously *read* them. As they write (at once consciously and unconsciously), they form mental images of their characters by referring to paradigms of gender difference. Given that future readers will more or less share the same cultural models, their readings will tend to resemble a writer's initial readings. So when writers characterize, they "quote" textual fragments drawn from received knowledge regarding males and females. These citations in turn work as signals that direct readers along well-worn connotative paths, towards familiar texts inscribed in their minds.[5] Various already-written, already-read texts are therein summoned to a reader's mental stage where they cluster around a character's proper name. Such migrating textual fragments may derive from anterior readings of verbal texts—books, newspapers, and magazines—as well as from readings of experience, themselves preconditioned by verbal texts.[6] Or they may derive from visual texts—from the codified representations of men and women in painting, sculpture, photography, cinema, television, and advertising.[7] A multitude of heterogeneous (and often contradictory) texts inhabit the paradigms of gender that condition our imaginations, our thoughts, our readings, and our social practices.[8]

Julio, our dramatized reader, initially selects a single text—the Andrómeda painting and myth—through which to interpret his situation. His reading would seem immediately to fix our reading of the scene, to limit its powers of suggestibility by placing it in a specific mythological frame. Certainly the mythological reference directs us to complete to the last detail our own visualization of the scene; it instructs us to search our storehouses of received knowledge and to summon the Andrómeda myth along with images of Rubens's robust female figures. In addition, the reference may bring to mind countless other mythological or allegorial paintings that depict a nude woman in a natural setting; or it may evoke scenes from medieval romance, as when a knight encounters Temptation personified as a beautiful nude woman. But simultaneously, the reference creates ironic dissonance in readers' minds, for clearly we are not entirely within the realm of myth or romance. When a vacationing topographer in the mid-nineteen twenties finds a naked woman tied up in the woods, a purely mythological reading seems inadequate, and other less innocent interpretations may come to mind. Julio's reading of the victim as Andrómeda proves to be an ironic misreading. And the scene of the naked character becomes a "cuadro excesivo," for it generates connotations that spin out in various directions, evoking a surplus of incompatible intertexts (34).

As the narration continues, Julio unties the victim, wraps his jacket around her, runs into town for a car and driver, then returns and takes her to the city. Early the next morning, they proceed from shop to shop, and under instructions from the victim, whom he has named Star, Julio purchases hosiery, undergarments, shoes, a dress, a hat, and make-up. Gradually Star remakes herself as a modern fashion-plate and is finally ready to emerge from the car. At this point Julio recognizes her as Carmela, a well-known "creadora de danzas apócrifas de Oriente," and by coincidence, he had been carrying a publicity photo of her in his jacket all along (57). The story can be taken as a wry joke commenting on traditional narrative, for rather than gradually unveiling the truth, this story performs a striptease in reverse.[9]

Clearly the intent and tone of the text is humorous and ironic, but in the beginning scenes, when readers are still searching for an interpretive frame, the humor may produce a jarring effect. For readers still reading somewhat "realistically," Julio's wisecracks may seem rather inappropriate to the occasion, given that the victim is obviously distressed. When out of modesty she cries out "¡No avance! ¡No avance!," Julio thinks to himself: "La cautiva le impedía acercarse, como el cicerone detiene al turista a alguna distancia del cuadro de Rubens, para explicarle que 'aquella mujer atada es Elena Fourment.' O quizá se le incitaba a prolongar la contemplación" (17). And after introducing himself, Julio asks jokingly, "¿Dónde está el dragón?" (18). When she fails to comprehend the mythological allusion, Julio responds, "Perdone. Era un tropo" (18). Later as they consider the next course of action, Julio jokingly suggests, "Me desnudaré yo," to which she exclaims, "¡Caballero!" (23).

Notwithstanding the signals to read the novella as a comic modern myth, the image of a naked and bound female inevitably incites erotic connotations, which are explicitly invoked both in Jarnés's "copy" and in Rubens's "original" text. In the painting the naked, vulnerable flesh of Andrómeda fills the canvas: her arms are chained above her head, forcing her breasts and torso forward; her head is thrown back, her mouth is open, her eyes are rolled upward in distress. Behind her a hungry (lascivious) sea dragon approaches, ready to devour (ravish) her, while in the far background Perseus approaches. Contrary to expectation, her body is not tense and rigid in terror, but languid, as if to invite ravishment. The signs in the painting simultaneously evoke two scenarios—a heroic as well as an erotic one—and this same *double entendre* is maintained in Jarnés's text.[10] As we read, regardless of whether we know the painting, the image of a naked woman in bondage may evoke scenarios of sexual fantasy, perhaps of sado-masochism and rape—scenarios drawn from other visual, fictional, and journalistic texts, as well as from the text of "real life." Indeed, this fictional text seems to encourage such speculations, for not until the fourth chapter do we learn that nothing untoward has occurred, that thieves merely robbed her of money, jewelry, and clothing, then tied her to the tree, and escaped with her car and driver.

The narrator, then, maintains a veneer of propriety by banishing all explicit sex and violence from his narration, while continuing to flirt delicately and ironically with eroticism.[11] We can almost see the narrator winking as he describes a series of naughty vignettes. In recounting Julio's attempts, while blindfolded, to untie Star, the narrator comments with ironized relish: "Los dedos de Julio, al avanzar, según el módulo de Edipo, iniciaron su faena, tropezando, cínicamente, con la vanguardia pectoral de la cautiva" (19). And as Julio continues feeling his way, "recorría la más ondulante trayectoria que es posible recorrer, desde el pecho a los tobillos" (20). Protesting this impropriety, Star permits him to remove the blindfold. After Julio unties her arms, she folds them over her breasts, and the narrator comments on: "la actitud tradicional que tan deliciosamente subraya, al intentar velarlas, las parcelas más sugestivas del desnudo" (20-21). In all these descriptions there is a curious double-voicing: certainly the narrator, through the exaggerated delicacy of his language, imposes an ironic distance and reinforces the humorous characterization of Julio; but simultaneously we may detect an undertone of complicity, an evident relish on the part of the narrator as he gazes through his character's eyes and suggestively evokes the scene. These naughty vignettes are spaced intermittently throughout an otherwise quite "proper" narration. Each incident of forwardness is followed by a retreat, and we sense an authorial hesitency, a self-censorship, imposed perhaps by a sense of propriety, or by the requirements of an ironic characterization.

This playful flirtation with the erotic continues as the narrator recounts the long ride to the city. As Star sleeps, the blanket occasionally slips down: "la tela roja fue deslizándose por hombros, brazos y senos, descubriendo, por etapas inesperadas, todo el cuerpo, condenado aquella noche a exposición permanente" (39). In one of these "paréntesis de inocencia edénica," Julio performs a topographical survey of the female body: "Después de confinado el terreno, prefería considerar los desniveles. Ahora, el torso desnudo de Star apenas era para Julio sino cierta reducción, escala de 1: 25.000 de una parcela ondulante, que podría suministrar dos mojones al levantar el acta legal de catastro femenino" (39, 41). At one point Julio goes so far as to lift the blanket and peek under: "Realizaba él, topógrafo de la tierra, todo lo que hubiera podido realizar un médico, topógrafo de la piel. Se comenzó a inventar fórmulas de aproximación. Buscaba pretextos para seguir desembarazando a Star de su envoltura roja" (45). Such behavior in a *redentor* of a female victim cannot be condoned—unless of course her virtue is called into question. So in attempting to read her, to find her identity, Julio leaves open the possibility that she may be a whore, perhaps to justify his ungentlemanly behavior. As she sleeps she murmurs words, which Julio strains to hear, hoping for an erotic revelation:

> Se descubrió, en un revuelo de la manta, uno de los senos.
> Por fin, balbuceó:
> —Doscientas, doscientas.
> Nada más. Enmudeció totalmente después de aquella frase aritmética. Quedó allí truncada su revelación, y Julio nunca pudo saber si aquellas doscientas eran el precio de una factura o de una entrega. (40-41)

Certainly, one effect of these erotic vignettes is to portray Julio humorously as the consummate voyeur. Indeed, in a previous vigil with a sleeping female he had heard "el pintoresco relato de su desfloración," and had then fled, but only "después de haber sacado de la anécdota una minuciosa copia" (40). But undeniably a supplemental effect is to titillate a presumably male reader; I say *male* because the only viewing position provided by the text is that of the masculine voyeur, who may gaze through Julio's eyes upon the naked female character and take his pleasure at her expense.[12]

For the moment, however, my concern is not whether readers, male or female, might find this innuendo-filled narration to be either titillating or offensive. What interests me here is that in narrating the events and in characterizing Julio and Star, the narrator appropriates the common scripts of sexual fantasy, and rewrites them in high literary style. Beneath the somewhat precious language we hear the voices of men in barrooms recounting sexual adventures, or telling off-color jokes. As we read, these various appropriations serve as triggers that lead us to envision scenarios drawn from *novelas rosa* or perhaps from our own sexual fantasies—themselves inscribed in our imaginations by a long tradition of erotic texts, from the *serranas* to farmer's daughter jokes. But always alongside these appropriations from "low art" are those drawn from "high art"—the Rubens painting, the Andrómeda myth, and many others. From the initial scene when Julio "read" nature intertextually, until the end of his night-long adventure with Star, he continues appealing to intertexts to comprehend his situation. At one point, after untying Star, Julio is momentarily stymied, unable to decide upon a course of action until he finds an appropriate textual model: "El diálogo se prolongaba sin sentido alguno. Julio revisaba su álbum de recuerdos, sin hallar en él un trance, mítico o real, que pudiera sugerirle una gallarda continuación de la escena. No encontró modelo, y desconfiaba mucho de su propia originalidad" (22). But more frequently, before each act he performs, Julio succeeds in finding a fitting textual model. When he considers giving Star his jacket, he comments, "Rivalizaré con San Martín" (23). He then contemplates "las impertinencias del terruño, poco dispuesto a servir de alfombra, mientras no se tratase de una égloga" (23). As Star is unable to walk barefoot on the rocky ground, Julio tries but fails to carry her Rubenesque bulk—"un fardo de sesenta kilógramos de belleza, peso neto" (25). He excuses himself saying, "no estoy preparado para un grupo escultórico, ni para una fuga romántica" (25). And in reply, Star also alludes to a literary model, "Pudo aprender en el Tenorio" (25). Both characters then engage in a dialogue replete with hackneyed phrases. Star despairs:

—¿Qué va a ser de mí?
—Si logra no acatarrarse, nada.
—¡Sola, en medio de la noche!
—No apele a dialectos extraños. Esa frase es de un melodrama.... Ni usted está sola, porque yo estoy aquí, ni en medio de la noche, porque estamos más cerca del alba que del ocaso. La noche no es un mar de sombras. Es un túnel: nada más.
—Para mí, es un laberinto. (25-26)

In reading themselves and their situations both characters fall into stereotype and follow a script drawn directly from melodrama.
    This comic inability to speak or act without following a script is further dramatized in the scenes within the car. As Julio wraps the blanket around Star and tries to comfort her, he follows nurturing scripts learned from women in his past: "Acumuló en ella todas las dulzuras

maternales que recordó haber recibido en la infancia. Agotada su niñez, reprodujo las tiernas efusiones de una hermana mayor, recibidas en su adolescencia y, por fin, los púdicos mimos de la primera novia" (31). Julio continues to reenact "caricias de todas las épocas de su vida," but he quickly exhausts his repertoire: "la memoria de Julio, sometida a presiones extremas rezumó pronto todos sus juegos sentimentales. Nada le quedaba por reeditar, ya que todas las demás mujeres intercaladas en su juventud le sugerían gestos idénticos, algunos de impertinente reproducción" (31). Star in turn begins following another script, borrowed from the art of coquetry. With the blanket as her only prop, she remakes herself: "Estudiaba para cada miembro su rítmico embozo, se cincelaba interiormente el bloque total" (31). Robbed of the modern weapons of *coquetería*—"ametralladoras y bombas de mano, se encontraba con una catapulta" (32). In remaking herself with the "primitive" weapon at hand —the blanket—Star refers to well-known artistic representations: first she casts herself as a sculpture by Tanagra, featuring an intricately pleasted toga—"el vivo pedestal de un torso de Afrodita"; and later, with her bare arm emerging from the blanket, she appears as an "infanta goyesca a quien le acaban de robar las joyas" (32, 33).

Of course, when we observe Star in the act of imitating these artistic models, we are reading Julio as he reads her reading herself. The narrator consistently directs his gaze through Julio's eyes, whereas Star remains the object to be read—enigmatic Woman. However much Julio, this "héroe a regañadientes," may comically misfit the role of "redentor," he stands for the archetypal seeker of knowledge (59). Just as he has read the sounds of nature intertextually, he reads this woman by referring to manifold scripts and representations. The quoting of intertexts from high and low art may be read as a parody of the *aventura amorosa* in all its diverse articulations. But in a broader sense the novella also parodies the act of reading as a knowledge-seeking enterprise. This pursuit of knowledge is ever allusive and elusive. We can only seek Truth by alluding through an infinite web of signs, loosely arranged in categories containing texts, meanings and images; yet absolute, grounded meaning forever eludes us. Julio, in a sense, stands allegorically for Everyman, or Everyreader who, in seeking to know Nature/Woman, can only wander infinitely through intertextual space. Somewhat aware of his predicament, at one point Julio contemplates the inadequacy of two of his readings of the enigmatic woman: "la llorona hija de los dioses, y el pícaro golfillo de americana. Ninguna era aún la mujer. Y era preciso decidirse, antes de continuar la aventura, por crear un tipo intermedio entre el Olimpo y el Arroyo" (30). Throughout the episode, even as he summons a multiplicity of literary and nonliterary prototypes, none is sufficient, none identifies the Woman. Her nakedness is her nothingness. In her nudity he finds not Naked Truth, but a void, yet he feels compelled incessantly to seek various intertexts in an attempt to know her, and thus clothe her. Even his initial reading of the victim as Rubens's nude "Andrómeda" is an attempt to clothe her. For in Western painting, nudity, as opposed to nakedness, refashions the female body into idealized and conventional poses.[13]

At the end of "Andrómeda," as the fully-clothed Star applies makeup, Julio finally recognizes her as the cabaret dancer, Carmela: "una lenta máscara comenzó a revelar a Julio el secreto de su bella redimida. Un fino antifaz fue cayendo sobre la tez de Star, descubriendo, poco a poco, su verdadero rostro" (57). Believing that at last he has read her correctly, he tells her:

> Para mí, comenzó usted a existir ahora.
> —¿Vestida?
> —Sí, Carmela.
> —Por fin me reconoció.
> —Cuando recuperó usted su verdadera cara.
> —Es la de la calle, la del teatro. No la mía.
> —La única. Porque es la única que usted se ha elaborado. La otra, es sólo una vulgar herencia. La que usted llama *suya,* es la cara de todas las demás bellas mujeres, como el traje. Por fortuna, usted no lo viste, lo asimila. (58)

But Julio's insistence that her made-up face, her theatrical/social mask, is her "verdadero rostro" can only be taken ironically. For albeit with some measure of artistic latitude, Carmela has made herself in conformance with the modern fashion code, by compressing her Rubenesque bulk into the narrow, straight silhouette of the nineteen-twenties:

> Cada prenda le añadía agilidad y desenfado. Iba perdiendo en peso y en volumen. A cada nueva opresión, ondulaba y decrecía toda la rolliza musculatura. Star iba sometiendo su sugerente anatomía a las normas del último figurín. El pecho, ceñido y alto; los muslos y caderas, alargados, estilizados. Todo estaba en aproximar al cilindro algunas superficies casi esféricas. Pronto la insolente opulencia de Elena

Fourment se trocó en una grácil heroína de la pantalla. (56)

After she is fully clothed, "Julio no lograba ver de nuevo la mujer atada al tronco, ni la mujer acurrucada en el coche, frío y lacio despojo del alba, sino una nueva mujer, de plasticidad aderezada, según los principios inquebrantables de la moda" (57). Although Julio may momentarily believe that he knows her by recognizing her as "*La Bella Carmela,* la *genial* creadora de danzas apócrifas de Oriente," the narration makes clear that he continues to read her by referring to codified representations—to "el último figurín" of contemporary fashion, or to "la heroína de la pantalla" (57, 56). The contemporary codes that govern a woman's representation (and self-representation) can be no less a "vulgar herencia" her "godgiven" face (58).

If we take inventory of the various representations of woman that Julio quotes in his attempt to read Star/Carmela—the mythical and Rubenesque Andrómeda, Aphrodite, Pygmalian's Galatea, the Tanagra sculpture, the "infanta goyesca," "la liviana esposa de vodevil, sorprendida en el preludio de una infidelidad" (55), and finally a fashion mannequin—the cumulative effect becomes somewhat dizzying. In addition, Julio invokes the common feminine stereotypes—the innocent victim, the coquette, the whore—as well as conventional allegorical personifications —woman as Nature, as Beauty, as Art, as Enigma, as Truth. Each of these representations—whether artistic, stereoptypical, or allegorical— comes freighted with connotations, including images, traits, and scripts. Together they assemble on a reader's mental stage, swarming and colliding around the empty form of this impossible character. Too diverse and incompatible, these freighted representations cannot coalesce; nor can her figure contain them all. If we are alert to this semantic excess, we might envision this character as a cubist portrait of woman: as a combination of juxtaposed perspectives, as a collage of disparate representations. What is ultimately revealed by this excess is not woman's identity, but her *impossibility*—that culturally speaking, Woman is none of these and all of these. This text defamiliarizes and destabilizes our cultural practice of reading woman intertextually, by simply overdoing it—by mobilizing from our reservoir of received knowledge a surfeit of feminine representations.

I am calling attention to a surplus of evoked meanings that in a more conventional reading might be suppressed. Whether in reading the world or in reading books, we are trained to filter the excess signification produced by any utterance or image. Our interpretations tend to follow narrow connotative paths. We are conditioned to be oblivious to what disrupts received knowledge.[14] Certainly a more conventional reading is possible, but I argue that in this novella Jarnés makes it difficult (or impossible) for readers to suppress the excess. And given its problematic reception, which Jarnés will later address (in the addendum of 1939), his contemporary readers found it quite disturbing.

Until now I have avoided the question of the gendered reader, even as I have asserted that characters are always gendered. Indeed, the question of a feminine reading (or writing) is a thorny issue that has generated a vast body of critical commentary.[15] It is possible that a woman would read this text less complicitously, with more resistance, particularly to the discourse of male fantasy.[16] Although a female reader must gaze through the eyes of the male voyeur (as no other view is offered), and although she is denied access to Star's consciousness, her allegiance may be somewhat divided. Even as she assumes the position of voyeur, she may simultaneously read from another site, one slightly off-center, resulting in a doubled or contrapuntal reading.[17]

But speaking in very general terms about conventional reading practices, I tend to doubt a substantial difference between a female's reading and a male's. After all, we are officially offered only one perspective, that of a narrator speaking in a language suffused with patriarchal terms, and within a culture long governed by patriarchal assumptions. I see the feminine as a patriarchal invention, as a composite of masculine needs, desires, and fears—as a manufactured other. So even if I am feminine, (in a sense) I am still masculine. If there is a true "other than masculine," it is as yet an unthinkable and unnamed space, perhaps neither masculine nor feminine.[18] I am suggesting, then, that speaking in absolute terms, a *feminine* reading is logically impossible.

However, as readers, whether male or female, we can seek that unthinkable other-than-masculine space by accepting only partially (as the condition of intelligibility) the terms offered by a text. We can develop a critical awareness of how our readings—our ventures through intertextual space—are governed by cultural paradigms and conventional reading practices. As we read, we can simultaneously rewrite the paradigms of gender and loosen their constraints upon our interpretations as well as our experiences. We can become more attuned to the noise of signification and, unlike Julio, resist the tendency to filter and discipline the cacaphony.[19] And in reading this particular text, "Andrómeda," rather than suppressing the noisy clashing of disparate representations of the feminine, we might aspire to a multiperspectival reading that reveals the untenability of the representational uses and misuses of woman and points to their dissolution.

The Discourse on Woman

If indeed "Andrómeda" interrogates and destabilizes the representation of woman in Western culture, it might be worthwhile to inquire how this text participated in the "cultural conversation" of its time and place.[20] I borrow the conversational metaphor from Kenneth Burke, who in 1941 wrote,

> Imagine that you enter a parlor. You come late. When you arrive, others have long preceded you, and they are engaged in a heated discussion, a discussion too heated for them to pause and tell you exactly what it is about. . . . You listen for a while, until you decide that you have caught the tenor of the argument; then you put in your oar. Someone answers; you answer him; another comes to your defense; another aligns himself against you, to either the embarrassment or gratification of your opponent, depending upon the quality of your ally's assistance. However, the discussion is interminable. The hour grows late, you must depart. And you do depart, with the discussion still vigorously in progress. (qtd. in Mailloux 58)

To what extent does "Andrómeda" converse with other contemporary texts, responding to the dominant issues "in the parlor" during the nineteen-twenties, in particular, the "woman question"? How does the work "stage" these issues, by providing a terrain for their elaboration and interrogation? The results of such an inquiry can only be provisional, given the impossibility of reconstructing accurately and completely the cultural dialogue of a given time. But even more incomplete would be any consideration of a work in isolation from its discursive matrix.

The obvious starting point for such an examination would be the circle of writers and intellectuals, among them Benjamín Jarnés, who associated with the *Revista de Occidente* during the nineteen-twenties.[21] In this context "the cultural conversation" becomes more than mere metaphor, for indeed, the *Revista's* founder, Ortega y Gasset, presided over nightly *tertulias* at the *Revista* offices. Ramón Gómez de la Serna colorfully (and obsequiously) described these tertulias:

> Ortega, que aplica la brújula de su nariz a cada conversación mientras olfatea los lejanos horizontes percibiendo la caza lejana, ofrece pastas con levadura de pensamientos y con el piñón de una frase amable. Y en ese medio azulado, la improvisación es ágil, y nos queremos acordar después de lo que hemos dicho, favorecidos por esa agilidad que da el agua propicial a los movimientos y a los desperezos frenéticos de la imaginación. Sólo un grande hombre que posee las llaves de las grutas maravillosas ha podido permitirnos ese goce de la levitación. . . . Parecía la "Revista de Occidente" la casa eterna, y el capitán con su brújula orientada hacia occidente nos llevaba detrás del sol sin que entrase en su ocaso, siguiendo su salto de horizontes. Sin rezagarnos en ningún valle. (431-32, 434)

For Ortega and the members of his circle, the *tertulias* served an important function within their broad project: to overcome Spain's backwardness by integrating its intellectual life with the latest currents of Western thought.[22] Evelyne López Campillo, in her study of the *Revista*'s history and content, argues that the journal itself emerged as the product of conversations:

> La *Revista* da la sensación de ser la prolongación de un diálogo, de un intercambio, que se producían probablemente durante las reuniones de discusión previas a la elaboración de los números. A partir de su contenido, no puede ponerse en evidencia una línea ideológica estrecha: no cabe duda de que siempre es posible, dada la variedad de las posiciones expresadas, atribuirla una línea ideológica determinada (aristocrática, por no decir prefascista, como se afirma a veces), pero esto no puede hacerse más que mutilando todas las otras posibilidades presentes en la revista. (250-51)

Despite the lack of a unified ideological orientation, the "other possibilities present in the *Revista*" were surely not unlimited. Arguably, the *tertulias* and meetings, led by Ortega, exerted significant but unmeasurable power in legitimizing or delegitimizing various intellectual and artistic currents, as well as literary styles and themes.[23]

To some extent we can surmise the content of these conversations based upon the editorial decisions reflected in the *Revista de Occidente* itself.[24] Upon surveying its content, one is first struck by the remarkable variety of subject matter and the high quality of the writing. Clearly, the *Revista* placed itself squarely within the newest intellectual and artistic currents of Europe and America. Its purpose, as stated (presumably by Ortega) in the inaugural issue, was to provide select readers in Spain and Latin America with "noticias claras y meditadas" of intellectual events beyond their national frontiers (1).[25] The *Revista* would respond to "la vital curiosidad que el individuo de nervios alerta siente por el vasto germinar de la vida en torno y . . . el deseo de vivir cara a cara con la honda realidad contemporánea" (1). Although Ortega, as his biographer Rockwell Gray points out, was not solely responsible for the *Revista's* editorial policy, "the general tendencies of the magazine constituted a kind of cultural topography of Europe as he perceived it" (139). Among the literary selections, works by contemporary Spanish writers predominate, including Baroja, Pérez de Ayala, Lorca, Machado, Diego, Guillén, Aleixandre, Salinas, Ayala, Gómez de la Serna, Alberti, Alonso, and Jarnés. But also represented are works (or reviews of works) by modernist writers from thoughout Europe and the Americas, including Conrad, Joyce, Huxley, Lawrence, Kafka, Cocteau, Gide, Valéry, Proust, Giraudoux, Svevo, Pirandello, Ocampo, Torres Bodet, Reyes, Crane, Anderson, O'Neill, and Dos Passos. Essays and reviews on the "non-literary" arts—music, cinema, architecture, and painting—abound, including numerous studies of cubism and Franz Roh's famous essay on contemporary art, "Realismo mágico." Many issues contain scientific articles describing the new physics and cosmology, including two by Albert Einstein. Also included are essays on philosophy (with an emphasis on phenomenology), history, archeology, geopolitics, anthropology, psychology, and sociology.

Undoubtedly, this listing of content reveals to some degree the dominant topics in the cultural conversation of the time. But such a listing of inclusions may warp our understanding of that dialogue by exaggerating the importance of those intellectual and artistic currents most favored by Ortega and his editorial board. Presumably, the currents in disfavor were also discussed frequently and fervently; and perhaps, certain "taboo" topics, never discussed, applied a pressure upon their discourse that is impossible to measure. Among the artistic currents less favored, and therefore under-represented in the *Revista,* were futurism, Dada, constructivism, surrealism, and expressionism; whereas cubism, whose heyday had already passed, received constant attention. In the realm of philosophy, the *Revista* neglected Bergson, Croce, Heidegger, James, and Dewey, but frequently included essays by Russell, Ortega, and various German phenomenologists. The *Revista* also tended to ignore two of the most influential discourses in the Occident: Freudian psychoanalysis and Marxism. Although Freud's ideas were then at the height of influence in the Continent, the journal generally slighted his works.[26] However, the *Revista* published and promoted those schools of psychology more compatible with Ortega's views—the archetypal and essentialist strands of Carl Jung, Georg Simmel, and Gregorio Marañón, along with pseudoscientific tracts on "characterology."[27] The neglect of Marxism and anarchism is not surprising, given Ortega's political views, but descriptions of life and the arts in the Soviet Union occasionally appeared. Most notably absent are articles that address contemporary social and political issues in Spain, again not surprising, given that the original statement of purpose had declared the *Revista* "de espaldas a toda política, ya que la política no aspira nunca a entender las cosas" (2).[28]

Among the most widely debated social and political issues of the day was the "woman question." Women had recently obtained the vote in a number of Western countries, and in Spain the growing feminist agitation would lead to the full extension of women's rights under the Republican Constitution of 1931.[29] In line with its policy "de espaldas a toda política," the *Revista* never explicitly addressed the demands of the feminist movement (Ortega, "Propósitos" 2). Granted, the journal gave a small measure of attention to women writers: the inaugural issue included an essay by Ortega on the French poet Ana de Noailles, and subsequent issues occasionally included short fiction by Victoria Ocampo, Rosa Chacel, and the Russian writer Lidia Seifulina. But certainly, the *Revista* circle never granted its female contributors full membership status, although, by the late twenties, Chacel contributed regularly and attended the *tertulia* upon occasion.[30]

Despite these biases against women writers and feminist issues, the "woman question" evidently exerted significant pressure upon the *Revista* discourse. Throughout the nineteen-twenties, numerous literary, philosophical, and psychological articles revealed a general preoccupation with the woman's "nature"—"el alma femenina." Among the most frequent contributors on this topic was the German sociologist Georg

Simmel, whose work Ortega considered "[e]l análisis más agudo y penetrante de las diferencias entre la psicología del hombre y la mujer" (qtd. in Bordons and Kirkpatrick 288).[31] Simmel's work ostensibly provided the scientific basis for the traditional identification of the masculine with the knowing, acting subject and the feminine with the realm of undifferentiated nature and life force. In the essay, "Cultura femenina" (1925), Simmel states unequivocally, "Nuestra cultura, en realidad, es enteramente masculina," and he promotes the participation of women in cultural production. But because our culture is entirely man-made, he believes that women who work and create in that culture are doomed to fail; for "la índole femenina—cuyos contenidos vitales existen por la energía de un indivisible centro subjetivo y permanecen siempre fundidos en el foco de la personalidad—es inadecuada para actuar en el mundo de puras cosas que la naturaleza diferencial del varón ha edificado" (1: 285). At the same time, Simmel sees no reason to consider "la objetividad varonil como lo más perfecto y la vida indiferenciada [femenina] . . . como lo más débil, lo 'menos desarrollado' " (1: 285). The only means of overcoming the "ingenuo prejuicio" that confuses masculine values with human values, is to affirm "un dualismo radical, reconocer que la existencia femenina tiene otras bases, fluye por cauces radicalmente distintos que la masculina, construir dos tipos vitales, cada uno con su fórmula autónoma" (1: 286). For a genuine "cultura femenina" to evolve then, women must dedicate themselves to those spheres of cultural activity in which they undertake "lo que los hombres no pueden realizar" (1: 288). Through these twists and turns in his argument, Simmel manages to promote women's participation in cultural life, while imposing absolute restrictions—based on unexamined assumptions about woman's essential, irrevocable difference from man. Simmel's writings on the woman question reveal that curious combination of progressive and retrograde notions that characterizes many of the contributions to the debate over "el alma femenina."

Another frequent contributor to this dialogue is the endocrinologist and sexologist, Gregorio Marañón. In "Notas para la biología de Don Juan" (1924) and "Nuevas ideas sobre el problema de la intersexualidad y sobre la cronología de los sexos" (1928), Marañón presents ideas that at first glance seem quite advanced for their time. He argues that, based upon recent findings in biology, strict sexual differentiation does not exist; rather, each individual displays a mixture of masculine and feminine traits. But at the same time, Marañón tries to salvage essential sexual difference by claiming that both the overly feminized male and overly masculinized female are abnormal and potentially pathological.[32] Whereas a normal male finds satisfaction in his work, in political, social, or artistic labors, a feminized male, a "Don Juan," is consumed by the sexual function and (like women) he is prone to lying. While a normal female finds her satisfaction in domestic duties, a masculinized female— one endowed with exceptional intellectual capacity or athletic ability—is driven to achieve in the outside world.[33]

Other contributors also developed elaborate justifications for sexual polarity. Carl Jung in "La mujer en Europa" (1929) concurs with Marañón in affirming that all humans contain a mix of masculine and feminine traits. And like Marañón, Jung insists that one or the other should dominate in a given individual: "El varón debiera vivir como varón, y la mujer como mujer" (9). In defining woman, Jung continually defers to Nature as the absolute authority, for by nature woman is passive, motivated by love, and indirect in her wiles:

> [E]lla, por regla general, se instala en el costado íntimo del hombre. .:. . Está en su verdadera naturaleza el recatarse. ... [P]or virtud de su actitud pasiva ... ayuda al hombre a su realización y le sujeta. ... Un rasgo esencial de la mujer es que puede hacerlo todo por amor a un ser humano. ... El amor a las cosas es una prerrogativa masculina. ... La mujer, como la Naturaleza, se sirve de caminos indirectos, sin expresar anticipadamente la meta. Reacciona de un modo teleológico a lo insatisfactorio invisible con caprichos, afectos, opiniones y hechos. (6, 7, 8, 31)

Jung also reaffirms the timeworn oppositional associations of *eros* with woman and *logos* with man:

> La psicología femenina tiene como principio el *eros*, el que ata y desata, mientras al varón le está adscrito desde tiempos remotos el *logos* como principio supremo. ... El *eros* es para el hombre un país de sombra, que le enreda en lo inconsciente femenino, en lo anímico, y, a su vez, el *logos* es para la mujer un razonamiento mortalmente aburrido, cuando no temible y aborrecible. (17,19)

While reaffirming these ancient "truisms," Jung addresses the disagreeable consequences of the progressive "masculinización del alma femenina" in Western societies: neurosis, frigidity, sexual aggressiveness, homosexuality, and the destabilization of marriage (11). While Jung seems to regard these developments as irreversible, he maintains a weak hope that woman's affinity to *eros* will mitigate the ill effects of modern life.[34]

Waldo Frank in "La mujer norteamericana" (1929), likewise addresses the social effects of the changing relations between the sexes. As in the articles by his fellow-experts on women, Frank begins by expressing rather advanced ideas on the woman question. He systematically debunks various myths about the American woman—that her independence results from the industrial revolution, that she is responsible for Amercan puritanism, that American society is a matriarchy—and he criticizes American men for their obsession with power, for their fear of letting women be women. But in conclusion, Frank, like Jung, restores woman to the realm of Nature and celebrates a new trend that he perceives among American women. No longer do they imitate men, but rather they are returning to the "fuentes de su feminidad: a una femininidad nueva, dura, astuta, sagaz, sin pizca de sentimentalidad, al estado de hembra" (82).

In another clever combination of progressive and traditionalist views of woman, "El espíritu filósofico y la femininidad" (1929), Manuel García Morente welcomes the emancipation of woman, but only as a step towards a greater goal: "para que comience a formarse la cultura femenina, es decir, una cultura que concrete, en productos objetivos—actividades, obras, descubrimientos, arte, ciencia, formas de vida, instituciones jurídicas, políticas, etc.—, las peculiaridades del alma femenina, de la feminidad eterna" (290).[35] García Morente wonders if philosophy can find a place in this feminine culture of the future, and he posits the question: What is it in the feminine soul that prevents her from taking pleasure in philosopical meditation? He attributes woman's lack of philosophical aptitude first to "el unitarismo del alma femenina"—to her preference for homogeneity and lack of attention to diversity (300). Second, he contends that "la mujer es mucho más sujeta al proceso vital que el hombre" and "más adherida a las formas sentimentales de la vida"; therefore, she finds it difficult to engage in the cold, objective examination of reality (300). But despite these deficiencies, woman may one day find a vocation in philosophy, given that femininity is evolving in directions that make possible

> un tipo maravilloso de mujer, una forma exquisita de cultura femenina que reúna la intensa preocupación vital

y personal, la unidad profunda del ser, con la diversidad de los más tenues, sutiles y apartados intereses ideales, un tipo de mujer hecho a la medida de la meditación filosófica, que sea capaz de alternar la intimidad de la vivencia con la claridad de la especulación. Es posible entonces que la filosofía reciba de las mujeres una última y más sublime depuración. (303)

García Morente here expresses perhaps the most unqualified support for women's full participation in public life, while still wrapping his argument in the dusty platitudes of the eternal feminine.

Ortega wrote frequently, though less magnanimously, on the nature of woman, consistently defending essentialistic views of sexual difference.[36] In "Para una caracterología" (1926), he distinguishes three "ingredients" that combined in varying quantities constitute the human personality: *vitalidad*—the inferior stratum of the psyche associated with physiological and sensorial impulses; *alma*—made up of feelings, desires, fantasies; and *espíritu*—comprised of the intellect, will, logic, and aesthetic sensibility. One or another of these components may predominate in individuals, as well as in groups—races, nationalities, and the sexes. In woman, for example, "predomina el alma, tras de la cual va el cuerpo, pero muy raramente interviene el espíritu" (242). Ortega attributes woman's lack of logic to her capriciousness,

> consecuencia inevitable de esa arquitectura natural a la psique femenina, que ha obligado siempre a Eva a vivir *desde* su alma. . . . Al ser caprichosa la mujer cumple su destino y se mantiene fiel a su estructura íntima. Hemos visto cómo es imposible querer—en el sentido de la voluntad—dos cosas opuestas; en cambio, se pueden desear cosas antagónicas, sentir simpatía y antipatía hacia lo mismo. Así se explica que, siendo la mujer de ordinario menos rica de contenido interno que el hombre, su actitud ante un mismo objeto puede parecer a éste de una complejidad desesperante. El espíritu propende al *sí* o al *no* rotundos, que mutuamente se excluyen. La mujer suele vivir en un perpetuo y deleitable *sí-no*, en un balanceo y columpiamiento que da ese maravilloso sabor irracional, ese sugestivo problematismo a la conducta femenina. (243)

Ortega's views in this essay seem moderate compared to those he expressed in an earlier essay, "La poesía de Ana de Noailles" (1923). With a strange blend of praise and scorn, Ortega describes de Noailles's poetry as "espléndida" and "voluptuosa," while deriding her "lirismo vegetal" (35, 32, 34):

> El alma que en esta poesía se expresa no es espiritual; es más bien el alma de un cuerpo que fuera vegetal. Si intentamos imaginar el alma de una planta, no podremos atribuirle ideas ni sentimientos: no habrá en ella más que sensaciones, y aun éstas, vagas, difusas, atmosféricas. . . . La voluptuosidad femenina es acaso, de todas las humanas impresiones, la que más próxima nos parece a la existencia botánica. (32)

To reinforce his claim for women's kinship with plants, he quotes a line of verse and then posits the rhetorical question: "¿No es ésta una idea que cabe muy bien en el corazón de una amapola?" (33). Ortega's botanical analogies support his thesis that "la mejor lírica femenina, al desnudar las raíces de su alma, deja ver la monotonía del eterno femenino y la exigüidad de sus ingredientes" (38). Then denying women's capacity to write true lyric poetry, Ortega argues:

> Sólo en el hombre es normal y espontáneo ese afán de dar al público lo más personal de su persona. Todas las actividades históricas del sexo masculino nacen de esta su condición esencialmente lírica. Ciencia, política, creación industrial, poesía, son oficios que consisten en dar al público anónimo, de dispersar en el contorno cósmico lo que constituye la energía íntima de cada individuo. La mujer, por el contrario, es nativamente ocultadora. (36)

Because of this innate domesticity, Ortega avers, women have excelled in only one literary genre: in epistolary writing, "la única forma privada de la literatura" (37). But when women's writing is exposed to the public glare, "descubrimos que esa intimidad femenina, tan deliciosa bajo la luz de un interior, puesta al aire libre resulta la cosa más pobre del mundo. La personalidad de la mujer es poco personal, o, dicho de otra manera, la mujer es más bien un género que un individuo" (38). At this point, a reader might logically ask: If indeed women have excelled in private literary genres, such as diaries and letters, does this not result from women's historical confinement to the home, which limited their opportunities for worldly experience and public expression? But interestingly, here at the weakest point in his argument, Ortega becomes most vehement: "Es vano oponerse a la ley esencial y no meramente histórica, transitoria o empírica que hace del varón un ser sustancialmente público, y de la mujer un temperamento privado. Todo intento de subvertir ese destino termina en fracaso" (37). And on the next page he again states in no uncertain terms, "Me parece vano querer cegarse ante esta evidente realidad que explica tan bien la labor de la mujer en la historia y la perpetua mala inteligencia interpuestas entre ambos sexos" (38). Ortega goes to such extremes in this essay that he draws suspicion to his argument. One wonders if behind the "ingenious" tropes meant to disguise commonplace ideas, behind the fist-thumping vehemence aimed at banishing all doubt, perhaps there lurks some voice daring him to ask if things could be otherwise, a question from which he recoils in horror.

It is evident from Ortega's arguments, along with those of his likeminded colleagues, that the woman question had become a general preoccupation in the cultural dialogue of the nineteen-twenties, undoubtedly linked to the growth of feminism and the increasing participation of women in public life. These leading intellectuals—Ortega, García Morente, Frank, Marañón, Simmel—responded by producing a seemingly new discourse on the nature of woman. The very excessiveness of the response seems peculiar, given the quite moderate character of the Spanish feminist struggle, which was led by Catholic women's organizations. Each of these thinkers, either cleverly or clumsily, espoused a few progressive ideas in favor of feminine advancement, while repeating ad infinitum the fossilized arguments that for centuries have justified woman's subordination to man. In the words of Teresa Bordons and Susan Kirkpatrick, their arguments formed part of "the anti-rationalist discourse that sought to preserve established social categories by exalting difference and hierarchy as the keys to a 'natural' vitality that could resist the 'weakening' and 'degenerative' effects of the revolutionary erasure of traditional distinctions" (288).

Jarnés himself made a small contribution to this discourse in a book review of Juan Larnac's *La historia de la literatura femenina en Francia*. In the review, "Musas de Francia" (1929), Jarnés follows in his colleagues' footsteps by alternately asserting progressive and traditional views on the Woman Question. At first, Jarnés expresses advanced ideas on women's writing, observing, "Siempre ha intrigado excesivamente a los hombres el hecho de que la mujer escriba," and debunking the conventional notion that only an abnormal woman, a "caso patológico," attempts to write (138). He refutes the hackneyed argument that, based on "natural" law, men create machines, philosophical systems, and works of art; but since woman's entire being is dedicated to creation of life, "¿Cómo, entonces podría nacer en ella el deseo de crear otra cosa?" (139). Ridiculing these ideas, Jarnés argues:

> Si el concepto de creación lo hacemos extensivo a la producción de todos los fenómenos del cielo y de la tierra, la importancia de crear se va reduciendo mucho de tamaño. Pero no importa lo mismo asistir en una selva a la lactancia de un cachorro que en un estudio al nacimiento de un cuadro. ¿Cómo la cuna y la intuición artística pueden ser barajadas como fuentes de creación? Es excesivo. Sólo una extrema longanimidad puede asignar a un vientre fecundo los mismos atributos creadores que al cerebro. (139)

Jarnés asserts: "Continúa la incomprensión de la mujer; probablemente nunca llegaremos a corregirnos. Varones ilustres, de clarísima visión en tantas cuestiones, se condujeron siempre en ésta lamentablemente" (140). He cites examples from views of the Ancients on woman and suggests: "la historia de las opiniones del hombre acerca de la mujer sería la más pintoresca entre todas las historias pintorescas del pensamiento humano" (140).

But here Jarnés's argument abruptly turns, and he suddenly invokes the conventional wisdom regarding the *function* of woman in the arts—woman as muse or as object of contemplation and desire:

> Sería preferible que los hombres se decidiesen a escribir la historia de la influencia femenina—tan decisiva—en toda la literatura de los hombres; libro magnífico, inacabable, tan voluminoso como toda la literatura. Porque toda la ha creado, con su presencia unas veces, con su ausencia otras, la mujer. ¿Habría que repetir que la coquetería de una hembra fue la llave de toda nuestra literatura occidental? (140)

His argument takes another regressive turn in the conclusion, where he returns to the question of women's writing. He asserts that the proper question is not *whether* woman can write, but *what* she writes and for *whom?* Deferring to Ortega, Jarnés quotes from his essay on Ana de Noailles, reaffirming the claim that women can excel only in private literary endeavors, whereas "[e]sa intimidad femenina, tan deliciosa bajo la luz de su interior, puesta al aire libre, resulta la cosa más pobre del mundo" (141). So after initially expressing quite progressive views, Jarnés suddenly backtracks, and bows before the master: "en estas sagaces palabras del maestro se nos revela el verdadero punto de vista desde donde hay que atisbar las letras femeninas" (141).

By calling attention to Jarnés's participation in this cultural conversation on the nature of woman, I make no claims for conscious intentionality in his novella, "Andrómeda," or in his other works of fiction. However, I want to affirm that he shared these preoccupations and to point out certain analogical relationships between Jarnés's works and this discourse on woman. That the "problem" of woman had become a dominant issue in the intellectual dialogues of the nineteen-twenties seems indisputable. And it goes without saying that fictional works serve as sites for examining problematic issues—be they aesthetic, existential or social. Certainly, as Jarnés noted, in Western works of art woman has for centuries been the object of contemplation, examination, and desire. But I argue that, not only in "Andrómeda," but in many vanguard works of the nineteen-twenties, the conventional representations of the feminine are called into question, and woman appears as a *problem*, as a puzzle in pieces to be reconstructed by a narrator, protagonist, or reader.[37] I am thinking of works such as Azorín's *Doña Inés*, Gómez de la Serna's *Senos* and *La Mujer de ámbar*, Salinas's *Víspera del gozo* and "35 bujías," Díaz Fernández's *La Venus mecánica*, and other novels by Jarnés, including *El profesor inútil* and *El convidado de papel*. Often in these works the woman-seeking enterprise is humorously ironized, by a narrator or anti-hero who, like Julio, mocks himself and acknowledges his ineptitude or failure at "solving" the problem of woman.

The questions posed in "Andrómeda"—What is the nature of woman? How do we read her? How can we know her?—all relate to the central problem that each of the illustrious thinkers addresses in the essays cited from the *Revista de Occidente*. "Andrómeda" playfully dramatizes the same woman-seeking enterprise that Ortega, Marañón, Simmel, García Morente, Jung, and Frank undertake. Like these seekers of knowledge, the fictional hero, Julio, examines woman categorically and relationally as *other* than man: in Jung's words, as his "absoluto contrario," as an object to be studied, devoid of subjectivity and rationality (1). Just as these thinkers read/define woman as bound to nature, as the embodiment of *eros*, as the unconscious agent of vital and irrational forces, Julio encounters Andrómeda bound to the earth. Like these essayists, Julio can read (and rewrite) woman only by alluding intertextually through the vast storehouse of prototypes, stereotypes, and metaphors that constitute received knowledge. He, like them, is compelled to read on endlessly, re-citing the timeworn tropes that comprise the category of the feminine, quoting from proverbial knowledge, as well as Biblical, mythological, and literary sources. The representation of woman that emerges from their work is, like Andrómeda/Star/Carmela, a dissonant, hybrid composite of traditional archetypes and modern prototypes, of idealizations and denigrations of woman—an impossible "tipo intermedio entre el Olimpo y el Arroyo" ("Andrómeda" 30).

Even Ortega's curious association of woman with the vegetable kingdom—ostensibly to explain "la monotonía del eterno femenina"—finds an echo in "Andrómeda" ("La poesía" 38). Significantly, this occurs at a moment when Julio almost recognizes "Carmela," but decides not to question her about her past, since it is bound to be a monotonous tale: "De las mujeres, desdeñó siempre el pasado, tan semejante. Prefería comenzar la historia de cada mujer desde el punto en que él las conocía, para evitarse monótonas repeticiones" (47). At that moment they are passing the Escuela de Agricultura, and they launch into a lively discussion of trees and plants. With great entusiasmo Julio discusses all the varieties of radishes and turnips—their sizes, colors, shapes. When Star mocks him saying, "Conoce usted íntimamente a todos los rábanos del mundo," Julio responds: "No se burle, Star. Es que me cautiva un matiz inesperado de las cosas. . . . He visto exposiciones, he leído revistas. Nunca vi pintados estos rabanitos deliciosos, estos nabos de oro y violeta" (49). Clearly, this absurd conversation produces an analogy between vegetables and woman as object of art and desire. And whether intentionally or not, it parodies Ortega's ridiculous assertions in "La poesía de Ana de Noailles."

But however absurd their arguments, Ortega and Company took quite seriously their "heroic" rescue operation: to salvage "the eternal feminine" in an age when its viability was in jeopardy. Julio, in contrast, is quite aware of his ineptitude and mocks his own clumsy attempts at rescue, his "balbuceos de héroe" (44). Early in the encounter, Julio explains his stilted and long-winded speeches with the quip: "A mal héroe, buena arenga. Es ley de redentores y caudillos" (19). And later he confesses, "como redentor de cautivas, me siento fracasado" (46). Star at one point also remarks on his awkward performance: "Poco le entusiasma su

papel de héroe" (25). The narrator, whose voice seldom diverges from Julio's thoughts, continually draws attention to his character's embarrassment: Julio, whose "estilo nunca suele lograr el nivel de la hazaña," "desconocía totalmente la actitud justa de un salvador de bellezas
 . . . . Estaba avergonzado de tal desnudez de iniciativas" (37, 23).

By simultaneously dramatizing these mock-heroic efforts to *rescue* Star and to *know* her, the text conflates two venerable metanarratives—the heroic rescue and the knowledge-seeking enterprise. This conflation in turn renders the rescue itself ambiguous: Is Julio freeing "Andrómeda" from bondage to Nature and delivering her to culture? Or is he reinforcing her bondage to culture by continuing to read her through endless layers of tropes? I suggest that "Andrómeda" collapses the nature/culture opposition itself, and it does so by staging in burlesque fashion the contemporary project to rescue and redefine the nature of woman. By evoking a multiplicity of prototypes, stereotypes, and metaphors of woman, it demonstrates that all these definitions of woman's nature—whether produced by Julio, or by the venerable essayists of the *Revista*—are ultimately rereadings and rewritings of an already tropological construction. The "nature" of woman is a cultural artifice produced through the centuries by a patriarchal culture; it is composed of a vast network of associations etched into our consciousness. What Ortega and Company professed to "define" was not woman's identity, but the age-old representation of woman as a composite of masculine needs, desires, and fears. They sought to "reveal as essence" the very artifice that was most in their interests to preserve.

On this terrain where woman is constructed, where nature and culture converge, the art/life antithesis—so sacred to Ortega—also collapses. In attempting to define woman's nature, Julio, Ortega and Company, can only cite from art—"the supreme code, the basis for all reality" (Barthes, *S/Z* 167). Another Julio, in Jarnés's *El convidado de papel*, expresses his frustration at this same predicament:

> Siempre la hembra, convidada perenne, ceñida de tropos antiguos, coronada de símbolos nuevos, que se acerca desnuda a enlazarse ardientemente con nosotros, torpes simuladores, eternos escolares, esclavos de fórmulas, de ritos, de metáforas polvorientas. ¡Papel, todo papel, en silencio abrazado, reducido a pavesas por estas ocultas centellicas del instinto! (74)

No man can *see* woman without reading what is culturally inscribed around her, without interpreting her in *other* terms: He must read her by alluding through endless layers of tropes. It follows that no woman can *see* herself, or *be* herself, without reading and writing herself with the cultural materials at hand, just as Star, with the blanket, represents herself as "un torso de Afrodita" and as an "infanta goyesca" (32, 33). A woman, in viewing herself, in representing herself, must refract her gaze through the mirror of the masculine symbolic order and dress herself in the available tropes.

But Jarnés's texts are usually read as shining examples of Ortega's descriptions (or prescriptions) of the *arte nuevo* as stated in "Deshumanización del arte," most importantly, the separation of life and art.[38] According to Ortega, modernist texts declare their autonomy from the world by drawing attention to their own artifice. This new art reveals "respeto a la vida y una repugnancia a verla confundida con el arte. . . . repugna ante todo la confusión de fronteras" (40, 41). But in my readings of "Andrómeda," as well as of the *Revista*'s treatises on woman, I find a most radical "confusión de fronteras" between art and life. Perhaps I am mistaken. I have situated "Andrómeda" within a cultural dialogue on the nature of woman, and I have read this text as a dramatization of the impossibility of discovering her nature. But Jarnés's texts also participate in a cultural dialogue on the New Art, as defined in large measure by Ortega. Considered within this discourse, perhaps "Andrómeda" should be read—not as an allegory of impossibility—but as a parable, a didactic allegory, that presents a defective character, unable to distinguish art from life, and his struggle to learn the difference?[39] Such an interpretation would more aptly fit Jarnés's rather didactic coming-of-age novel *El convidado de papel* (1927). Indeed, in the quotation just cited from that novel, Jarnés, or at least his character, seems to suggest that instinct and sensuality offer some exit from the layers of tropes, some direct, immediate access to Nature, to the "real woman."

"Andrómeda," however, lacks the narrative distance usually present in fiction that ironizes a defective character. The voice of the narrator and Julio are almost inseparable; both employ the same stilted and precious language. It is often impossible to discern whether the narrator is mocking Julio, or conveying Julio's thoughts as he mocks himself. Moreover, unlike the Julio of *El convidado de papel*, the protagonist of "Andrómeda" never learns his lesson.[40] The novella ends rather ambiguously with the departure of Andrómeda/Star/Carmela from the car.

And Julio, still "un héroe a regañadientes," decides not to continue the relationship: "sería muy penoso volver del revés este pequeño lance de vestir a Carmela. Tendría que retroceder a un punto de partida donde, a su avidez de topógrafo, nada le quedaba ya por descubrir" (59). But this last phrase can only be taken ironically, for Julio has "discovered" nothing. Upon viewing her nakedness, he could allude only to countless literary and artistic models of nudity in all their diverse articulations. His topographical survey of the body of this woman converges with his tropological survey of the "figure" of woman. Physical space and semantic space are rendered indistinguishable.

Allegorical Woman

As Julio the topographer reads the semantic terrain of woman, as he alludes intertextually to various texts, images, and meanings, allegory serves as his map, marking out the connotative paths and destinations. And when readers, in turn, read Julio reading woman, they too refer through their reservoirs of received knowledge and employ the same allegorical cartography. From the very beginning, the novella activates an allegorical frame of reference by associating woman with Nature—perhaps the most pervasive allegorical personification in Western culture. As Julio walks through the woods, reading the natural world for literary meanings, he discovers Woman bound to Nature, and thereafter, she becomes the object of his interpretations. From that point on, throughout his night-long journey, Julio will refer to a multiplicity of allegorical narratives, personifications, and meanings in his attempt to read and to know the enigmatic woman.

Allegory, in its most elementary definition, involves a textual doubling, a superimposition (in readers' minds) of one text upon another, as when we read a Biblical text through a modern articulation.[41] Allegorical writing elicits predictable responses from readers by pointing them towards commonly known narratives or to specified abstract meanings; it rests assured that readers will generally share the same cultural knowledge—the same set of assumptions, associative fields, and narratives. Since ancient times, allegory has been commonly defined as the temporal extension of metaphor. But many allegories—such as literary or visual emblems and personifications—are, as Joel Fineman observes, "primarily perpendicular, concerned more with structure than with temporal extension" and making "only the slightest gestures towards full-scale narrative progress" (31). Other allegories are primarily horizontal, "such as picaresque or quest narratives, where figurative structure is only casually and allusively appended to the circuit of adventures through time"; and "of course, there are allegories that blend both axes together in relatively equal proportions, as in *The Canterbury Tales*, where each figurative tale advances the story of the pilgrimage as a whole" (Fineman 31).[42]

The novella "Andrómeda," after initially conflating woman and nature, continues to elicit allegorical readings on both the perpendicular and horizontal axes. Figuratively, the repeated allusions to Julio's profession, topography, and its application to the female body reinforce this association of Woman with passive space—*physis*—and man as the active seeker, explorer—*techne*. And temporally, within the narrative structure Andrómeda/Star/ Carmela stands for the Enigma, for Truth to be unveiled (although in this wry inversion of narrative convention, the Enigma is already bare). Immediately upon seeing her, Julio begins to dress her in allegorical clothing by invoking the myth of Perseus and Andrómeda. At this moment a "secondary" fully drawn narrative is superimposed upon the "primary" text, and from this point onward, the mythical narrative will coexist with the modern version. But whereas in traditional allegory the relation between the two narrative lines generally remains harmonious, in this novella the relationship is troubled, muddied by ironic dissonance. For Julio clearly misfits the hero's role, and the exotic dancer Carmela hardly typifies the helpless virgin in distress.

The dissonance is amplified by the multiple allegorical possibilities of the Andrómeda myth itself. As a common subject for artists from the Renaissance through the nineteenth century, the Andrómeda myth has evoked numerous allegorical meanings. Adrienne Munich cites some of these articulations in her study of nineteenth-century English literature and painting: Andromeda has variously stood for Woman rescued by Man from Error, Faith assailed by Lewdness, Barbarism rescued by Civilization, the Church rescued by Christ, and Emotion rescued by Reason. So Jarnés, in allegorically "doubling" his narrative by explicitly invoking the Andrómeda myth, simultaneously opens multiple possibilities for additional allegorical readings. I, for example, in a critical-allegorical operation, have doubled Jarnés's novella with a historical narrative—the rescue enterprise undertaken by Ortega and Company to reconstruct and preserve the "eternal feminine."[43] The text, "Andrómeda," on both its figurative and temporal axes, is capable of spawning additional allegories in promiscuous reproduction. Once we enter allegorical terrain, the possibilities are potentially endless, and herein lies the paradox of allegory: its attempt to pin down meaning by pointing to specific abstractions and narratives may lead to a loss of control as readers freely write their own allegories.

But in addition to the the Perseus-Andromeda myth, Jarnés's text explicitly brings numerous other narratives into play. As we have already seen, Julio, in his allusive search for interpretive frames, refers to Adam and Eve, to the pastoral églogas, to the *novelas de cabellerías*, to Don Juan, to Pygmalion, and to the biographies of Rubens and Elena Fourment. Readers are thus overtly asked to read this story allegorically by alluding to other narratives. Moreover, as it weaves (in readers' minds) a tangle of narrative strands, the text also mobilizes a succession of allegorical personifications. Andromeda/Star/Carmela, as a "cuadro excesivo," converts herself "por sucesivas depuraciones, en un sugerente retrato," capable of signifying multiple meanings (34). Initially standing for Nature, she comes to personify Culture—the incarnation of Art—as when she constructs herself first as a statue of Aphrodite and then as a princess in a Goya painting. As Julio observes her observing herself, "contemplando su propia creación," he invokes the pictorial tradition of *Vanitas*: the depiction of a beautiful woman, often nude, observing herself in a mirror and thus personifying Vanity (33).[44]

Through an ongoing game of substitutions, various allegorical meanings continue attaching themselves to her form, only to be subsequently replaced by others. At one moment Julio sees Andrómeda/Star/Carmela as the representation of "inocencia edénica" (39). But in another moment she will embody not Virtue, but Vice: when she murmurs in her sleep, "doscientas, doscientas," Julio wonders if she is naming her "price"; and later, when he sees her partially dressed in stockings and a corset, he imagines her as an adulterous wife in a vaudeville comedy, "sorprendida en el preludio de una infidelidad" (40-41, 55). In addition, she stands for Temptation, to which Julio nearly yields at various times, as when he takes the opportunity to fondle her breasts while untying her, and when he peeks under the blanket while she sleeps. Andrómeda/Star/Carmela also partakes in the allegorical associations of Woman with Bounty, Plenitude, and Fertility: when they pass the School of Agriculture Julio praises the sensuous beauty of radishes and turnips; and later when Star chooses her ensemble, she selects the colors of fruits— *albaricoque, guinda, cereza, grosella*. Julio remarks, "Prefiere las frutas," and she replies, "Soy mujer de estío" (56).

In her one permanent allegorical role, Andrómeda/Star/Carmela stands for the unsolved Enigma, in that she ultimately escapes Julio's foolish attempts to know her, to grasp her. Although we can never gaze through her eyes, we "see" Julio watching her gaze back at him through "pupilas irónicas," with a "sonrisa burlona" (47, 45). Unlike Perseus, Julio does not "keep" Andrómeda as a reward for his rescue. Rather, he returns her to her social milieu, believing to have "cumplido en ésta, decorosamente, sus funciones de héroe con sólo restituir a Augusta uno de sus más voluptuosos elementos decorativos" (59). Julio thus takes credit (albeit tongue-in-cheek) for restoring Carmela in her decorative capacity as a cabaret dancer in the small city of Augusta. But if we read his claim "decoratively," or figuratively, he has merely restored her "clothed" in the tropes—the allegorical meanings—that have traditionally adorned and constrained woman.

When all of these allegorical personifications are comically assembled in the space of a brief narrative, their absurdity becomes evident. Swarming together, these heterogeneous meanings converge and collide, creating a field of disturbance that raises broader questions about Woman's allegorical function in Western culture. How can Woman stand for Truth, Wisdom, and Knowledge when through most of history, she was denied access to knowledge? And how can she stand for Art and Creativity, when traditionally, she could not *be* an Artist? How is it that in certain contexts woman embodies untamed Nature, Chaos, Barbarism, Irrationality, and in others she stands for Art, Culture, Order, Justice, and the Nation?[45] How can she simultaneously represent Virtue and Vice, Solace and Danger, Vanity and Charity? How can she stand for Bounty, Plenitude, Fertility when she also embodies Lack—lack of the phallus and all that it represents—power, knowledge, action? How can she represent both life and death? And how can the figure of woman bear the weight of so many contradictory meanings?[46]

Normally, each of these allegorical meanings is activated within a discrete context, kept in a separate categorical niche. Each allegorical personification generally stands alone and guards its own semantic realm—just as each of the myriad statues of Liberty, Justice, Knowledge, Victory, the Motherland stands alone and guards an institutional realm. Based on centuries of tradition, each personification "makes sense" within its assigned context. But when so many allegorical meanings are moblized in a single work of art, the absurdity and untenability of an entire signifying practice becomes apparent. It becomes evident that Woman, as a category, as a cultural construct, performs an allegorical function in Western culture.[47] Her figure serves as the repository, a categorical dumping ground, for everything desired, feared, and loathed by Man.[48] Woman, as a "character" in fiction or in life, is therefore a logical impossibility. Her alleged unity and coherence as either an aesthetic or social being is a lie.[49]

As an allegorical personification Woman is asked to represent "things in themselves," to make visible Truth, Knowledge, Virtue, Vice, Art, Nature, Reason, Chaos, Charity, Vanity.... Her nude body is called upon to concretize (albeit fictitiously), to *masquerade* as a multiplicity of unattainable abstractions, including the impossible abstraction of Woman itself.[50] She must provide an infinite terrain on which the masculine subject can inscribe an endless series of incompatible meanings. But along with each allegorical act of making woman stand for the unattainable goes the tacit admission of the failure and impossibility of the project—not only because her figure must bear an impossible burden of heterogeneous meanings, but also because this "dumping ground" called woman is actually groundless, a *mise en abyme* through which meaning ever recedes.[51]

Allegory, then, through its ongoing game of displacement and substitution, forever points towards presence, towards things in themselves, even as it acknowledges absence and privation. For this reason theorists such as Derrida and de Man, have "allegorized allegory," employing it as a metaphor for the human linguistic predicament—for our privative access to the world. Stephen Greenblatt summarizes this view:

> Allegory... is quite the opposite of what it often pretends to be: the recovery of the pure visibility of the truth, undisguised by the local and accidental. Allegory may dream of presenting the thing itself—not particular instances of sin or goodness, but Sin and Goodness themselves directly acting in the moral world they also constitute—but its deeper purpose and its actual effect is to acknowledge the darkness, the arbitrariness, and the void that underlie, and paradoxically make possible, all representations of realms of light, order and presence. Insofar as the project of mimesis is the direct representation of a stable, objective reality, allegory, in attempting and always failing to present Reality, inevitably reveals the impossibility of this project. This impossibility is precisely the foundation

upon which all representation, indeed all discourse, is constructed. (vii-viii)

I read Jarnés's "Andrómeda" as an allegory of impossibility, in that it stages in all its excess and absurdity the allegorical quest for Woman in our regime of representation. Julio stands parodically for Everyman, a mock-hero who, while acknowledging his impotence, is compelled to seek Woman allusively, by invoking and inscribing on her figure an endless series of terms. Through its strategy of excess, by imposing upon woman a surfeit of allegorical meanings—nature, truth, virtue, vice, temptation, etc.—this text effectively *de-natures* woman, revealing that her bondage is not to Nature as essence, but to nature as a cultural artifact: she is bound to a vast semantic regime of assumptions, categories, associations, and tropes.

Earlier, I remarked that if we visualize Andromeda/Star/Carmela not mimetically but semantically—as a composite of the heterogeneous blocks of meaning that cluster around her—she might resemble a cubist collage.[52] In a cubist reading, according to Barthes, "the meanings are cubes, piled up, layered, juxtaposed, and yet feeding on each other, whose shift produces the entire space of a painting and makes this very space into a supplementary meaning" (*S/Z* 61). This collage-like effect of Andrómeda/Star/Carmela's characterization may not be accidental.[53] The strategies that Jarnés employs in "Andrómeda"—fragmentation, accumulation, juxtaposition, along with the general troubling of representation and denial of closure—all align him not only with cubism but also with what I will loosely term the vanguardist project of his time. In "Arte al cubo" (1927), an influential essay published in the *Revista de Occidente*, Fernando Vela commented on the tendency of the new art to expose the problematics of representation without offering a solution:

> Como el andamiaje muestra que el edificio está en construcción, así el cuadro cubista deja ver el andamiaje puesto para obtener el volumen. Y en realidad, más que el volumen verdadero del objeto están dados los elementos para construirlo. Lo que desde luego no encontramos es la solución. Esta es nuestra anormalidad: que sentimos fruición cuando la obra de arte nos presenta problemas y no soluciones. (84)

Franz Roh expressed similar views in another influential *Revista* article of the same year, "El realismo mágico" (1927), where he asserted that cubism depicts "las preformas, las formas primordiales, las categorias de toda percepción humana, al mismo tiempo que la materia percibida" (286). In like manner, the text "Andrómeda" paints (in semantic space) a female character by accumulating and juxtaposing heterogeneous meanings: it reveals the problematics of representation by exposing the ramshackle, semantic framework, the "andamiaje," that supports and organizes the representation of the feminine.

This strategy of semantic excess also aligns Jarnés with the renegade surrealist writer, Georges Bataille, who in his "Critical Dictionary" (1929) posited a category that would allow all categories to be unthought, the *informe*. Refusing to assign a definition to the *informe*, Bataille assigned it a task: to undo the "mathematical frock coats" that divide sense into neat packages, "to deny that each thing has its 'proper' form, to imagine meaning as gone shapeless" (Bataille, *Visions* 31, Krauss 64-65).[54] In "Andrómeda," Jarnés's excessive allegorization—the inscription of multiple meanings upon the female form—creates the effect of the *informe*. The juxtapositions of these heterogeneous terms—of everything desired, denied, or feared by man—produces a semantic cacaphony. These allegorical terms collide and converge, obliterating boundaries and short-circuiting the transmission of discrete meanings. Suddenly, if only for a moment, an entire representational regime based on the continuous manufacture of a feminine other collapses under the weight of absurd excess.

The representations of the feminine by the historical avant-garde, in both literature and the visual arts, are often deemed misogynistic.[55] In their attempt to dismantle the Western regime of representation, the avant-garde artists frequently, if not obsessively, "made use" of women's bodies as a means of achieving their effects. Cubist painting and collage violently chopped up the feminine form, while surrealist photography obsessively portrayed dismembered or deformed female bodies.[56] Less frequently, this same tendency appears in literary works: Ramón Gómez de la Serna wrote a lengthy tome on women's breasts, *Senos*; Jarnés included in *El convidado de papel* a humorous description of dismembered female bodies; and in "Andrómeda," as we have seen, the masculine voice/vision (of Julio and the narrator combined) partakes ever so slightly in sadistic relish at the sight of a bound naked woman.[57]

The representations of the feminine that emerged in vanguard art are, not surprisingly, hybrid images. At once disturbed and disturbing, these images in varying degrees bear traces of eroticization, idealization, and debasement. But the vanguardists, to their credit, were attempting to interrogate and disrupt an institutionalized mode of representation, in which for centuries woman has stood for absolute Beauty, Unity, Art, Solace, Life, Death, etc. Arguably, they kept woman pinned beneath their gaze, but in part they relinquished control, they refused to order and unify those images, to allow woman's body to convey unproblematically the venerable allegorical meanings.[58]

Until now I have written rather unproblematically of this male gaze: I have presumed the existence of a masculine center from which that gaze originates, from whence it projects a feminine other—a composite of masculine needs, desires, and fears.[59] Although Woman as a manufactured other, represents what Man cannot admit, although she stands allegorically for the unobtainable Other, she cannot be truly other-than-masculine, for she is still made of his debris, and therefore belongs to him. Either the other-than-masculine lies elsewhere, as something yet unknown, or else it is undifferentiation itself, Bataille's *informe*: a vast field of undifferentiated difference, the entire range of possibilities of being and performing as (dare I say) human animals.

But in writing this I have written under false pretenses, for this masculine center can only be a fiction: Man stands allegorically for a center which no historical man can occupy, although, under the pretenses of the patriarchal system of signification, a center is presumed to exist. Vast symbolic and institutional hierarchies emanate from this fictional center, organizing and governing the tropes, categories, and sequences of our thoughts, our writing, our speech, as well as our social practices. Although historical men cannot stand dead-center on this non-site, certainly they, to varying degrees, partake in maintaining and reproducing this Man-made system of representation. And although historical women cannot stand on the non-site of the impossibly heterogeneous other, certainly they too shape (as they are shaped by) this system of representation. Just as men read and write women through its terms, in art as well as in "everyday life," women read and write themselves through these same terms. But if we, as men and women, stop operating under false pretenses, if we stop believing in Man as center and Woman as other, are we therefore free? Perhaps if we acknowledge the ultimate impossibility of these gendered positions, we are *free-er*. But we still can work only with the terms provided by our regime of representation, finding a measure of freedom by disrupting, rearranging, rewriting, and playing among the fragments of an impossible allegorical puzzle.

Addendum

Writing across a historical gap, I impose upon this excessive allegorical text, "Andrómeda," my own excessive allegory, one informed (perhaps deformed) by poststructuralist and feminist theory, an impossible reading for Jarnés's contemporary readers. But apparently, his readers of the nineteen-twenties found the work quite disturbing, for Jarnés addressed the problematic reception of the original "Andrómeda" in the first of two sections that he appended to the novella in 1939 and published as *La novia del viento* in 1940. In this section, "Digresión de Epimeteo" the author emerges from behind his narrator and recounts the complaints of various readers of the original "Andrómeda." First he cites the exemplary reading of "algunos expertos, ya cansados de leer esas historias pasionales que se detienen golosamente en el punto y hora en que el héroe acaba de desnudar al objeto amado" (67). These, Jarnés's *ideal* readers, had enthusiastically praised this "nueva modalidad en desenlaces novelescos," saying, "Es admirable ese modo de no dar fin a una novela. El epílogo queda a cargo del lector. El lector colabora imaginando epílogos" (67). Jarnés then humorously describes the readings of less exemplary readers who insist on knowing the "zonas reales" of the adventure: they complain of the unrealistic and inconcrete protagonist; they want to know about Carmela's anterior and posterior life; and they ask why the driver did not intervene in the story (68). One "lector impertinente" complains of the indecency of the novella:

> Y parece mentira que un hombre a quien suponíamos tan cabal se haya complacido en pasear de tal modo a una lozana mujer, a juzgar por la pintura, después de abandonarla desnuda, quién sabe cuánto tiempo, a merced de las más lúbricas miradas. Ese paseo, a solas, por una carretera, toda una noche, provocando con sus malignas reticencias la sensualidad de muchos jóvenes incautos que seducidos por la novedad . . . Porque lo peor del relato no es lo que se cuenta, sino lo que se insinúa. (69)

Jarnés concludes his account of these cantankerous readers with the sardonic comment, "Pero el lector zoilesco es así, y también es preciso complacer al lector zoilesco" (69). Then offering his sequel to this unhappy reader—named after Homer's censorious critic, Zoilo—Jarnés assures him: "Las páginas que siguen pretenderán calmar las ansias de verdad histórica que suelen acometer al buen lector—y censor de novelas" (69). With plenty of irony and a touch of cynicism, Jarnés thus declares his intent to capitulate to readers whose judgments he has just discredited. At this point in the text it is difficult to tell if he truly intends to capitulate, or if he is "setting us up." But as he continues, it seems evident that, however ironically he declared his capitulation, he does indeed mean to carry it through. He then resumes the narrative by recounting Julio's thoughts as he returns to the summer resort, having restored Carmela to the city of Augusta. This new Julio launches into an angry mental diatribe against the tendency of men and women to focus exclusively on surface appearance: "¡La piel, siempre lo exterior, sólo la hembra! No podemos librarnos de esa encantadora superficie. . . . ¡La piel! Mutuo conocimiento, base de un fecundo equilibrio, ¡es tan poco frecuente!" (71). Somehow this vehement Julio of 1939 is not quite the same "hijo de capricho," and "joven insensato" that we encountered in the "Andrómeda" of 1926 (68). And neither is the narrator of 1939 the same voyeur of 1926, who along with his character relished the sight of a naked woman in bondage. This new narrator, more intrusive and judgmental, suddenly interrupts Julio's thoughts to comment ironically: "Hasta aquí llegan aquella noche las reflexiones de Julio, reflexiones escritas para lectores graves, enemigos de todo humorismo" (72). Although the narrator here ironically undercuts the seriousness of Julio, as well as of the "lector zoilesco," he immediately takes over the diatribe himself and further develops his character's arguments: "En torno a la epidermis intacta se elaboraban dogmas y se acumularon versos. En torno a la profanada epidermis, urden su danza infernal los terribles ángeles caídos. . . . Como si algo fundamental para la vida humana pudiese arrancar de la mera fisiología" (76). The narrator continues in this didactic vein, expounding upon the three conceptions of love in our times —el *amor fetiche*, el *amor-concepto*, el *amor-instinto*—when he suddenly stops and again undercuts his own seriousness: "No hay espacio para detenerse a glosar cada uno de ellos. Que enmudezca Epimeteo [husband of Pandora], porque es preciso continuar la historia" (77).

I might generally agree with the rather progressive views so vehemently expressed here, yet I find their presence somewhat unsatisfying. Having delighted in the excess and ambiguity of "Andrómeda," I suddenly encounter an authoritarian narrator who is imposing a single interpretation upon what I have just read. His attempts at moderating his preachiness with intermittent self-mockery does not quite suffice (for irony can sometimes allow one to have it both ways). The narrative voice that had previously merged with Julio's vision now gazes down on him with a critical eye. After Julio has just resolved, "algún día, buscar la mujer dócil, sumisa, individuo más débil, que no aspira a llegar a la plena región de las ideas, ni siquiera en los actos decisivos de la vida," the narrator remarks with a patronizing tone: "No posee Julio ese profundo conocimiento de cuanto en la intimidad debe entrar en juego. Porque sin la sabiduría del hombre respecto a la mujer, y viceversa, ¿podrá la intimidad ser felizmente duradera?" (78). Julio, who in the "Andrómeda" of 1926 stood allegorically for "Everyman" caught in the allusive, elusive quest for the impossible Woman, now appears in a didactic parable as a defective character who must be taught a lesson.

In the third and final section of the novel *La novia del viento*, Julio learns his lesson. He encounters, not the docile, mindless woman he is seeking, but rather an extraordinarily independent woman, Brunilda, a painter of female nudes who is also on vacation in the summer resort of Valleclaro. A "mujer señorial" of considerable "estatura mental," Brunilda continually spars with Julio in a witty dialogue of courtship that comprises most of the narration (90, 89). Andrómeda/Star/Carmela does not reappear "in person," but her presence is palpable through the gossip of the townspeople, through the continual insinuaciones of Brunilda, and through a letter and photo she sends to Julio. In this letter Carmela informs Julio that "el dragón ha muerto," meaning that she has freed herself from a "viejo rentista" and wants to begin a new life, presumably with him (120). Julio decides to return to the city and answer her in person, but a very jealosa Brunilda convinces him to wait while she paints a gift for him. When at the end of the novel she unveils the painting before Julio,

> ¡Está allí fielmente reproducida la escena del olivo. Pero este cuerpo no es ya el maduro, el lozano cuerpo de Andrómeda, de Carmela, sino el fino, el delgado cuerpo de Brunilda. Pero estos ojos, este risueño rostro, no es el azorado, el patético rostro de Carmela . . . ¡Es Brunilda, en todo el esplendor de su clara, de su risueña desnudez! ¡Es Brunilda, la altiva! La que embruja con sus ojos de ascua, ¡estática en medio de la llama! (128).

Julio, forced to choose between two Andrómedas, chooses Brunilda and rushes to her arms: "Brunilda lanza un grito, el grito legendario que conmovía el tropel de las walkirias, el grito de la mujer victoriosa. Y ambos comienzan plenamente a arder en la misma llama" (128). After this romantic moment, Brunilda takes a knife and destroys the painting, leaving it in tatters. Presumably, Julio has now learned his lesson—how to distinguish between life and art: He has chosen the real flesh and blood woman, over the artificial one—the Andrómeda of art and literature.

The character of Brunilda seems designed to serve as a model of a modern woman, one who demands a more egalitarian relationship, and perhaps for this reason, Jarnés draws upon Germanic myth and Wagnerian opera for an aggressive feminine prototype. But this ploy merely inverts the traditional power relation as Brunilda takes the masculine role and Julio the feminine—an inversion made explicit when "Brunilda —siempre en actitud viril, decidida—abandona la terraza. Julio la sigue, dócilmente" (119). The fierce Brunilda declares to Julio her refusal to be "chiquilla a su lado": "No soy una mujer pasiva. A la muelle, a la indefensa desnudez, preferiría siempre la cota de malla. Al abanico, la lanza. A la silla de manos, un brioso corcel" (110, 126).

If Brunilda is meant to play the counterpart to the woman Julio wished for—"la mujer dócil, sumisa, individuo más débil"—certainly she fulfills this role admirably (78). But in doing so she merely conforms to another stereotype, the conniving "mujer-araña" who weaves a web to trap her mate. This image of the manipulative female is reinforced throughout the narration: at one point Brunilda feigns "el rojo vivo del pudor extremo, mientras oculta una maquiavélica sonrisa. Julio no llega a advertir el delicioso juego, y cae—avecilla incauta—en la red"; and at another point "Brunilda contempla fijamente al atónito Julio, que no encuentra ya el modo de huir de aquellos ojos tan ardientes, tan agresivos, tan seductores, detrás de los cuales una indomable voluntad sigue urdiendo su red" (99-100, 104). So although within the logic of the plot, Brunilda is designed to represent a "real" alternative to Andrómeda/Star/ Carmela—the woman inscribed with the desires of man—she cannot fulfill her purpose. Brunilda, like her antecedent, comes dressed in tropes: She is read by Julio (and by us) through a series of prototypes and stereotypes—drawn from German mythology, Wagnerian opera, and the popular image of the spunky, if not domineering, modern woman.

If Jarnés's addendum to "Andrómeda" is designed to provide narrative closure, to remove the disturbing ambiguities of the original text, to reinstate the boundary between life and art, it does not wholly succeed. Itself a heterogeneous text, it produces meanings that exceed its project. The intrusion by the author, who describes the various misreadings of "Andrómeda" and then imposes his own reading, initially confuses readers' expectations.[60] This confusion is compounded by the narrator's ambivalence towards his own thesis and his intermittent attempts at ironically undermining his own authority. Moreover, the central image —"la novia del viento"—perpetuates the theme from "Andrómeda" of the impossibility of discovering woman's true nature, and further undercuts Brunilda's ostensible role as the "real" counterpart to tropological woman. The image derives from a local legend about a "muchacha que se entrega al viento, como a un amante, hasta que el viento la desnuda y la arrebata" (97). If read as allegory, the legend echoes in reverse the story of Andrómeda, by suggesting that when the tropological inscriptions that clothe woman are blown away, she disappears, becoming nothing. But this legend, while lending the novel its title, fulfills no apparent function in the plot; and while replaying "Andrómeda's" theme —wherein woman as "essence" dissolves—Brunhilda's triumph in the end appears to cancel such an interpretation.

The outrageous heterogeneity and ambiguity of the earlier novella "Andrómeda," must have unsettled its own author. Writing years later in a much more somber time, Jarnés attempted to discipline his unruly text through an addendum that ostensibly would impose a "correct" interpretation and demonstrate the foolishness of not knowing the difference between life and art. But woman is already "art"; she is a cultural artifice comprised of either all that man lacks and desires, or, as in the novel I will next discuss, a repository for all that he loathes and denies.

NOTES

1. "Andrómeda" first appeared as a novella in a 1926 issue of *Revista de Occidente*. In 1929 Jarnés included the work in his collection of short fiction, *Salón de estío*. A decade later, while in exile in Mexico, Jarnés added two more sections and published it as a novel titled *La novia del viento* (1940). The first of these added sections, "Digresión de Epimeteo" consists of three essays in which the author satirically recounts the controversial reception of "Andrómeda" and then expounds upon his philosophy of the novel as well as upon relations between the sexes. The final section "Brunilda en llamas" bears little thematic or stylistic resemblance to the earlier story, and as we shall see later, it seems designed to cancel the very premises and effects of the original "Andrómeda." What results is a curious hodge-podge of a novel, and perhaps for this reason critics have generally ignored the work. However, if the novel in its entirety is an aesthetic

failure, it is certainly a very interesting one. To my knowledge, the only existing critical consideration of *La novia del viento* is found in Robert Spires, *Beyond the Metafictional Mode*. J.S. Bernstein and Emilia de Zuleta, in their monographs on Jarnés's works, summarize the plot but do not provide critical commentary. For general studies of Jarnés's works see: J.S. Bernstein, Victor Fuentes, Martínez Latre, and Jordi Gracia García. For studies of the avant-garde novel that include references to Jarnés's works refer to: Gustavo Pérez Firmat, José Manuel del Pino, Luis Fernández Cifuentes, Paul Ilie, and Ricardo Gullón in *La novela lírica*. See also the collection of essays edited by Darío Villanueva's, *La novela lírica*.

2. In Rubens's painting "Andrómeda," which is indeed owned by the Prado, the nude female figure nearly fills the canvas. As described in Jarnés's novella, her arms are raised and her wrists are tied to a tree. Far in the background, Perseus is rushing on horseback to the scene, and below him the sea-dragon approaches. Another painting by Rubens, "Perseus Saving Andrómeda," also in the Prado's collection, shows Perseus in full armor untying the nude and vulnerable Andrómeda, who is surrounded by Cherubim. Various copies of both paintings exist, all attributed to Rubens (or to his workshop). For a reproduction of "Andrómeda" and a list of museums holding versions of the painting, see Jan Kelch, *Peter Paul Rubens: Kritischer Katalog der Gemälde im Besitz der Gemäldegalerie Berlin* (29-36).

3. The notable study of androgynous characters is Carolyn Heilbrun, *Toward a Recognition of Androgyny*.

4. Cognitive psychologists would use the term "gender schema" to describe these textual composites. According to Sandra Bem, "a schema is a cognitive structure, a network of associations that organizes and guides an individual's perception" (355). She describes gender schema as "a diverse and sprawling network of associations encompassing not only those features directly related to male and female persons, such as anatomy, reproductive function, division of labor, and personality attributes, but also features more remotely or metaphorically related to sex, such as the angularity or roundedness of an abstract shape and the periodicity of the moon. Indeed, there appears to be no other dichotomy in human experience with as many entities assimilated to it as the distinction between male and female" (354). Wolfgang Iser in *The Act of Reading* also uses the term *schema* to describe the reading process: "social norms and contemporary and literary allusions all constitute schemata which give shape to the knowledge and memories which have been invoked—revealing simultaneously the overriding importance of the repertoire for the process of image building" (143). Teresa de Lauretis discusses this process of image-building as a semiotic practice: "If, then, subjectivity is engaged in semiosis at all levels, not just in visual pleasure but in all cognitive processes, in turn semiosis (coded expectations, patterns of response, assumptions, inferences, predictions, and, I would add fantasy) is at work in sensory perception, inscribed in the body—the human body and the film body. Finally, the notion of mapping suggests an ongoing but discontinuous process of perceiving-representing-meaning (I like to call it 'imaging') that is neither linguistic (dis-

crete, linear, syntagmatic, or arbitrary) nor iconic (analogical, paradigmatic, or motivated), but both, or perhaps neither" (*Alice Doesn't* 56).

5. These connotative paths are of course Barthes's codes. In *S/Z* he describes a code as "a perspective of quotations, a mirage of structure; we know only its departure and returns; the units which have resulted from it (those we inventory) are themselves, always, ventures out of the text, the mark, the sign of a virtual digression toward the remainder of a catalogue (*The Kidnapping* refers to every kidnapping ever written); they are so many fragments of something that has always been already read, seen, done, experienced: the code is the wake of that already. Referring to what has been written, i.e., to that Book (of culture, of life, of life as culture), it makes the text into a prospectus of this Book" (20-21). In "Textual Analysis of a Tale of Poe," Barthes defines the codes as "associative fields, a supratextual organization of notations imposing a certain idea of structure, the authority of the code, is for us, essentially cultural: the codes are certain types of *déjà-vu, déjà-lu,* and *déjà-fait*: the code is the form this déjà takes, constitutive of all the writing in the world" (93). See chapter I for a more complete discussion of Barthes' approach.

6. Here I oversimplify an exceedingly complex process of circular migration from books to life and from life to books. For Barthes, "the inter-text is: the impossibility of living outside the infinite text—whether this text be Proust or the daily newspaper or the television screen: the book creates the meaning, the meaning creates life" (*Pleasure of the Text* 36).

7. In the field of art criticism and history, recent critical and theoretical works examine visual art as text and as rhetoric. For collections of essays employing these approaches see: Norman Bryson, Michael Ann Holly and Keith Moxey, *Visual Theory: Painting and Interpretation*; Brian Wallis, *Art After Modernism: Rethinking Representation*; Wendy Steiner, *Image and Code* and *The Colors of Rhetoric*. Also useful are W.J.T. Mitchell's works, *The Language of Images* and *Iconology*. For an example of the application of narratology to visual arts, refer to Mieke Bal and Norman Bryson, "Semiotics and Art History." For recent studies of the representation of woman in visual arts, see: Marcia Pointon, *Naked Authority: The Body in Western Painting*; Linda Nochlin's essay in Bryson, Holly and Moxey; and also Kate Linker's essay in Wallis. For a study of both iconic and verbal representations of woman in nineteenth-century Spain, refer to Lou Charnon-Deutsch, *Gender and Representation: Women in Spanish Realist Fiction*.

8. See Teresa de Lauretis, *Technologies of Gender* for a discussion of the social construction of gender. She argues that gender, "both as representation and as self-representation, is the product of various social technologies, such as cinema, and of institutionalized discourses, epistemologies, and critical practices, as well as practices of daily life" (2).

9. Striptease as a metaphor for the unveiling of narrative truth has become commonplace. Roland Barthes in *The Pleasure of the Text* contrasts the gradual unveiling in classical narrative with the intermittent erotic flashes of the avant-garde text (10-11). A well-known fictional critic, Morris Zapp of David Lodge's

novel *Small World*, develops this same idea in his conference paper, "Textuality as Striptease" (20, 24-27).

10. Adrienne Munich in *Andromeda's Chains* explores the Andromeda myth as an obsessional subject for male painters and writers in the nineteenth century. For Munich, each representation of the naked and bound female figure yields multiple and apparently irreconcilable meanings, a mixture of pornographic and allegorical elements. She suggests that the Perseus-Andromeda myth "became a coded account of male conflicts about the sex-gender system" and that men "used the Andromeda myth not only to celebrate the rewards of a patriarchal system but also to record their discomforts with it" (2).

11. For a discussion of eroticism in Jarnés's works see Víctor Fuentes, "La dimensión estético-erótica y la novelística de Jarnés" and "Jarnés: Metaficción y discurso estético-erótico."

12. Robert Hershberger provides an insightful analysis of masculine voyeurism in Jarnés's *El convidado de papel*.

13. This nude/naked dichotomy has been most notably addressed by John Berger in *Ways of Seeing* and Kenneth Clark in *The Nude*. Marcia Pointon uses the term nude "in the sense of the conventions within which the naked body is represented within high art forms, observing unwritten rules concerning such matters as pose, gesture and the absence of body hair" (83). (Spanish, unlike English, does not provide two terms to express the nude/naked distinction). Later in the novel Julio contemplates the contrast between the idealized nude in Art and the naked body in the flesh: "Ese repliegue bajo los senos opulentos, que siempre escamotea el escultor, en ella lo escamoteaba la misma indecisión, del amanecer. Ese convexo perfil de la cadera, cortada en ángulo, producido por la adiposidad de la modelo, que suele eliminar el buen pintor, en ella lo rectificaba la misma sombra del coche" (43).

14. An interesting study of this conditioned obliviousness in our readings of artistic representations of Christ is Leo Steinberg, *The Sexuality of Christ in Renaissance Art and in Modern Oblivion*. Steinberg argues that we are "educated into incomprehension," and fail to read the erotic signifiers in religious representations (108).

15. For thoughtful essays on this question, see: Elizabeth Flynn and Patrocinio P. Schwieckart, Eds., *Gender and Reading*; and Shari Benstock, ed., *Feminist Issues in Literary Scholarship*. Jonathan Culler offers a summary of feminist thought on this issue in "Reading as a Woman," *On Deconstruction*. See also: Judith Fetterley, *The Resisting Reader*; Teresa de Lauretis, *Alice Doesn't*; Gayatri Spivak, "Finding Feminist Readings: Dante-Yeats"; and Shoshana Felman, "Rereading Femininity."

16. The well-known work by Judith Fetterley, *The Resisting Reader*, argues that the major works of American fiction have "designs" upon woman readers. She calls for women to resist those designs through a kind of re-vision.

17. Teresa de Lauretis discusses this double identification by a female reader: simultaneously or alternately with the masculine subject (through his gaze), and with feminine object or image (the body or the landscape) (*Alice Doesn't* 143-44).

18. I will quote at length a thoughtful statement by Julia Kristeva from an interview published in *Tel quel*, 1974: "The belief that 'one is a woman' is almost as absurd and obscurantist as the belief that 'one is a man.' I say 'almost' because there are still many goals which women can achieve: freedom of abortion and contraception, day-care centers for children, equality on the job, etc. Therefore, we must use 'we are women' as an advertisement or slogan for our demands. On a deeper level, however, a woman cannot 'be'; it is something which does not even belong in the order of being. It follows that a feminist practice can only be negative, at odds with what already exists so that we may say 'that's not it' and 'that's still not it.' In 'woman' I see something that cannot be represented, something that is not said, something above and beyond nomenclatures and ideologies. There are certain 'men' who are familiar with this phenomenon; it is what some modern texts never stop signifying: testing the limits of language and sociality—the law and its transgression, mastery and (sexual) pleasure—without reserving one for males and the other for females, on the condition that it is never mentioned. From this point of view, it seems that certain feminist demands revive a kind of naive romanticism, a belief in identity (the reverse of phallocratism), if we compare them to the experience of both poles of sexual difference as is found in the economy of Joycian or Artaudian prose or in modern music—Cage, Stockhausen. I pay close attention to the particular aspect of the work of the avant-garde which dissolves identity, even sexual identities; and in my theoretical formulations I try to go against metaphysical theories that censure what I just labeled 'a woman'—this is what, I think, makes my research that of a woman" (in *New French Feminisms: An Anthology*, eds., Elaine Marks and Isabelle de Courtivron (137-38).

19. See William Paulson's study, *The Noise of Culture*. By noise, Paulson means "anything that gets mixed up with messages as they are sent"—those elements that muddle, exceed, or interfere with the transmission of information (ix, 67). Literature "functions as the noise of culture, as a perturbation or source of variety in the circulation and production of discourses and ideas" (ix). Paulson argues that "by recognizing the irreducible presence of noise in literature, and in turn literature's function as the noise of culture, we can understand how literary meaning can be neither authoritative nor nonexistent, how literature's cultural function can be positive and yet not conservative" (181).

20. In *Rhetorical Power* Steven Mailloux proposes a historical criticism that examines how a given text participates within the cultural conversation at the moments of its production and reception. Mailloux bases his approach, not only on Burke, but also on the neopragmatism of Richard Rorty who sees conversation as "the ultimate context within which knowledge is to be understood" (Rorty 389). In *Philosophy and the Mirror of Nature* Rorty argues for an "edifying philosophy" that "aims at continuing a conversation rather than at discovering truth" (373).

21. The *Revista de Occidente* began publication in July, 1923. Ortega invited Benjamín Jarnés to contribute in 1925. Shortly thereafter, Jarnés joined the staff as a paid contributor of fiction and book reviews. His novella, "Andrómeda" appeared in the August, 1926, issue. His reviews appear in nearly every issue between 1925 and 1936, when the *Revista* suspended publication. According to Evelyne López Campillo's calculations, Jarnés was the most prolific contributor to the *Revista*, with 89 contributions appearing between 1925 to 1936 (72).

22. In stressing the importance of "live dialogue" in Ortega's life, Rockwell Gray cites and then refutes the English historian Raymond Carr's "curt judgment of prewar Madrid culture." In Carr's view, "this emphasis on conversational exchange and journalism was one of the main weaknesses of Spanish intellectual life: conversation was the essential foundation of Ortega y Gasset's work." Gray responds, "Carr is certainly right in one sense, precisely as Ortega's portrait of mediocre salons indicates; but when those endless conversations bore fruit, the result was the provocative, polished, and quasi-colloquial essay at which Ortega became a master" (175).

23. In these remarks and those that follow, I do not want to overstate Ortega's authority over the *Revista* circle and its content. According to López Campillo. "la *Revista* no fue la revista de Ortega, en un sentido estrecho: Ortega es el iniciador, el mecenas. No es su ideólogo, ni siquiera su mentor, y puede decirse, . . . que él colaboró menos en la revista que otros muchos. Fundó esta revista para formar lectores que tuvieran su cultura, para crear una atmósfera cultural en la que él pudiera ser leído, discutido y apreciado por sus iguales" (251). However, from my survey of *Revista* content, it seems evident that the aesthetic, philosophical, and psychological contributions for the most part coincide with Ortega's views. And it is striking how often various contributors cite Ortega and reiterate his opinions.

24. I base these observations upon a survey of the *Revista's* contents from 1923 through 1930. For a more extensive summary of the its content, see Evelyne López Campillo, *La Revista de Occidente y la formación de minorías (1923-1936)*. For a discussion of the aesthetic and philosophical underpinnings of the *Revista*, see Andrés Soria Olmedo, *Vanguardismo y crítica literaria en España*. Also see Rockwell Gray, *The Imperative of Modernity: An Intellectual Biography of José Ortega y Gasset*, which situates the *Revista* within the social-political context in 1920's Spain..

25. Although undoubtedly the *Revista* wielded great influence in Spanish intellectual life, we should remember that the journal reached a fairly restricted public. Between 1923 and 1936, its press run was three thousand copies per issue, of which more than half went to Latin America (Gray 137, López Campillo 66). However, López Campillo points out that the *Revista* readers were strategically situated in the universities in the professions (66).

26. Evelyne López Campillo discusses the *Revista's* neglect of Freud. From 1923 to 1925 three articles critical of Freud appear along with one favorable review of *The Interpretation of Dreams*. Rockwell Gray asserts that after 1925,

Freud's name never appears. I should point out, however, that Ortega provided a prologue to an Spanish edition of Freud's works, published in 1922.

27. For example, the first issue contains an article, complete with illustrations, by the German psychiatrist Ernst Kretschmer, in which he connects certain body types with specific mental disorders. His arguments seem quite compatible with those of the German eugenicists who later provided "scientific" support for the Final Solution.

28. Certainly, the *Revista de Occidente* was subject to censorship under the dictatorship of Primo de Rivera. But as yet, I have encountered no evidence that the journal tested the censorship laws. Rockwell Gray discusses at length Ortega's ambivalence about the role of the intellectual in political life. Ortega argued that "men of ideas" should be given greater "social power" and influence without being obliged to involve themselves directly in partisan politics (172). Also see pp. 136-50.

29. Not until the mid-nineteen-twenties did a feminist movement become organized and politically significant in Spain. Whereas feminism in other Western countries generally aligned itself with liberal and secular politics, the Spanish movement was dominated by Catholic women's organizations, most prominently the Asociación Nacional de Mujeres Españolas, which concerned itself with humanitarian and charitable causes. Under the dictatorship of Primo de Rivera, women were granted the vote only in municipal elections, and only if they were over twenty-three, unmarried or widowed, and independent of parental support. During the *Cortes Contituyentes* that ratified the Republican Constitution, women's suffrage was hotly debated and eventually approved in 1931. Those who most strongly opposed women's suffrage came from the radical left, while many conservatives, along with liberals and moderate socialists were in favor. Interestingly, many from the left as well as the right assumed that Spanish women, given their limited education and adherence to the Church, would vote more conservatively. In the elections of 1933, the first in which women participated, conservatives indeed won the majority of seats in Parliament, and the leftists blamed their loss on the women's vote. The new Constitution guaranteed women equal access to education and employment, equal rights within marriage, and the right to divorce. The following year, the *Cortes* passed one of the most progressive divorce laws in Europe. Nearly all these rights were abrogated in 1938 by the Franco regime. For a detailed history of the feminist movement in Spain, see Geraldine M. Scanlon, *La polémica feminista en la España contemporánea (1868-1974)*. For a history of the Spanish women's suffrage movement, refer to Concha Fagoaga, *La voz y el voto de la mujeres: El sufragismo en España, 1877-1931*. A broader historical overview, from the Middle Ages to 1936, may be found in González, Anabel, et al., *Los orígenes del feminismo en España*.

30. See Teresa Bordons and Susan Kirkpatrick for an interesting account of Rosa Chacel's troubled professional relations with Ortega and her tenuous status in the *Revista* circle.

31. During *Revista's* first year of publication, four of the five issues contained installments of extended essays by Georg Simmel, "Filosofía de la moda," and "Lo masculino y lo femenino: Para una psicología de los sexos." The essay I discuss here, "Cultura femenina" appeared serialized in two issues of 1925. In the following year, the *Revista* published, "Fidelidad y gratitud," which without explicitly treating the psychology of gender, examines the phenomenon of fidelity in love, marriage, friendship, and patriotism. All of these articles were translated from the original German and published in Spanish after his death in 1918.

32. Geraldine Scanlon, in her history of Spanish feminism, provides a useful summary of Marañón's views (183-87).

33. See also Marañon's article "Sexo y trabajo."

34. After 1929 Jung became a more frequent contributor to the *Revista*. Rosa Chacel in "Esquemas de los problemas prácticos y actuales del amor" (1931), engaged Jung's arguments, in particular his assertion that Eros and Logos serve as the foundation respectively of feminine and masculine psychology. Rejecting Jung's essentialist differenciation between genders, Chacel "argues that the two principles cannot be assigned a gender, that Eros and Logos manifest themselves in all human subjects, female or male" (Bordons and Kirkpatrick 289). For a more complete summary see Teresa Bordons and Susan Kirkpatrick, "Chacel's *Teresa* and Ortega's Canon."

35. Manuel García Morente served as the first managing editor of the *Revista* and frequently contributed articles and reviews.

36. Other works by Ortega on the essence of femininity include: "Divagación ante el retrato de la Marquesa de Santillana" (1918); "Esquema de Salomé" (1921); "Epílogo al libro *De Francesca a Beatrice*" (1924); "Paisaje con una corza al fondo" (1927); "La percepción del prójimo" (1929); and *El hombre y la gente* (1949-50). For summaries and commentaries on Ortega's views of women, see: Flora Guzmán, "La mujer en la mirada de Ortega y Gasset"; Darcy Donahue, "Mujer y hombre en Ortega"; Maryellen MacGuigan, "Is Woman a Question?"; and Geraldine Scanlon, *La polémica feminista*, 188-89. For short excerpts from Ortega's more extreme antifeminist writings, see Linda A. Bell, ed., *Visions of Women*. For an exhaustive, topically indexed bibliography on Ortega, refer to Anton Donoso and Harold C. Raley, *José Ortega y Gasset: A Bibliography of Secondary Sources*.

37. Maryellen Bieder in "Woman and the Twentieth-Century Spanish Literary Canon: The Lady Vanishes," discusses the absence of female protagonists and authors from 1900 to 1936. She observes that whereas "female protagonists as created by the nineteenth-century narrative tradition—women not only of flesh and blood but of thoughts and desires—are written out of fiction, the twentieth-century novel closes in on itself to privilege male experience" (305). While I agree in large measure with her argument, I believe Bieder overstates the degree to which female characters in novels—such as *Fortunata y Jacinta, La Regenta, La de Bringas, Madame Bovary, Anna Karenina*—are truly endowed with subjectivity. Although they are central characters, they remain objects of examination,

pinned under the supremely confident gaze of a presumably male narrator, who documents their behavior within the stranglehold of a fictional society. I agree with Bieder's view of the novels from 1898 to 1920, in which the narrative gaze turns inward as the male subject examines himself—evidenced in the early novels of Unamuno, Azorín, Valle Inclán, and Baroja. But Bieder gives short shrift to the novels of the twenties in her analysis. During the vanguard period, woman returns as the object of examination, but she herself, her "nature," becomes the problem rather than the society that constrains her. And arguably, the supreme confidence of the male narrator or character disappears. Often the masculine subject is ironically drawn, like the comic, bungling antihero of silent film.

38. Most critics—including Eugenio G. De Nora, Víctor Fuentes, and Gustavo Pérez Firmat—concur with Paul Ilie in viewing Jarnés as "one of the most conscientious practitioners of Ortegan theory" (247). Robert Spires generally agrees, but notes: "Somewhat challenging to a dehumanized reading, however, is one that stresses the sensual and erotic aspects of Jarnés's novels" (*Transparent Simulacra* 118). In reference to the art/life issue, Emilia de Zuleta denies that Jarnés subscribed to their "separation": "no hay pugna entre vida y arte. Por el contrario, las relaciones del arte con la vida, a los ojos de Jarnés, son recíprocas y profundas, y a lo largo de los años se complace en describirlas recurriendo, a veces, a símbolos expresivos de la inextricable integración entre ambas esferas" (34). De Zuleta quotes Jarnés, "¿Qué es el arte? La ruta de un hombre hacia la profunda realidad de los seres y de las cosas." . . . "Lo difícil no es crear de la nada, sino crear de lo que nos rodea" (40). She contends that Jarnés's quarrel with realism was not that it failed in its attempt to capture the real, but that "se conformaba con las apariencias, con los signos superficiales de la verdadera realidad" (40). Roberta Johnson also takes issue with the notion that the works by Jarnés, as well as by Salinas and Chacel, are embodiments of Ortega's aesthetic ideas. She argues that "these writers' literary-philosophical origins are considerably more heterodox" and that they entered in dialogue not only with Ortega's aesthetics, but also with "the Generation of '98's metaphysical novels and the serious phenomenological prose of Juan Ramón and Miró" (173).

39. This is indeed how *El convidado de papel* has been read; and thematically and stylistically, "Andrómeda" resembles that work in many respects. See Robert Spires, *Transparent Simulacra*, pp. 118-30.

40. I must emphasize once more that I refer to the 1926 version of "Andrómeda." The addendum of 1939 attempts to provide the closure that the original novella lacked.

41. Etymologically, in ancient Greek, *allos* means "other" and *agoreuei* "to speak," in other words, "to speak other" (Owens 205). Going beyond the etymological level, definitions of allegory are extremely problematic. A survey of prominent works on allegory reveal a wide range of definitions, from "strict construction" to "loose construction," in which the concept becomes impossibly broad. For the purposes of this study, I require only the most traditional definition of allegory: "a story or visual image with a second distinct meaning partially hidden behind

its literal or visible meaning. The principal technique of allegory is personification, whereby abstract qualities are given human shape—as in public statues of Liberty or Justice. An allegory may be conceived as a metaphor that is extended into a structured system. In written narrative, allegory involves a continuous parallel between two (or more) levels of meaning in a story, so that its persons and events corrrespond to their equivalents in a system of ideas or a chain of events external to the tale" (Baldnick, *The Concise Oxford Dictionary of LIterary Terms* 5). For discussions of the history and definition of the term, from a more traditional viewpoint, see: Angus Fletcher, *Allegory, The Theory of a Symbolic Mode*; Edwin Honig, *Dark Conceit: The Making of Allegory*; and Maureen Quilligan, *The Language of Allegory*. Walter Benjamin's study, *The Origin of German Tragic Drama*, has influenced poststructuralist discussions of allegory, among them Paul de Man's *Allegories of Reading* and the collection of essays edited by Stephan Greenblatt, *Allegory and Representation*. For a discussion of allegory in postmodernist art, see: Craig Owens, "The Allegorical Impulse: Towards a Theory of Postmodernism."

42. Fineman is relying on Roman Jakobson's linguistic formula, according to which "allegory would be the poetical projection of the metaphoric axis onto the metonymic, where metaphor is understood as the synchronic system of differences which consititutes the order of languages (*langue*) and metonymy as the diachronic principle of combination and connection by means of which structure is actualized in time and in speech (*parole*)" (Fineman 31).

43. Northrop Frye argues that "all commentary is allegorical interpretation, an attaching of ideas to the structure of poetic imagery. The instant that any critic permits himself to make a genuine comment about a poem . . ., he has begun to allegorize" (89).

44. John Berger in *Ways of Seeing* discusses the *Vanitas* tradition rather accusatorially: "The mirror was often used as a symbol of the vanity of woman. The moralizing, however, was mostly hypocritical. You painted a naked woman because you enjoyed looking at her, you put a mirror in her hand and you called the painting Vanity, thus morally condemning the woman whose nakedness you had depicted for your own pleasure. The real function of the mirror was otherwise. It was to make the woman connive in treating herself, as first and foremost, a sight" (51). Marcia Pointon, departing somewhat from Berger, considers the mirror in the *Vanitas* tradition as "a mechanism within a discourse on art and nature. Woman looking at herself whether in a mirror or in the form of a sculpted bust of herself is locked into a cycle of re-presentation outside which she has no existence. She is defined exclusively within the closed system of circulating reflection. The mirror in post-sixteenth-century culture . . . corresponds to art as a practice; it is the artefact through which nature is viewed and processed, art becoming a mirror to the world" (29).

45. Sherry Ortner, in "Is Female to Male as Nature Is to Culture?," discusses the symbolic practices whereby woman is identified with nature and man with culture. At the same time, however, woman in her domestic role has traditionally

been reponsible for the acculturation of children. According to Ortner, the unstable intermediate position of woman between nature and culture accounts for those cultural and historical inversions in which woman sometimes become aligned with culture and man with nature. For example, in the mythology of the American Wild West, in the ideologies of Nazi Germany and Franco's Spain, women were viewed as the guardians of civilization and morality.

46. For works on the allegorical function of woman, see Marine Warner's *Monuments and Maidens*, an exhaustive compendium of feminine allegorical personifications. For case studies and analyses of feminine personification in nineteenth-century scientific culture, refer to Ludmilla Jordanova, *Sexual Visions*. In *Spurs: Nietzsche's Styles* Jacques Derrida discusses the implicit allegorical function of woman in Nietzsche's thought. See also: Londa Schiebinger, "Feminine Icons: The Face of Early Modern Science"; Marcia Pointon, *Naked Authority*; and Pilar Pedraza, *La bella: Enigma y pesadilla*.

47. The term *fetishism*, derived from Freudian discourse, is more commonly used by feminist theorists to describe the function of woman in our system of representation. In Diana Fuss's words, "A fetish (typically a woman's legs, breasts, face, or other body part) is a substitute for the missing maternal phallus, a prop or accessory fashioned to veil its terrifying absence" (720). Clearly, in both allegory and fetishism a "prop" is made to stand in for the unobtainable Other.

48. According Luce Irigaray, "The rejection, the exclusion of a female imaginary certainly puts woman in the position of experiencing herself only fragmentarily, in the little-structured margins of a dominant ideology, as waste, or excess, what is left of a mirror invested by the (masculine) 'subject' to reflect himself, to copy himself" (*This Sex Which is Not One* 30). Diana Fuss also appropriates this metaphor: "femininity is itself an accessory: it operates as a repository for culture's representational waste" ("Homospectatorial Fashion Photography" 720).

49. In "God and the *Jouissance* of The Woman," Lacan wrote: "*The* woman can only be written with *The* crossed through. There is no such thing as *The* woman, where the definite article stands for the universal. There is no such thing as *The* woman since of her essence—having already risked the term, why think twice about it?—of her essence, she is not all" (144).

50. The metaphor of masquerade derives from Jacques Lacan, "The Meaning of the Phallus," pp. 84. See also Ellie Ragland-Sullivan, "The Sexual Masquerade: A Lacanian Theory of Sexual Difference," and Jacqueline Rose's introduction to *Feminine Sexuality: Jacques Lacan and the école freudienne* (edited by Juliet Mitchell and J. Rose), pp. 43-44.

51. I am indebted here to the work of various feminist theorists. Sherry Benstock describes the feminine other as "the vanishing point of representation," that "any system must posit *and* exclude in order to achieve a fiction of self-consistency" (*Textualizing* xxx). According to Luce Irigaray, the desire that creates woman as object is just another failure of the subject; "for where he projects a something to absorb, to take, to see, to possess . . . as well as a patch of ground to stand upon, a mirror to catch his reflection, he is already faced by another specu-

larization. Whose twisted character is her inability to say what she represents. The quest for the 'object' becomes a game of Chinese boxes. Infinitely receding" (*Speculum* 134). In Shoshana Felman's view, "the conventional polarity of masculine and feminine names woman as a *metaphor of man*.... Man alone has thus the privilege of proper meaning, of *literal* identity: femininity, as signifier, cannot signify *itself*; it is but a metaphor, a figurative substitute" (25). Gayatri Spivak contends, "As the radically other [woman] does not *really exist*, yet her name remains one of the important names for displacement, the special mark of deconstruction" ("Displacement" 184). Jacques Derrida suggests: "Perhaps woman —a non-identity, a non-figure, a simulacrum—is distance's very chasm, the outdistancing of distance, the intervals' cadence, distance itself" (*Spurs* 49).

52. A more explicitly cubist description of a character can be found in *El profesor inútil*, where the first-person narrator, contemplating a female character, comments: "A las fórmulas ascéticas, prefiero las fórmulas cubistas. A Valdés Leal, Picasso, el humorista. Rápidamente los brazos de Carlota se me truecan en cilindros; los senos en pequeñas pirámides, mejor que en casquetes esféricos de curva peligrosa; los muslos en troncos de cono, invertidos... Traslado al cuerpo de Carlota todo el arsenal de figuras del texto. Todo en ella es ya un conjunto de problemas espaciales.... Es una pura geometría, lo más cercana posible a una pura estatua" (104-05). Paul Ilie discusses similar cubist descriptions of the female form in *Locura y muerte de nadie* (Ilie 251-53).

53. Various critics have commented on Jarnés employment of cubist technique, particularly his "geometrización del cuerpo femenino" (Gullón 116). Generally, they attribute this tendency to the project of "deshumanización." For discussions of literary cubist technique in various works by Jarnés, see: Ricardo Gullón, 116-17; Paul Ilie, 251-53; Victor Fuentes, 7-8; María Pilar Martínez Latre, 66; and Emilia de Zuleta, 53-54.

54. I rely on Rosalind Krauss's astute commentary on the *informe* in *L'Amor Fou: Photography and Surrealism*.

55. Xavière Gauthier makes this argument in *Surréalisme et sexualité* (1971). More recently, various literary and art critics have engaged in a polemic over the issue of misogyny in surrealism: In *Surrealism and Woman* May Ann Caws, Rudolf Kuenzli, and Gwen Raaberg, emphasize the mysogynistic elements in surrealism. (See also Caws' essay in Suleiman's collection, *The Female Body in Western Culture*). In *L'Amor Fou*, Rosalind Krauss argues that surrealism attempted to transgress the categories of gender; Susan Rubin Suleiman in *Subversive Intent* seems to take the middle ground. I would suggest that both sides are correct and that many images from avant-garde art and literature are (like "Andrómeda") hybrids of complicitous and transgressive elements.

56. For examples of these images, see Rosalind Krauss and Jane Livingston, *L'Amor Fou: Photography and Surrealism*.

57. In *El convidado de papel*, this wickedly ironic passage occurs when Julio, the protagonist, is in the room of a "Venus Mercantil," or prostitute. He observes her contemplating herself in the mirror: "envuelta en su traje de faena, es decir,

en su piel. Aunque en plena integridad exterior, no como otras mujeres que Julio había visto desnudas, pero siempre hechas pedazos; mutiladas por el verdugo o por el bisturí" (37). The narrator then continues revealing Julio's thoughts, citing numerous images of mutilated and dismembered female bodies: "aquella matrona colgada de las trenzas, ante Apolo, sobre un rojo braserillo, donde, lentamente, se le iban los pies dorando a fuego. Y aquella otra atada a dos árboles violentamente aproximados que, al recobrar su normal postura, partían por dos con toda exactitud el virginal dividendo.... Recuerda senos de doncellas cercenados sobre un plato; niñas aserradas por el talle; ... frentes de muchacha atravesada por un clavo; piernas, brazos, dedos sueltos" (37-38). At the end of this lengthy description, the narrator reveals the source of these gory images—"un ejemplar ilustrado de las Actas de los Mártires recomendado por el cura y por un texto antiguo de ginecología desechado por el médico" (38).

58. Rosalind Krauss argues that although surrealism took "the love act and its object—woman—as its central, obsessional subject, it must be seen that in much of surrealist practice, woman . . . is nowhere in nature. Having dissolved the natural in which 'normalcy' can be grounded, surrealism was at least potentially open to the dissolving of distinctions that Bataille insisted was the job of the *informe*. Gender, at the heart of the surrealist project, was one of these categories. If within surrealist poetry *woman* was constantly in construction, then at certain moments that project could at least prefigure a next step, in which a reading is opened onto deconstruction. It is for this reason that the frequent characterizations of surrealism as antifeminist seem to me to be mistaken" (95).

59. The now commonplace term "male gaze" derives from Laura Mulvey's influential essay, "Visual Pleasure and Narrative Cinema" (1975), included in the collection *Visual and Other Pleasures*.

60. See Robert Spires's discussion of the metafictional implications of these authorial intrusions in *Beyond the Metafictional Mode*, 50-57.

III. CHARACTER DEFECTS:
MIGUEL DELIBES'S *CINCO HORAS CON MARIO*

> [T]he false death, the atrocious death, is what has no end, the interminable. ("For God's sake!—quick!—put me to sleep—or, quick—waken me!—quick!—I say to you that I am dead!") The stereotype is this nauseating impossibility of dying. (Roland Barthes, *The Pleasure of the Text* 43)

Reading through Received Knowledge

Miguel Delibes's novel, *Cinco horas con Mario* (1966), asks readers to envision a woman sitting alone before a coffin, talking to her dead husband, Mario, throughout the night.[1] Holding Mario's Bible, Carmen reads the passages that he had underlined, each serving as an ironic prelude to a litany of complaints, accusations, and unhappy memories.

> *Casa y hacienda, herencia son de los padres, pero una mujer prudente es don de Yavé* y en lo que a ti concierne, cariño, supongo que estarás satisfecho, que motivos no te faltan, que aquí, para inter nos, la vida no te ha tratado tan mal, tú dirás, una mujer sólo para ti, de no mal ver, que con cuatro pesetas ha hecho milagros, no se encuentra a la vuelta de la esquina, desengáñate. Y ahora que empiezan las complicaciones, zas, adiós, muy buenas, como la primera noche, ¿recuerdas?, te vas y me dejas sola tirando del carro. Y no es que me queje, entiéndelo bien... (39)

This repetitive, disjointed, somewhat comic harangue continues for five hours, or 244 pages, and constitutes the body of the novel.[2] From it we construct a portrait of a character notable for her utter lack of redeeming characteristics.

But before we begin reading Carmen's soliloquy, we have already formed a decidedly negative opinion of her character. A prologue, narrated in third person, functions to "set" in readers' minds an initial impression of Carmen that will govern our interpretations of her chaotic monologue. When the narrator introduces Carmen, she is resting on the bed, exhausted after receiving a long stream of visitors come to *dar los pésames*. Through her head flash images of a multitude of "bultos obstinados, lamigosos," their "rostros inexpresivos como palos"—each of whom she has mechanically kissed, although "en realidad, no se besaban, [sino que] cruzaban estudiadamente las cabezas, primero del lado izquierdo, luego del derecho, y besaban al aire, tal vez a algún cabello desmandado, de forma que una y otra sintieran los chasquidos de los besos pero no su efusión" (16, 10, 11). Through her ears echo their formulaic condolences: "Cuando me lo dijeron, no podía creerlo"; "Lo dicho"; "Salud para encomendarle a Dios"; "El corazón es muy traicionero"; "Cuídate, Carmen, los pequeños te necesitan" (18, 13, 14, 10). She recalls the day's events in confused, disordered sequence: her attempt to awaken her husband, the doctor's arrival and pronouncement of death, her children's "inappropriate" reactions, her preparation of the corpse, and the presentation of the casket in Mario's study.

Upon reading each of Carmen's narrated actions, thoughts, and comments, we allude to our storehouse of received knowledge and infer each of the traits that will name, or *characterize* her.[3] In Roland Barthes's words,

> thus begins a process of nomination which is the essence of the reader's activity: to read is to struggle to name, to subject the sentences of the text to a semantic transformation. This transformation is erratic; it consists in hesitating among several names. . . . The connotator refers not so much to a name as to a synonymic complex . . . thus, reading is absorbed in a kind of metonymic skid, each synonym adding to its neighbor some new trait, some new departure. (*S/Z* 92)

As we continue attaching traits to her proper name, Carmen gradually expands in our minds as a swarm of signs, ever expanding, ever changing, each sign in turn capable of attracting additional signs as we read and imagine. In this process of nomination, we employ a culturally learned psycho-logic based on received ideas about the significance of various human behaviors.

Consider, for example, the following set of behaviors: Carmen begs to have the honorific "Ilustrísimo Señor" inscribed on the *esquela fune-*

raria (included in the novel), but is told that the title can be granted only to directors, not to *catedráticos de instituto*. During the wake Carmen exiles Bertrán to the kitchen, explaining in an aside, "Un bedel no debe estar nunca donde estén los catedráticos" (13). After shaving and dressing the corpse, Carmen takes great pride in its appearance, commenting to a friend, "Nunca vi un muerto semejante, te lo prometo. No ha perdido siquiera el color" (12). Repeatedly, she expresses annoyance that her son Mario refuses to wear mourning and that he cried only in private. And she obsessively worries about the propriety of her large breasts swelling the too-tight sweater, saying, "Estos pechos míos son un descaro, no son pechos de viuda" (29). From this series of behaviors and utterances, we deduce that Carmen is overly concerned with appearances and assign her the traits of superficiality, vanity, and shallowness.

Based on another set of related behaviors, we continue this process of naming Carmen's traits: she spends the afternoon in Mario's study laboriously turning around all the books with "cubiertas chillonas que sobresalían del crespón negro" (13). After noticing her hands covered with dust, she remarks to Valen, "para eso es para lo que sirven los libros" (17). Later, as she listens to Mario's friends, grouped around the coffin, she cannot understand them, because "aquellos hombres hablaban en clave" (24). She admits at one point: "yo para eso de las palabras soy un desastre" (30). And of course, we notice her ungrammatical speech patterns—the endless run-on sentences interrupted with colloquial expressions. From this set of information, we infer that Carmen lacks formal education and places little value upon book-learning. We might assign her the trait ignorant or, more generously, uneducated; and we might surmise that her anti-intellectual stance betrays defensiveness about her educational deficiencies.

From Carmen's response to her children's "inappropriate" reactions to their father's death, we further develop our image of her character. When her teenage daughter Menchu refuses to look at her father's corpse, pleading, "¡por favor, que me horroriza, dejadme!," Carmen, with the maid's help, "la había obligado a entrar y la había forzado a abrir los párpados que ella se obstinaba en cerrar" (12). Later that day, Carmen complains to Valentina that her daughter "no hacía más que chillar, como una histérica"; and while admitting, "Yo pienso que la hice daño," she insists that "algún día me lo agradecerá" (23). When her six-year-old son, Borja, comes home from school shouting "¡Yo quiero que se muera papá todos los días para no ir al Colegio!," Carmen "le había golpeado despiadadamente, hasta que la mano empezó a dolerle" (17). From this information we assign Carmen additional traits—insensitive, tyrannical, and perhaps brutal.

Just in case readers might be leery of jumping to conclusions about Carmen, the narrator at times intervenes to *tell* us what to think of her. For example, as Carmen is expressing to Valentina her pride in the corpse, the narrator suddenly interrupts and informs us that "Carmen experimentaba una oronda vanidad de muerto, como si lo hubiese fabricado con las propias manos. Como Mario, ninguno; era su muerto; ella misma lo había manufacturado" (12). In another instance, when Carmen is expressing embarrassment about her large breasts, the narrator again interrupts in order to drive home the significance of this detail: "El suéter negro de Carmen clareaba en las puntas de los senos debido a la turgencia. En puridad, los pechos de Carmen, aun revestidos de negro, eran excesivamente pugnaces para ser luto" (16).

If we are thus compelled to construct a rather negative image of Carmen, we form quite a different impression of her husband, who although deceased, will "live" in our minds through Carmen's evocations of the past.[4] Beginning with the prologue, the comments of mourners, of Carmen and her son lead us to infer the traits that will mark him as a character. Our first impression of Mario is formed when one of his friends says repeatedly to the deaf Bertrán, each time progressively louder: "Se mueren los buenos y quedamos los malos" (13). We are thereby led provisionally to name this dead character, "Mario the good." This judgment is corroborated soon after, when we learn of Mario's concern for the poor: Carmen, lamenting the arrival of some low-class mourners, remarks that Mario "tenía un gran cartel entre la gente baja" (20); and the typesetter, who printed the *esquela*, also testifies, "don Mario defendió a los pobres sin hacerse rico" (22). Next, we surmise that Mario was an intellectual, judging from the size of his library and his son's protest upon finding that Carmen had turned his books around: "los libros eran él" (26). However, Mario may not be entirely without flaws, for it seems that this teacher, intellectual, and progressive thinker never tried to teach his wife. The narrator, relating Carmen's thoughts upon hearing Mario's friends speak "en clave" affirms that "ni Mario, en vida, se tomó la molestia de explicarle su lenguaje" (24). Other remarks lead us to infer that Mario was unhappy and even to question the naturalness of his death.[5] A mourner intones, "No es un muerto, es un ahogado," and Carmen's friend, Valentina, suspiciously asks about the bottle of tranquilizers on Mario's night stand (24). We therefore form a conception of a miserable marriage of absolute incompatibles. Later, during

Carmen's long disorderly discourse we will reconstruct the history of their courtship and married life.

In the prologue we have been thereby "instructed to construct" images of two opposing characters: Mario, for the most part an exemplary figure—a compassionate, long-suffering liberal intellectual, and his wife Carmen, a flawed character—vain, superficial, elitist, ignorant, insensitive, and tyrannical. By the time we begin Carmen's soliloquy, our opinions have more or less "set," and we tend to distance ourselves from her. Although in the prologue the narrator consistently focalizes through Carmen, revealing her thoughts, and although through the body of the novel we "hear" only her voice, we will most likely choose *not* to inhabit her consciousness. Readers tend to identify with more "appealing" characters, particularly in first-person narrations: we may say, "yes, I am like that!" and willingly merge our subjectivities with theirs. But in the case of Carmen we may say, "Thank God I am not like that!" And while we may recognize her, finding her somehow familiar, we will not identify with her; she is too repellent. Instead, we maintain a comfortable distance, "watching," "listening" and judging her.

If the aversion we have formed towards Carmen is not sufficient to distance ourselves from her, the narrator carefully positions us at the end of the introduction. Left alone in the room with the body, Carmen "cierra la puerta y se sienta en la descalzadora. Ha apagado todas las luces menos la lámpara de pie que inunda de luz el libro que ella acaba de abrir sobre su regazo y cuyo radio alcanza hasta los pies del cadáver" (37). This theatrical description places Carmen "on stage" under a spotlight.[6] As we read the next 244 pages, we will maintain this distance as we "watch" her there before the coffin, and as we envision the flashbacks she evokes.

Carmen's long monologue consists of a finite set of resentments, accusations, dogmatic opinions, and (largely) unpleasant memories—each repeated over and over in chapter after chapter. She complains about Mario's lack of passion and their unsatisfactory sex-life, boasts of the *piropos* she receives from other men, and accuses Mario of having an affair with his sister-in-law. She reproaches him for not providing her with certain amenities—a silver service, a larger apartment, more servants, and a modest (indeed tiny) automobile—a "Seiscientos."[7] Carmen also lambastes Mario for his progressive political views and the resulting upon punishments visited upon the family. In the process she incessantly quotes the dogma of the Franco regime: expressing xenophobia and racial prejudice, opposing the reforms of Vatican II, condemning *los rojos y los Masones*, and insisting upon *autoridad* and *disciplina*.[8] Carmen also quotes the proverbial wisdom of traditionalist Spain, constantly repeating the same *refranes*: "a los hombres nunca os falta un remiendo para un descosido y, como diría la pobre mamá, a falta de pan, buenas son tortas" (214-15). In evoking the past, her only happy memories coincide with the war years, "unos años estupendos, los mejores de mi vida" (73). She avers, "Yo lo pasé divinamente en la guerra," but with one sore point: An Italian soldier, a boarder, brought shame on the family by impregnating her sister—although Carmen insists that "a Galli le gustaba yo cien mil veces más que a Julia" (214).

It is important to note that Carmen's monologue is not monologic, for other "voices" implicitly undermine her authority. We "hear" the voice of Mario, either quoted by Carmen or implied by her discourse, and his powerful presence resonates through the novel as a sign of integrity, as "la conciencia del mundo" (85). Although, after the prologue, the omniscient narrator officially absents himself, we sense his moral presence behind her voice; we sense some agency pulling the strings, making her talk while undermining her, and subtracting authority from her authoritarian discourse. His "God-like" presence is evoked in the Bible verse that introduces each chapter with a moral touchstone—a point from which Carmen launches her hypocritical, at times blasphemous, counterpoint.[9] In league with this narrative agency, we as readers "watch" her perform (on our mental stages) with amusement, smiling condescendingly as she makes a fool of herself. Having been "set-up" by the narrator in the prologue, we maintain a distant, superior, ironic attitude, as we catch her in all her little hypocrisies. And throughout her long diatribe, we continue attaching traits to her figure.

One reader, the critic Arnold Verhoeven, assigns to her an impressive listing of traits:

> Carmen es una cínica materialista; es una (re)celosa; es una burguesa asocial y explotadora de los menos privilegiados; chismosa, maliciosa y malpensada; hipócrita; criptoanalfabeta; tradicionalista a machamartillo, por no decir retrógrada; zenófoba; Carmen está dispuesta a claudicar en cuestiones de justicia y honradez, y disculpa la injusticia; es cruel, vengativa y rencorosa; es insensible y poco compasiva, intolerante e intransigente; ufana y creída; cursi y remilgosa; autoritaria; llena de prejuicios y, sobre

todo, regañona, como prueba en cinco horas de acusaciones. (68)

All of these traits and more could aptly characterize this character—all of them migrating to her proper name and making her an ever-expanding assemblage of signs. There is a danger here that Carmen may become overdetermined, overly nominated. So many negative traits have attached themselves to her figure that she risks becoming too ugly, too monstrous, so extreme that she destabilizes: for all of the defects that name her, that define her character, add up to a *lack* of character. What serves to rein in this threatening profusion of signs is the release of a very powerful sign in the final cathartic moment of Carmen's monologue—*adultery*. At the end of her soliloquy, Carmen finally musters the courage to confess an infidelity (or more precisely, she *almost* confesses a *near* infidelity). She had accepted a ride in Paco Alvarez's Tiburón and found herself "hypnotized" by his flattery, by a glimpse of his bullet-scarred chest, and by the sensation of speeding in a much-coveted car.[10] When Paco made advances, she was powerless to stop him. But she swears that he stopped just in time—although, had he not done so, she of course would have acted. At the end of her monologue, Carmen is crying hysterically, begging Mario to show her a sign of forgiveness:

> pero escúchame, que te estoy hablando! ¡no te hagas el desentendido, Mario!, anda por favor, mírame, un momento, sólo un segundo, una décima de segundo aunque sólo sea, te lo suplico, ¡mírame, que yo no he hecho nada malo, palabra, por amor de Dios, mírame un momentín, aunque sólo sea un momentín, ¡anda!, dame ese gusto, qué te cuesta, te lo pido de rodillas si quieres, no tengo nada de qué avergonzarme, ¡te lo juro, Mario, te lo juro! ¡¡te lo juro, mírame!! ¡¡que me muera si no es verdad!!, pero no te encojas de hombros, por favor, mírame, de rodillas te lo pido, anda, que no lo puedo resistir, no puedo, Mario, te lo juro, ¡mírame o me vuelvo loca! ¡¡Anda, por favor . . . !! (282-83)

Carmen's guilt for this violation of her only moral scruple—the sexual taboo—suddenly explains a great deal. It explains the incessant repetition of the same resentments and reproaches: if Mario had only bought her a car, if he had shown more romantic fervor and sexual passion, if he had enriched himself like Paco, rather than writing obscure books and standing on principle—then none of this would have happened. In other words, Carmen's dramatic confession suddenly introduces a powerful explanatory logic; it unifies and orders the heterogeneous jumble of recriminations that were let loose, begging disbelief. Suddenly all the outrageous nonsense makes sense. Most important, the confession introduces an element of pathos. Carmen's expression of pain, grief, and guilt rings "true to life" and "humanizes" her, making her less monstrous.

The epilogue to the novel functions to rein in further the expansive swarm of signs and thus reduce Carmen to size. Once more the third-person narrator appears to reassert control over readers' interpretations. Once again a "stagey" scene works to distance readers:

> Carmen se sobresalta al oír el gemido de la puerta. Gira la cabeza, se sienta sobre los pies y hace como que busacara algo por el suelo. Sus ojos y sus manos expresan un nerviosismo límite. Aunque la luz del nuevo día entra ya por la ventana, la lámpara continúa encendida, proyectando su mortecino cerco luminoso sobre la descalzadora y los pies del cadáver:
> —¿Qué pasa, mamá? ¡Levántate! ¿Qué haces ahí de rodillas?
> Carmen se incorpora sonriendo tontamente. Se siente indefensa, blanda y maleable. Sus párpados han adquirido un color rosa fuerte, casi violeta, y cuando mira, mira de soslayo, como amedrentada. "Rezaba," murmura, pero lo dice sin convicción, para que no la crean, "sólo rezaba," añade, y el muchacho se adelanta hacia ella, la arropa los hombros con su brazo joven y nota que se estremece. (284)

Here an immense shrinkage suddenly takes place in this monstrous character. Suddenly, Carmen becomes very small, weak, pitiable, and readers are made to see her as a victim.

Only once more does the narrator enter into Carmen's consciousness and convey her thoughts. Before leaving the room, Carmen looks through the window, and in a lyrical passage the narrator describes what she sees and hears:

> Por la ventana se divisa ya nítidamente la casa de enfrente, con sus balcones verdes, de gresite, y sus cerradas persianas pintadas de blanco. Y cuando, de pronto, se abre

una—una persiana—con un ruido de matraca, seco, de tablillas que se juntan parece como que la casa bostezara y se desperezase. Antes de terminar de abrirse la persiana, petardea, abajo, en la calle estrecha, el primer motocarro. Y cuando el estrépito cesa, se perciben rumores de conversaciones y crujidos de pisadas de las gentes madrugadoras, que marchan al trabajo. Un gorrión cruza el poyete de la ventana, a saltitos rápidos, como si botase, gorgeando alborozadamente, como en primavera. Tal vez le llama a engaño el fragmento de cielo que cierra como un telón de fondo el taller de Acisclo del Peral y que ha pasado del negro al blanco y del blanco al azul en unos minutos, apenas sin transición. (285-86)

With this evocation of the typical sights and sounds of a Spanish morning, the narrator provides a too-obvious message—"life goes on." And with the image of the window, he provides a too-obvious metaphor, which all readers should obediently interpret as a call to open their minds. After this point in the novel, Mario Jr. takes command and speaks authoritatively for the narrator, as well as for his father. As the voice of morality and truth in the novel, he hammers home the message of the open window:

—El mundo cambia, mamá, es natural.
—A peor, hijo, siempre a peor.
—¿Por qué a peor? Sencillamente nos hemos dado cuenta de que lo que uno viene pensando desde hace siglos, las ideas heredadas, no son necesariamente las mejores. Es más, a veces no son ni tan siquiera buenas, mamá. (288)

Carmen, speechless, looks at him without comprehending, as he continues: "Sencillamente tratamos de abrir las ventanas. En este desdichado país nuestro no se abrían las ventanas desde el día primero de su historia, convéncete" (288-89). Against Carmen's incomprehension, against her repeated insistence that the old days were better, Mario becomes more vehement: "¡Por Dios, mamá! Ya salió nuestro feroz maniqueísmo: . . . ¡los buenos a la derecha y los malos a la izquierda! . . . Todos somos buenos y malos, mamá. Las dos cosas a un tiempo. Lo que hay que desterrar es la hipocresía" (290). But he gives up trying to communicate with his mother, realizing that further effort is futile. When Carmen finally speaks, she asks him how he slept, and Mario replies:

"Me ha sido imposible. Una cosa rara. Cada vez que lo intentaba parecía que se me hundía el jergón. ¿comprendes? Un vértigo" (291). At this point, Carmen screams, "¡¡No!!"—for these are the very words that the elder Mario had used to describe his own sleepless nights.

The moral of this *novela de tesis* thus comes through loud and clear: Spaniards must open their windows, open their minds, question "las ideas heredadas," and overcome their Manicheism. But the future looks bleak, for the inert masses of closed-minded people, represented by Carmen, cannot or will not comprehend. So the absurd, Manicheistic history of Spain may continue repeating itself, and Mario Jr., a liberal intellectual like his father, will probably self-destruct.[9] The novel ends with the *conducción*, as the mourners leave the home and follow the coffin to the church. Carmen, helpless and meek, pulling at her tight sweater, allows herself to be led by her savvy, reactionary friend Valentina: "[s]e estira el suéter de los sobacos y mansamente deja que Valentina la pase un brazo por los hombros y la atraiga hacia sí" (296). A shrunken semblance of her formerly monstrous self, Carmen thus exits from our mental stage.

This account of "our" reading of this novel is of course ultimately "my" reading. If I have presumptively insisted upon the readerly "we," it is to draw attention to readers' reliance (within a given culture) upon the same body of received knowledge, not to deny the possibility of variant readings. And if I have belabored the obvious, it is to demonstrate that characterization, whether deriving from a writer's instructions and clues *in the text*, or from readers' construction of the character *in their minds*—relies absolutely upon culturally shared and codified knowledge. Certainly, not all readers read exactly alike; variant readings are possible and indeed desirable. Far more troubling than variance is how much alike our readings tend to be. Upon reading a fragment of text, we all refer immediately to specific bits of information and thereby complete the text, supplementing, and vastly expanding it. If this knowledge were not so generally shared in a given culture, characterization, indeed, reading itself, could not take place—which in turn makes reading a profoundly social activity. This novel, in particular, seems to posit a contemporary *Spanish* reader, one who shares Carmen's world, one who is intimately acquainted with her expressions and references, one who will automatically follow the coded paths of connotation triggered by the text. It is a novel with a compelling project, largely driven by a "command structure." The prologue compels readers to construct at a distance a decidedly undesirable and repellant character; the epilogue then asks readers to pity her, to see her as a victim.

Perhaps, as a non-contemporary non-Spanish reader, I read this novel somewhat less cooperatively, more at variance. But upon finishing the text, I remain disturbed by a certain residue left behind. Carmen's character-image had so expanded in my mind, through the attachment of so many negative traits, that she had grown to monstrous proportions. I had surrounded her figure with a profusion of trait-names—petty, vain, nagging, selfish, ignorant, snobbish, hypocritical, vengeful, tyrannical, reactionary, cruel, xenophobic, prudish, . . .—all of which, suddenly, under the aegis of the epilogue, should be subordinated to one name, *victim*. This attempt by the narrator to halt the expansion of this over-determined character by eliciting readers' pathos somehow fails. What has been "let loose" by Carmen's chaotic and excessive monologue cannot be wholly contained by the conclusion. There remains at the close of the novel a certain dissonant echo, a disturbing supplement; and herein lies the potential for variant readings.

As an attempt to explain, to sift through this troubling residue, let me next describe three somewhat variant readings of this novel. Borrowing from Charles Sanders Peirce's typology of signs, I will provisionally name these readings iconic, symbolic, and indexical.[10] Each reading opens a different "window" on this novel, through which I will examine this sign (or composite of signs) named Carmen. Each perspective operates within a different logic and reveals a different function of this exorbitant character: insofar as readers construct a mental portrait of a "person-like" character, Carmen functions as an icon; insofar as she stands for something *unlike* herself, she functions as a symbol; and insofar as she points to the time and place of production—to the moment the author inscribed her on the page—and to the possibilities and contingencies of that moment, she functions as an index.[11] Each of these readings produces a web of meanings in readers' minds; and together they work in harmony and dissonance—converging and diverging, overlapping and colliding.

An Iconic Reading: The Uses of Stereotype

As conceived by Peirce, an iconic sign is a fixed image that *resembles* its object, for example, a painting, drawing, diagram, or cinematic image. We have no such fixed images of characters in a fictional text. But as we read the marks on the page, meanings and images spontaneously leap out, and we *envision* Carmen in our mind's eye. This mental portrait can be thought of as an iconic sign, or more precisely, as an elusive collage of signs, ever-expanding and changing. Carmen "works" as a character, as a "believable" fictional being, only by virtue of the person-like image constructed in readers' minds.[12]

Carmen's iconicity thus rests upon her verisimilitude, upon the "reality effect" produced by the act of reading (Barthes, "Reality" 16). As we read, we *recognize* her as a familiar character. It seems that we have read, seen, or heard her before, that we already know her. When we search our memories of already-read literary texts, we find her predecessors in Spanish literature: Doña Perfecta, Bernarda Alba, the mother of Pascual Duarte.[13] Carmen clearly conforms with the literary stereotype of the archconservative, tyrannical mother, rigidly following the formulas of Christianity, if not its ethics. When we refer to our knowledge of social stereotypes, we find the ready-made image of the ignorant, tradition-bound, shrewish wife. And if we refer to our memories of "direct" experience, we may recall flesh-and-blood women who are "Carmen-like," who have adopted and lived the same stereotype. Gonzalo Sobejano, for example, would vouch for the ubiquity of such women: "Carmen no es meramente ella: es la española normal, regular, habitual . . . tan corriente que no hay más que abrir los ojos para verla" (187).

Until recent decades, the assumption has prevailed in Spanish society that many, or even most, Spanish women closely resemble this stereotype. The power of this deep-seated belief led many leftist, and even feminist, delegates to the *Cortes Constituyentes* of 1931 to oppose women's suffrage for fear of losing the up-coming elections; and conversely, many conservatives, in hopes of winning, supported the vote for women. Margarita Nelken voiced the leftist point of view:

> Si no fuese demasiado atrevido, yo me permitiría rogar a Ud. que, antes de volver a pedir el voto femenino, viajase por varias regiones de España, por todas ellas, para ver

cómo todo cuanto en España significa atraso, estrechez de miras y cortedad espiritual es—como en muchos países— obra de mujeres. (qtd. in Capmany 95).

Nelken goes on to say that women themselves are not to blame for this situation, for in Spain they have not been prepared to be "espiritualmente iguales al hombre" (95). Before granting women the vote, the level of feminine culture must be raised to that of the masculine.

Whether the vast majority of Spanish women from the various social classes have, like Carmen, exemplified "atraso, estrechez de miras, y cortedad espiritual" may be open to question. Sometimes the universal acceptance of a stereotype blinds members of a culture to all evidence to the contrary. But certainly, women in many societies have been restricted from educational opportunities and participation in public life, and such restrictions often produce a traditional, conservative mindset.[14] It is therefore not surprising that women have to varying degrees adopted and lived social stereotypes, often using them to obtain a modicum of power in a male-dominant society.

Undoubtedly, stereotypes function in more subtle and complex ways within a given culture than our simplified notions of the term would suggest. We see Carmen as "like" living women we have known, because we tend to fit characters into the typologies and paradigms stored in our minds; we "match" them with ready-made images and accordingly "manage" our interpretions of the complex beings we encounter in books and in life. Moreover, as we acquire language, become conscious of self and others, and proceed to live out our lives, we fit ourselves into those same typologies and paradigms, thereby managing our conceptions of self. Stereotypes thus constantly circulate between life and art, between living and fictional characters: as members of society we learn the rules, the gestures, and the "looks" of various stereotypes; to varying degrees we employ or reject them in our social and interpretive practices; and those practices in turn function to reinforce, develop, and potentially to alter the "original" stereotypes.

As a given, all stereotypes, along with their corresponding traits and behaviors, form part of a cultural reservoir of received knowlege. For Carmen to emerge as an iconic, or verisimilar, figure in readers' minds, she must *rearticulate* a piece of that common knowledge. In writing her, Delibes drew from that reservoir of texts and images, making her a "copy of a copy," one more articulation of a familiar social character (Coward and Ellis 52). Then upon reading the marks on the page that characterize her, readers refer to that same cultural reservoir, seeking "like" figures from literary, historical, sociological, psychological, and journalistic texts, as well as from the "text" of remembered experience (itself already conditioned by the aforementioned texts). All of this corroborating information lends authority, believability, and power to a character and enables readers to fill out the image developing in their minds. We tend to think of stereotype as something false, inauthentic, too simplified, or exaggerated to be "real." But to a large degree our very notion of truth depends upon correspondence to the "received wisdom"—that ensemble of stereotypical thinking. If Carmen seems true-to-life, it is because her "truth," to borrow from Nietzsche, "is only the solidification, of old metaphors" (qtd. in Barthes, *Pleasure* 42-43).

Carmen's iconicity depends not only upon her resemblance to an accepted cultural stereotype, but also upon the "naturalness" of her speech. Her language, while absolutely stereotypical, rings "true"; we would swear that we have heard women talk that way. Indeed, Delibes has long taken an ethnographer's interest in capturing the authentic popular language of Castile.[15] As he explains, "me interesó sobre todo el lenguaje de este tipo de mujer; ese lenguaje vacío, hecho de timitos, de vulgarismos, y de frases hechas. Luego tuve que estudiar la manera de encajar el lenguaje dentro de ese tipo para dar luz a la novela" ("Miguel Delibes" 102).

Carmen's speech is a pastiche of quotations, a sociolect, made up of bits of the received wisdom of Franco's Spain during the nineteen-sixties:

> Desengáñate de una vez, Mario, el mundo necesita authoridad y mano dura. . . . es preciso callar y obedecer, siempre, toda la vida. . . . que libertad de expresión, ¿puede saberse para qué la quiere? ¿Quieres decirme qué pasaría si a todos nos dejaran chillar y cada cual chillara lo que le viniera en gana? Que no, Mario . . . la Inquisición era bien buena porque nos obligaba a todos a pensar en bueno, o sea en cristiano, ya lo ves en España, todos católicos y católicos a machamartillo, que hay que ver qué devoción, no como esos extranjerotes que ni se arrodillan para comulgar ni nada, que yo sacerdote, y no hablo por hablar, pediría al gobierno que los expulsase de España, date cuenta, que no vienen aquí más que a enseñar las pantorras y a escandalizar. Todo esto de las playas y el turismo, por mucho que tú digas, está organizado por la Masonería

y el Comunismo, Mario, para debilitar nuestras reservas morales y, ¡zas!, deshacernos de un zarpazo. (152)

Although exaggerated and garbled for comic effect, Carmen speaks the *official* language of her society, described by Agnes Gullón as "el lenguaje con carga de prejuicios, frases hechas, fórmulas hipócritas, tics, modas autosatisfechas" (19). Roland Barthes would call Carmen's speech "Encratic language"—the language "produced and spread under the protection of power" (*Pleasure* 40). By definition, it is "a language of repetition; all offical institutions of language are repeating machines: school, sport, advertising, popular songs, news, all continually repeat the same structure, the same meaning, often the same words: the stereotype is a political fact, the principal aspect of ideology" (*Pleasure* 40).

Through her stereotypical discourse, Carmen engenders herself as a "typical" Spanish housewife and mother, as she believes a woman is "supposed to be" in her society.[16] She "impersonates" the contemporary model of Spanish womanhood by quoting a multiplicity of texts—rules, clichés, proverbs—circulating in the culture at large: "para una mujer la pureza es la prenda más preciada" (187); "una mujer es un ser indefenso" (175); "para una mujer es agradable notar que el hombre repara en su debilidad" (120); "la mujer o novia deben ser sagradas" (125); "¿para qué va a estudiar una mujer? . . . Hacerse un marimacho, ni más ni menos, que una chica universitaria es una chica sin femineidad . . . una chica sin sexy" (75); la "vocación de madres, lo más noble que puede haber" (147). On the one hand, Carmen claims to "enjoy being female," to accept gladly her subordinate status. But on the other hand, her outpouring of resentment would seem to belie her acceptance of her status. She complains incessantly of her lot: "los hombres . . . sois soberbios, os creéis en posesión de la verdad y a nosotros ni caso" (107-08); "que no soy de tener muchos hijos, por lo que sea, que si yo soy una de esas artesanas conejas que los echan a pares, para qué te voy a contar" (153); "que me gustaría a mí verte dando a luz" (46).

But all this resentment falls within a "psycho-logic" of how women are supposed to feel, how they are supposed to behave, given their situation. And it is this conformity to a cultural logic that arguably makes Carmen seem most true-to-life: Yes, it is to be expected that a housewife is frustrated, that she misdirects the energies she might expend in public life to tyranny over her children, that she nags and whines, mouthing a slavish discourse.

> Pero de estas cosas los hombres no os dais cuenta, cariño, que el día que os casáis, compráis una esclava, hacéis vuestro negocio, como yo digo, que los hombres, ya se sabe, no tiene vuelta de hoja, siempre los negocios. ¿Que la mujer trabaja como una burra y no saca un minuto ni para respirar? ¡Allá se las componga! Es su obligación, qué bonito, y no es que te reproche nada, querido, pero me duele que en más de veinte años no hayas tenido una palabra de comprensión. (42-43)

All this is codified emotion, produced and channeled through a system of cultural beliefs and institutions. Carmen desires only what a woman is *permitted* to desire—man as the center, as source of strength, as protector.[17] Since in her society, a woman is not supposed to express openly her sexual desire, she must desire that man desire her, declare his love, and ravish her, so to exempt her from any responsibility.

We know all this already. This is the received psychological wisdom of how men and women in traditional roles have negotiated their relations. In Lacan's sardonic words, "the ideal or typical manifestations of behaviour in both sexes, up to and including the act of sexual copulation, are entirely propelled into comedy" (84). Upon Carmen's monologue, we refer to this *psycho-logic* of heterosexual interraction and reconstruct the tragicomedy of a courtship and marriage. As a child engendered as male, Mario accepts (he cannot refuse) a vast complex of assumptions, concepts, paradigms of gender. As a youth he performs (albeit badly) the ritual of courtship: his desires codified and structured so that he is drawn to a particular construct of the feminine—a traditional, well-brought-up Spanish girl. Certainly, she lacks formal education and chatters incessantly about nonsense—as girls are wont to do. But as a man, an intellectual, he finds stimulation in public life, in his all-male *tertulia*. In his home he seeks not intellectual companionship, but a refuge, with a traditional wife to keep house and raise his children.[18] On this point Carmen speaks cogently:

> ¿Estudié yo, además? Pues mira, tú no me hiciste ascos, que a la hora de la verdad, con todo vuestro golpe de intelectuales, lo que buscáis es una mujer de su casa, eso, y no me digas que no, . . . y, en el fondo, si me conoces en la Universidad hubieras hecho fu, como el gato, a ver, que a los hombres se os ve venir de lejos y si hay algo que

lastime vuestro amor propio es tropezar con una chica que os dé ciento y raya en eso de los libros. (75-76)

Carmen, trained only in *coquetería* and *hogar*, and conditioned to desire a man as ravisher, protector, and provider, accepts Mario's proposal, because he awakens her maternal instincts: "lo que más puede enorgullecer a una mujer es sentirse imprescindible, que recuerdo que yo me decía 'ese chico me necesita, podría matarse, si no' " (58).

But within this oppositional system lie the seeds of pathology. Mario will find it less than satisfying to share a household with someone so intellectually limited. Prone to depression, he feels absolutely alone. In his moments of anguish and doubt, she is incapable of understanding and cannot provide companionship. When he stands on principle against the petty corruptions and injustices of the regime, Carmen cannot support him, and increasingly, she resents the "costs" of Mario's principles, as well as his shortcomings. Mario falls short (as all men must) of the cultural presumption of man as center, as source of absolute strength and authority. Carmen, feeling betrayed by these shortcomings, goes so far as to memorize passages from Mario's books and to recite them to her friends so they can laugh and ridicule him. Finally, she takes her revenge in (near?) adultery, fulfilling her desire to be ravished by a man, only to be later tormented by guilt. And Mario, in the final months of his life, becomes increasingly passive and tormented.

We have in this oppositional psychology a familiar cycle of thwarted, deformed human potentiality. Barthes could have been speaking of Mario when he writes of Sarrazine: "psychology—pure social discourse—thus appears as a murderous language which conduces . . . the subject to the final castration" (*S/Z* 148). Mario finally is "murdered," either "henpecked" to death, or destroyed by his own failure and impotence. And Carmen is so victimized that she is incapable of changing, of learning, of comprehending the cultural logic that entraps her. Depending on how pessimistically one reads the ending, this novel leaves no way out. Their children and namesakes, Mario and Carmen, seem to be dutiful copies of their parents, doomed to repeat the same dreadful cycle.

If the characters are caught in a reactive cycle of codified emotions, so are we as readers. We respond on cue, predictably, with a succession of responses triggered by Carmen's monologue. At first, during the initial pleasure of recognition, we are amused by Carmen's garbled language and her foolish shenanigans; later we become irritated; and ultimately, we are repelled by the grotesque banality of it all. The nonstop repetition of resentments, accusations, and clichés, the "over-exposure" of a pathological relationship—it all induces boredom and nausea. Then at the end, after Carmen's cathartic confession, we are left with a sense of revulsion mixed with pity.

All of these codified responses comply with the novel's critical project: to induce readers to *recognize* this as a "true-to-life," prevalent social pathology, to see its deadly absurdity, and then to repudiate it. Since this critical mission relies upon the novel's iconicity, the text must strike a difficult balance: it must reproduce a stereotypical character, language, and psychology that readers will recognize as "realistic" and "natural," while at the same time repeating and exaggerating until the real and the natural become repugnant. But if this exaggeration and denaturalization go too far, if Carmen becomes too grotesque and too monstrous, she loses her iconicity.[21] At times, Carmen becomes so extreme that she seems to cross the boundaries of her fictional world and to appear on *another* stage as a comedienne performing a parody of herself. For example, when calling for "una poquita de Inquisición," she remarks: "yo lo pienso muchísimas veces, que si la bomba atómica esa la perfeccionasen de tal modo que pudiera distinguir, que ya sé que es una bobada, pero bueno, y matase sólo a los que no tienen principios, el mundo quedaría como una balsa de aceite, ni más ni menos, ni menos ni más" (153). In order to refute Mario's notions of charity, she suggests that "si los pobres estudian y dejan de ser pobres, ¿quieres decirme con quiénes vamos a ejercitar la caridad?" (133).

As Carmen becomes increasingly outrageous, she begins "playing to her audience." She second-guesses the traits readers are assigning to her with such remarks as: "como si yo fuera una ignorante," and "como si yo te llevara a la tumba" (57, 46). After her friend Esther calls her insensitive for ridiculing Mario's books, Carmen responds: "pero sensibilidad, Dios mío, si es una de mis peplas, tú lo sabes, cariño, pero si cuando estoy indipuesta ni mayonesa puedo hacer, toda se me corta" (269). And at one point this increasingly offensive character suddenly asks pointedly: "¿ofendo yo? dime la verdad, ¿ofendo yo?, no, ¿verdad?, pues mira, bien de ello que hablo, que no paro, una tarabilla, tú me dirás, que a veces, si no tengo con quien, pues yo sola, fíjate qué risa, cualquiera que me viera, pero me importa un bledo" (208).

In this tendency towards self-parody (however amusing) lurks the danger of readerly disbelief, as Carmen expands beyond her stereotypical mold. The tenuous balance between parodic exaggeration and mimeticism creates a certain instability in the novel's internal logic—an instability made manifest in the recurrent image of Carmen's "over-sized" breasts. As we have seen, the narrator (in the prologue) explicitly draws attention to these breasts, describing them as "excesivamente pugnaces" and "agresivos," and Carmen returns to the topic in nearly every chapter: "La poitrine, mi gran defecto, un poco de más" (17); "no sé qué tendrán mis pechos pero no hay hombre que se resista" (217). Within the logic of an iconic reading, Carmen's breasts reinforce her iconicity, for in this novel, as well as in "real life," a woman's breasts come freighted with powerful social meanings: simultaneously they function as a sign of femininity, sexuality, and motherhood. For Carmen, her breasts serve simultaneously as a source of pride, shame, and sexual insecurity, and "trouble"—if we believe her claims that men are constantly admiring her bosom. But moving slightly outside the logic of her world, these enormous breasts also serve as an emblem of her overdetermination as a character. Just as her large breasts threaten to burst out of the tight black sweater, Carmen threatens to burst out of her iconic mold. But in pursuing this line of argument, I have already ventured into a symbolic reading.

A Symbolic Reading: The Uses of Blame

Insofar as Carmen becomes "bigger than life," she can no longer *resemble* our notion of a living being. At this point she loses her iconicity and becomes a symbol for something to which she bears no direct resemblance. For Peirce, the relation of a symbol to its meaning depends wholly upon convention, not upon any "natural" relation with its referent.[22] In Carmen's case, based upon the venerable convention of making feminine figures stand allegorically for nations (motherlands), readers will tend to associate her with Spain, or rather with the abstraction of a timeless, inert, and closed Spain.[23] Carmen will join the procession of feminine characters—la Cava, Doña Perfecta, Bernarda Alba—who have stood negatively for Spain, from its "rape" by the Moors through the failed *Ilustración*, the two ill-fated Republics, and the anachronistic Franco regime.[24] Within the logic of a symbolic reading, Carmen stands abstractly for "todo cuanto en España significa atraso, estrechez de miras y cortedad espiritual" (Nelkin qtd. in Capmany 95).

Both the iconic and symbolic readings are *authorized*, I believe, by the text. In order to comply with the novel's ethical project, readers must simultaneously accept Carmen as "la española normal, regular, habitual," and as an emblem of Spanish society (Sobejano, 187). The critics have spoken in chorus regarding the symbolic meanings of both Carmen and Mario. Gonzalo Sobejano, for example, immediately leaps from the individual case study to the national, seeing the novel as "el ejemplo del imposible entendimiento entre una mujer necia y simplista y un hombre inteligente y complejo, entre el dogma de fe y el amor de caridad, entre una España cerrada y una España abierta, entre la autoridad y la libertad, la costumbre inauténtica y el esfuerzo auténtico" (185). And for Edgar Pauk, "Mario y Carmen representan dos Españas, las eternas diferencias entre dos formas de enfocar la realidad" (99).

The novel actively encourages a symbolic reading, particularly in the epilogue, where, as we have seen, the image of the open window carries a quite obvious figurative meaning. There Mario, the younger, voices the novel's thesis: "Sencillamente tratamos de abrir las ventanas. En este desdichado país nuestro no se abrían las ventanas desde el día primero de su historia, convéncete" (288-89). But Carmen does not grasp the meaning of *España cerrada*, admitting, "No os entiendo—murmura, al fin—. Todos habláis en clave como si prentendieráis volverme loca. Leís demasiados libros" (289). Mario continues trying to reach her with his impassioned argument against Manicheism, but finally yields before her incomprending gaze:

> Carmen le mira asustada. Sus ojos son planos. Toda su cara es plana ahora. Le explora. Mario comprende que es inútil, que es como pretender que la pared de un frontón succione la pelota y ésta quede adherida a su lisa superficie. El rostro de Carmen es plano como un frontón. Y como un frontón devuelve la pelota en rebotes cada vez más fuertes. (291)

Clearly, Carmen here is likened to an inert, impenetrable substance, which in turn stands for an entire society that holds back progress by its inertia, ignorance, and stubbornness.

A symbolic reading is also suggested by Mario's own allegorical novels, those "novels within the novel" that Carmen holds up for ridicule. She wants Mario to write "libros de amor o libros con sustancia," and finds his *novelas de tesis* incomprehensible and distasteful (266):

> ¿quién iba a leer esas cosas tristes de gentes muertas de hambre que se revuelcan en el barro como puercos? . . .

¿quién iba a leer ese rollo de "El Castillo de Arena" donde no hablas más que de filosofías? . . . ¿tú crees, Mario, que le puede interesar a alguien un libro que pasa en un país que no existe y cuyo protagonista es un sorche al que le duelen los pies. (48-49)

Perhaps owing to the constraints of censorship, Mario's novels depict nameless, timeless worlds inhabited by "protagonistas estrafalarios," and they employ vague references printed in *mayúsculas*. Completely mystified, Carmen protests, "¿Dónde está ESA FUERZA? ELLA no tiene cabeza, ni forma, ni sabe nadie dónde se esconde," and later complains that in his novel *El Castillo de Arena*, "no hay castillos por ninguna parte" (50, 241). Esther, an intellectual who reads and enjoys Mario's novels, tries to explain that Mario's novels are symbolic, but Carmen scoffs at her, "como si ella supiera con qué se come eso" (50, 113). No doubt, the author is having some fun here, perhaps making sly references to the evasive techniques of writers under the Regime. But at the same time, these references to Mario's novels can be taken as signals that project Delibes's novel onto a symbolic plane.

Read symbolically, then, *Cinco horas con Mario* becomes a historical/political allegory about the failure and impotence of the liberal intelligentsia in Spain, about their futile struggle against the dead weight of tradition, ignorance, arch-conservatism, and stagnation. By design, Carmen's character displays all the supposed defects of the Spanish national character—pride, envy, close-mindedness, Manicheism, xenophobia, and over-adherence to appearances, formulas, and rituals.[25] To this list of national defects, long cited by liberal intellectuals, is added the central vice of the nineteen-sixties, consumerism. As Carmen "hams it up" for readers, and "delivers" her outrageous discourse, she unwittingly invites us to attach these negative traits to her figure. By playing to an audience anxious to expunge these stains from the national character, Carmen serves as the scapegoat in a ritual violence of blame and expulsion. As more and more defects are projected onto her figure, she becomes increasingly repellent until her cathartic confession reveals her utter hypocrisy and corruption. At the end she is expelled, led from the stage, a weak and pitiful figure, still furtively stretching her sweater.

By critical convention, such a symbolic (or allegorical) reading might be deemed incompatible with an iconic (or mimetic) reading. An iconic text relies on the presumed resemblance of characters, setting, and events to our conceptions of the "real world." A symbolic text, in contrast, maintains no pretense of mimesis: its characters are typically "unreal"—stylized, simplified, or exaggerated—often "standing in" for ineffable abstractions; its narratives typically retell mythic or historical events and convey moral lessons. However, these two modes, the mimetic and the symbolic, may not be so incompatible as we might think. In *Cinco horas con Mario*, both readings are encouraged and authorized by the text, and to some degree mutually reinforce each other.

Carmen's language fulfills a dual function by simultaneously supporting the novel's iconicity and its symbolism. Earlier I commented on how her colloquial speech reinforces an iconic reading, striking readers as natural, colorful and amusing. But as we read further, the incessant repetition of the same clichés, complaints, and accusations begins to wear on us. Carmen's language becomes "a nauseating mixture of common opinions, a smothering layer of received ideas" (Barthes, *S/Z* 206). According to Barthes, "Nausea occurs whenever the liaison of two important words *follows of itself*," and all of Carmen's words follow of themselves (Barthes, *Pleasure* 43). Ultimately, this very predictability works to drain her discourse of meaning. Her language, which at first impressed us with its "naturalness," later tires us with its repetitiveness, and eventually ceases to mean, becoming noise.[26] Within the iconic reading, this progression reinforces the social-political critique by denaturalizing her language, making the "natural" the "ultimate outrage" (Barthes, *Roland Barthes* 85). At the same time, the progressive meaninglessness of her discourse enhances the symbolic reading: the incantatory repetition, the liturgical rhythm of her litany of complaints—all contribute to a ritualistic effect that prepares readers for the final expulsion of the scapegoat. Carmen's "true-to-life" language thus works simultaneously to reinforce both the iconic and symbolic interpretations of this novel.

In other important respects, however, the iconic and symbolic readings fail to complement each other, but rather, work at cross-purposes, arousing in readers conflicting rational and irrational impulses. For example, the iconic reading calls for a rational political critique of Spanish society. Under its auspices, we are asked to see Carmen less as a perpetrator than as a victim; for presumably, once we rationally understand the sexual-social pathology that entraps her, we will (at least partially) forgive her and instead blame the male-dominant society and totalitarian regime. The symbolic reading, in contrast, compels readers to cast blame irrationally upon Carmen for all Spain's ills, to see her not so much as *víctima* but as *verdugo*.[27] While working iconically, the text calls for a rational repudiation of the Manicheism that has plagued Spain's history; but working symbolically, it makes "Manicheans" of its readers by leading us to label Mario as good and Carmen as bad.[26] Moreover, even as the text asks its readers to criticize Carmen's mindless obedience to formula and ritual, at the same time it makes us obey "mindlessly" by joining in a ritual of blame and expulsion. In other words, this text asks us to renounce "todas las ideas heredadas" made manifest by Carmen, and simultaneously to accept as given, the very ancient "inherited idea" of the scapegoat. In sum, the iconic reading leads us to condemn Carmen's hypocrisy, even as it makes us into hypocrites; for if, like Carmen, we are obedient followers of cultural (and narrative) codes and blind to our own duplicity, we will join in the ritual displacement of all that is loathsome onto the body of a manufactured other. But in raising the question of Carmen's *manufacture*, I have already ventured into an indexical reading.

An Indexical Reading: the Uses of Ventriloquism

Let me now suggest a third reading, one "unauthorized" by the text that focuses on its manufacture. An indexical reading would consider the text as an *event* and point to its "conditions of possibility" (including its freedoms and its necessities) at the time and place that it came into being (Foucault, "Order" 67).[27] According to Peirce, an indexical sign denotes a dynamic, usually physical relationship to its object. It frequently points back to a cause, which in turn functions as an index pointing forward to its effect. Art historians employ the term to denote the traces of the artist's hand: the brushmarks, chiselmarks, cuts, pastings, or the signature itself.[28] Index thus refers to a whole complex of decisions (not necessarily made freely or consciously by an artist), for example: the inclusions, exclusions, and choices of technique. In literature the indexical dimension of signs is often ignored, perhaps for fear of stumbling on the intentional fallacy and assigning greater agency to authors than they may possess. And perhaps, in literature—unlike in the plastic arts—the cutting and pasting is less visible and the exclusions (or silences) more difficult to identify.

But certainly, the choices writers make when leaving marks upon a page are not irrelevant. Delibes has discussed some of his conscious decisions, admitting his thesis, his allegiance to Mario's position, and his opposition to Carmen's:

> es una novela donde la viuda de un intelectual le reprocha todo lo que ha sido su vida. Lo que le reprocha es lo que yo quisiera que fuera la vida española, y eso en seguida lo nota el lector. Pero lo que dice la mujer, para el régimen de Franco era plausible, era digno de aplausos. ("Dialogando" 20)

He has also revealed certain decisions he made under the pressure of censorship:

> yo he procurado siempre decir lo que sentía. No me he sentido totalmente amordazado por la censura, lo que pasa es que tenía que recurrir al tiro por elevación o a la elipsis para decir lo que quería decir. Por ejemplo, en *Cinco horas con Mario*, mi primera idea fue presentar a Mario vivo, pero Mario hablando contra la sociedad que estábamos viviendo nunca hubiera sido aceptado por la censura. Recurrí a la argucia de que Mario estuviera muerto y fuera Menchu quien expusiera el credo de Mario para repudiarlo y rechazarlo. De esta manera, como el lenguaje de Carmen era plausible desde el punto de vista oficial, quedaba dicho lo que quería decir y no ofrecía pasto para que la censura se ensañase conmigo. A veces la censura ha operado de manera conveniente en cuanto que nos ha hecho sutilizar las fórmulas y la sutileza envuelve siempre un sentido estético. Esa sutileza se ha perdido al perderse la censura. ("Miguel Delibes" 105)

So to avoid censorship, Delibes opted to present Mario as a dead character, and happily, this endowed the work with greater aesthetic subtlety. But there are other options precluded by a very subtle form of "censorship": Delibes, like any writer, is constrained by "discursive limits"—by what is sayable, readable, thinkable, intelligible, or legitimate within the general discursive ensemble of a given culture in a given moment.

Let me embark on a rather unorthodox and speculative line of questioning. Without departing from his fundamental project—to present a critique of Spanish society that contraposes progressive and reactionary ideologies—what were the *other* possibilities for the manufacture of this text—those not chosen (or conceived of) by Delibes? What particular effects of these "other options" made them unacceptable, undesirable, or unthinkable? For example, what if the roles of these characters were reversed, making the dead liberal intellectual the wife and the arch-conservative cretin the husband? To most contemporary Spanish readers, such a marriage would be peculiar, if not freakish—possible but highly unusual in a society that generally restricted women's educational and political opportunities.[31] Such an unusual alignment would "stand out" as a special case and detract from the critique of "las ideas heredadas" (288).[32] What if, then, rather than a married couple, the two characters were brothers, or perhaps father and son? One dead, after years of suffering for his progressive views, and the other an opportunist with conservative views who has found success in a corrupt regime. In this case, the novel's thesis would not be radically altered. But what would be the effect of placing Carmen's traditionalist, reactionary discourse in the mouth of a male character? Would not the very fact of his maleness lend greater authority to that discourse, an authority that Delibes wants to undermine? By placing this discourse in the mouth of a character who is female and therefore lacks knowledge and authority in the society, Delibes subjects the discourse to greater ridicule.[33] In other words he invalidates this discourse by assigning it to a singularly *invalid* character.

In doing so, Delibes perhaps unwittingly repeats and reinforces a common cultural practice of manufacturing a feminine *other* to serve man's various purposes. As we have seen in "Andrómeda," the construction of the feminine as an *idealized other* represents all that man lacks and desires. In *Cinco horas con Mario*, however, the feminine is constructed as an *abject other*, as a repository for masculine debris—for all that is hated, denied, "inadmissable" within the supposed confines of the masculine. By using Carmen to subject a discourse to ridicule, he subjects his character to what Julia Kristeva terms a "ritual of defilement" (*Powers* 64).[34] This is consummately a Manichean rite of purification, based upon the demarcation and radical exclusion of the shameful, the loathsome, the horrifying (8).[35]

This textual/ritual event takes place late in the Franco regime, as all those who hope for a more open and democratic society begin the long wait for the Caudillo's death. At a time when "men of good sense" wish to dissociate themselves from a loathsome and already discredited discourse, what better way to do so than to cast it off onto the figure of woman. Such an "act of poetic purification"—making woman serve as the repository for masculine debris—evidently appears as the first impulse, the first available option, based on a long tradition, largely unquestioned, of making woman function as the abject, "jettisoned object," in other words, as excrement (Kristeva, *Powers* 28, 2). But how curious to have a woman character voice this man-made discourse, when *women* were denied a voice in the regime that wrote it![34]

This curious predicament lends multiple meanings to a colloquial phrase repeated by Carmen in the introduction, "Estoy hecha una facha" (16, 34). Idiomatically, the phrase means "I look like a sight," but literally it signifies "I am made a mess," or "I am made a fascist." To serve the logic of the iconic reading, Carmen is made a compliant subject, a fascist, and ultimately a victim by the regime and by the traditionalist culture that shaped her. To serve the logic of the symbolic reading, Carmen is "made a mess"—constructed as a grotesque scapegoat to stand in for all the national defects. And to serve the logic of an indexical reading, she is made a ventriloquist's dummy to mouth a discourse not her own.[35]

What, then, gives this ventriloquist's dummy even the provisional authority to utter an alien discourse? As a female character in a traditional society, Carmen has no authority to speak outside her domestic domain. Of course, within the logic of the iconic reading, Carmen is speaking *privately* inside her domain to one who cannot hear her, while surreptitiously, readers eavesdrop on her one-way conversation and judge her an unreliable speaker. But within the logic of the indexical reading, Carmen functions as a very *public* novelistic character—an utterly invalid character called upon to invalidate a discourse. So if she is so invalid, how can she be granted even the provisional, temporary right to speak this official language, however much she garbles it? Carmen signifies *lack*: lack of knowledge, power, and ultimately lack of "character." But interestingly, what she does not lack, indeed, what she has in great abundance are her breasts, which, as we have seen, function as the most powerful, significant, and recurrent image in the text.

An odd reference to Carmen's breasts appears in the prologue to the novel: suddenly the narrator interrupts a stream of direct quotes in order to announce, "Mario ya no estaba allí. Estaba en el libro y en el suéter negro que reventaban sus pechos agresivos" (29). Then immediately, without any transition, the narrator quotes Carmen's words from a phone conversation earlier in the day: "no me digas, Valen, estos pechos míos son un descaro, no son pechos de viuda, ¿a que no?" (29). Figuratively, it makes sense that Mario, now absent, "lives on" in the Bible he so carefully marked. But that he has transmogrified onto the tight black sweater that barely contains her "aggressive" breasts! What can this mean? Evidently, within the tenuous logic of this metaphor, the dead Mario is now present in the black sweater, emblem of her widowhood—a legal status which her bulging breasts defy. Carmen is now head of the family and acquires certain legal rights; so Mario has "transferred" to his widow some of the limited powers he enjoyed as a male under the regime. This leads me to associate these bulging breasts with a phallic authority, now by circumstance transferred to Carmen and lending her the provisional right to speak this masculine discourse. Her "pechos agresivos" and "pugnaces" thus serve as displaced, doubled phalli, producing a strange conflation of the masculine and the feminine. In this text Carmen's breasts—conventionally the cultural sign of the feminine *por excelencia*—become exaggerated to the point of absurdity. If I were to direct the stage version of *Cinco horas con Mario*, I would have the actress attach huge false appendages to her chest, like the absurdly large penises worn by actors in Aristophanes's *Lysistrata*.[36] For Carmen's phallic breasts dramatize the masquerade of femininity pushed to the absurd, woman made "a metaphor of man" (Felman, "Rereading" 25). If I may compare her to a very American version of the ventriloquist's dummy—the minstrel performer: Carmen resembles a black man compelled to wear blackface in order to fit the white stereotype of African-Americans, and then "allowed" to mouth a garbled, simple-minded, slavish imitation of the master's discourse.[37] To a degree, to be ventriloquized, to speak an alien discourse, is the lot of all marginalized groups. In Elaine Showalter's words, "all language is the language of the dominant order, and women, [as well as other subordinant groups] if they speak at all, must speak through it" (30).[38]

Ultimately, Carmen loses the provisional right to speak (even in comic, garbled fashion) this official discourse. At the close of the novel, having revealed her great sin, with her discourse utterly discredited, Carmen falls silent. Despite her "pechos agresivos" she becomes completely passive, reduced to a pitiable figure, and her breasts now weigh heavy: "Carmen está doblada por la cintura, como entregada, como si los pechos que empujan tercamente el entremado de lana negra, y que siempre ha soportado gallardamente la pesasen ahora demasiado. Se ahueca las axilas con disimulo" (287). Our final image of Carmen "shows" her being led away, still tugging uncomfortably at her armpits, trying to stretch her tight black sweater.

So who ultimately is the ventriloquist who manufactures and speaks through Carmen? Delibes? Certainly, I would not entirely discount authorial agency.[41] Delibes has made it very clear that he wrote this novel with a project in mind, as an ethical critique of his society and its belief system. He has discussed some of the choices he made, how he resorted to the "argucia de que Mario estuviera muerto y fuera Menchu quien expusiera el credo de Mario para repudiarlo y rechazarlo" ("Miguel Delibes" 105). But an author's range of choices is circumscribed by invisible limits. Even as he strains against those limits and seeks the as-yet unthought possibilities, he can only work with the cultural materials at hand. Simultaneously reading and writing, he selects from among those materials what is intelligible to him and to his readers. So Delibes, in the process of writing a social critique that would reveal the subjection of women, *subjects* a woman character to a ritual of defilement. He appropriates a host of ready-made negative images of woman already floating in the culture at large—the hag, the hen-pecking wife, the hysteric—and makes of her a repellent scapegoat. He thus unwittingly participates in a misogynistic cultural practice that he perhaps meant to denounce.

If Delibes were female, could he so blithely and blindly appropriate and reinforce these stereotypical constructions of woman? Perhaps, for we all share the same cultural materials; we all speak through the language of the dominant order and refer to the same reservoir of texts and images. But because women are somewhat further removed from the center where the masculine Subject is presumed to stand, and because many women see themselves as misfitting the social construction of the feminine, frequently, though not always, women writers employ the stereotypes somewhat less stringently, more ambiguously.

If Carmen could speak, what would she say? An absurd question—to posit an authentic voice in a mute, man-made construct.[42] Ventriloquism, as described by Brad Epps, "is an act of speech that hides its sources and throws itself, disembodied, into the bodies of others. As such it requires the dumb compliance, the submissive insignificance, of these other bodies. It is, hence, an act of speech that entails a violent silence on the part of another" (292). But I dare say, if Carmen could speak, she could only speak that excess, from that exorbitant site of disruption where so many heterogeneous meanings converge and become undifferentiated—her breasts. And the content of her speech, no doubt, would be utterly incomprehensible.

* * *

This excessive triple reading—iconic, symbolic, and indexical—has been merely a ploy: an artificial means of separating and examining three webs of meanings spun out simultaneously by this text.[41] As should be obvious, these configurations are impossibly entangled and interdependent. They interact in complex ways—adhering and interfering, merging and diverging. The excesses and disturbances created by these entangled webs of meaning might lead some readers to consider this text flawed and others to consider it enhanced by ambiguity and complexity. I would suggest that this novel provides a most interesting demonstration of the impossibility of any "pure" critical project and the inevitability of unwitting complicity. Delibes evidently set out to write a scathing critique of "las ideas heredadas." But in doing so, he made use of a very ancient inherited idea—the construction of Woman as a repository for all that man rejects, and his project became entangled in an ungovernable text.

The following chapter examines an equally ungovernable text, and undertakes a similarly tripartite reading of an excessive character. This fictional being, like Carmen, lacks "character"—but not in the sense of lacking an "ethical core." Rather, by virtue of his radical unintelligibility, he thwarts all attempts by readers to name and to know him as a character.

NOTES

1. Note-worthy general studies of Delibes's works include: Alfonso Rey, *La originalidad novelística de Delibes*; Agnes Gullón, *La novela experimental de Miguel Delibes*; Luis López Martínez, *La novelística de Miguel Delibes*; Edgar Pauk, *Miguel Delibes: Desarrollo de un escritor (1947-1974)*; Jesús Rodríguez, *El sentimiento del miedo en la obra de Miguel Delibes*; Manuel Alvar, *El mundo novelesco de Miguel Delibes*; Yaw B. Agawu-Karaba, *Demythification in the Fiction of Miguel Delibes*; and María Luisa Bustos-Deuso, *La mujer en la narrativa de Delibes*. See also the collection of *ponencias* in Cristóbal Cuevas García, *Miguel Delibes. El escritor, la obra, y el lector*. For studies that focus on *Cinco horas con Mario*, refer to relevant chapters from the following works: Gonzalo Sobejano, *Novela española de nuestro tiempo*; Bernardo Antonio González, *Parábolas de identidad: Realidad interior y estrategia narrativa en tres novelistas de posguerra*; Vicente Cabrera and Luis González-del-Valle, *Novela española contemporánea: Cela, Delibes, Romero y Hernandez*; and Fernando Morán, *Novela y semidesarrollo*. For articles focusing on the novel, see: Phyllis Zatlin Boring, "Delibes' Two Views of the Spanish Mother"; Teresa Boucher, "The Widow's Peak / The Widow Speaks: Carmen's Idle Talk in Miguel Delibes's *Cinco horas con Mario*"; H.L. Boudreau, "*Cinco horas con Mario* and the Dynamics of Irony"; Silvia Burunat, "Miguel Delibes y el feminismo"; Yaw Agawu-Kakraba, "Miguel

Delibes and the Politics of Two Women: *Cinco horas con Mario* and *Señora de rojo sobre fondo gris*"; Jack B. Jelinski, "Mario as Biblical Analogue in Miguel Delibes' *Cinco horas con Mario*"; Antonio H. Martínez, "Los códigos de la ironía en *Cinco horas con Mario* de Miguel Delibes"; Nina Molinaro, "Confessions of Guilt and Power in *Cinco horas con Mario*"; Isaac Montero, "El lenguaje del Limbo"; and Erik Camayd Freixas, "El monólogo literario y 'la novela de la posguerra': Miguel Delibes y Camilo José Cela"; Carlos Jerez Farrán, "Las bodas de doña Carnal y don Cuaresma in *Cinco horas con Mario*"; Matías Montes Huidoro, "Cinco horas con Carmen"; and Antonio Sobejano-Morán, " 'Dramatis personae' y manipulación narrativa en *Cinco horas con Mario y La cólera de Aquiles*."

2. Carmen's discourse has generated a great deal of critical discussion as to its appropriate classification. Most critics consider it an interior monologue (Alvar, López Martínez, Camayd Freixas). Delibes himself describes Carmen's speech as a "soliloquio mental que terminara por ser verbal" (*Conversaciones* 88). Alfonso Rey points out: "el discurso de Carmen tiene todas las características de un diálogo, aunque, al estar su pretendido interlocutor muerto, sólo hay un hablante" (181). Arnold Verhoeven defends the term "mono-diálogo" (61, 72n). Also see Silvia Burunat, *El monólogo interior como forma narrativa en la novel española (1940-1975)*.

3. I am indebted to Seymour Chatman's discussion of trait-naming in *Story and Discourse*.

4. In other words, to use Rimmon-Kenan's terminology, Mario is dead during the *text-time*—from the end of the wake to the *conducción* the following morning. But he is alive during the *story-time*—the period from his courtship and marriage to his death. Rimmon-Kenan has adapted these terms from Gérard Genette's distinction between the *récit* (text) and *histoire* (story). The *récit* refers to the events in the order narrated in the text, whereas the *histoire* designates the narrated events abstracted, reconstructed, and arranged in chronological order by the reader (Rimmon-Kenan 3, 16-17, 44-45).

5. See Arnold Verhoeven, "La muerte de Mario, ¿infarto o suicidio? la ambigüedad intencionada de Delibes."

6. Erik Camayd Freixas discusses the theatricality of Carmen's monologue in "El monólogo literario y 'la novela de la posguerra.' " Delibes collaborated on a stage version of *Cinco horas con Mario* and discusses it in an interview with Pilar Concejo.

7. Carmen comically expresses her longing for this mini-car, so ubiquitous in the sixties: "lo que más me duele, Mario, es que por unos cochinos miles de pesetas, me quitaras el mayor gusto de mi vida, que yo no te digo un Mercedes, que de sobra sé que no estamos para eso, con tanto gasto, pero qué menos que un Seiscientos, Mario, si un Seiscientos lo tienen hoy hasta las porteras, pero si les llaman ombligos, cariño, ¿no lo sabías?, porque dicen que los tiene todo el mundo. ¡Cómo hubiera sido, Mario!, de cambiarme la vida, fíjate" (106).

8. In Carmen's discourse, we sometimes hear echoes of Franco's speeches, for example: "No estamos en verdad pasando tiempos fáciles. Y es el tiempo difícil el

que exige mayor disciplina y orden para la resolución de los problemas.... Esta necesidad de orden y disciplina, que es en principio universal, afecta aún más a las instituciones y especialmente a aquéllas que representan un esfuerzo espiritual y moral capaz de ejemplarizar y orientar la vida de las gentes" (Franco 63). For further comparisons, see *Discursos y mensajes del Jefe del Estado, 1968-1970*.

9. For analyses of Delibes' use of Biblical references in *Cinco horas con Mario*, refer to: Angel Valbuena Briones, "Un diálogo de imágenes bíblicas en la narrativa de Delibes"; and Jack B. Jelinski, "Mario as Biblical Analogue in Miguel Delibes' *Cinco horas con Mario*."

10. Nina Molinaro discusses the complex relations between power and truth, and confessant and confessor at work in the confession. She argues that *Cinco horas con Mario* invites readers to assume the role of confessor—a complicity they may either accept or refuse. In the final analysis, the novel "eludes conclusive interpretation because its confessional strategy resurrects guilt and innocence as a perpetual weave of power relations" (609).

11. In interviews Delibes has shown discomfort regarding certain effects of his novel. He disagrees with pessimistic interpretations, arguing that "esta novela no es tan pesimista como algunos han querido ver," and that he meant for Mario Jr. to represent hope: "En fin, esta actitud del chico, de reconciliación, opuesta a nuestro tradicional maniqueísmo, comporta un rayo de esperanza. Si los jóvenes fueran así, es evidente que pasado mañana dejarían de existir Menchus en el país" (*Conversaciones* 92). Delibes may after the fact prefer a more hopeful reading, and even credit the exemplary critic who "discovered" it. But if he left a "ray of hope," it is nearly imperceptible, given that Mario fails in convincing his mother and that she lets herself be led away by the reactionary Valentina in the end.

12. I appropriate Peirce's triadic terms, not as absolute, universally applicable categories, but as a provisional scheme for elucidating various aspects of this character. According to Peirce, an *icon* resembles its object, either visually or analogically, sharing with it fundamental properties. Among the most obviously iconic signs are paintings, photographs, cinematic images, diagrams, and graphs, but Peirce also includes mental images in this category. By *symbol* Peirce means "a relationship between two dissimilar elements" (Silverman 20). A symbol arbitrarily refers to an object based upon conventional association, without any inherent relation or correspondence. (Peirce thus does not adhere to the Romantic and Symbolist conception of symbols based on natural correspondences). An *index* points to its object by virtue of a physical relationship, often of cause and effect. It forcibly generates in the mind of a viewer a referent which is ultimately another sign: smoke indicates fire; a signature indicates an "author"; a weather sock indicates wind direction; a symptom indicates a disease; a segment of a collage indicates a cutting and pasting by an artist. Peirce insisted that these categories of signs are not absolutely separable, but rather overlap, working together to make signification possible. As Richard Shiff explains, "Any individual sign—whether icon, index or symbol—will exhibit inherent qualities (like an

icon), connect one thing to another (like an index), and generate specific interpretations (like a symbol)" (83n). For further explanation of icon, index and symbol see the *Collected Papers of Charles Sanders Peirce*, Vol. II, pp. 156-73. Also see Umberto Eco's detailed discussion in A *Theory of Semiotics*. For a brief summary, see Kaja Silverman, *The Subject of Semiotics*, pp. 14-25. And for a detailed, thoughtful summation of Peirce's thought, see Karl-Otto Apel, *Charles S. Peirce: From Pragmatism to Pragmaticism*.

13. Vicente Cabrera and Luis González-del-Valle, in their analysis of ambiguity in *Cinco horas con Mario*, propose a somewhat different triadic scheme for interpretation: "en un primer plano [el texto] tiende a convencer al lector de que Carmen es esencialmente mala y de que Mario es esencialmente bueno. Es decir, tiende a que el lector incurra irónicamente en el mismo error que critica: en el maniqueísmo de Carmen que se arrogaba la calidad de ser buena acusando a su esposo de ser malo. En un segundo plano, más profundo, la obra apunta a una situación más ambigua, pero más universalmente válida: de que el ser no es ni bueno ni malo. Y en un tercer plano, la situación moral del ser frente al bien y el mal se vuelve una imposibilidad metafísica que, superando las de Carmen y Mario, tiene que ser confrontada por el lector. La estructura de la obra alcanza así una unidad sumamente efectiva, ya que el segundo plano (Mario) es una superación del primero (Carmen), como el tercero (lector) lo es del segundo" (48).

14. Ultimately, all communication depends upon iconicity, upon the predictable mental images that individuals will draw from a culturally shared "data base." According to Peirce, "The only way of directly communicating an idea is by means of an icon; and every indirect method of communicating an idea must depend for its establishment upon the use of an icon. Hence, every assertion must contain an icon or set of icons, or else must contain signs whose meaning is only explicable by icons"; an idea is a "mental icon" (Peirce II: 158, 167).

15. Gonzalo Sobejano likens Carmen, not only to Bernarda Alba, but also to Antonia Quijana, the book-burning niece of don Quijote (187). Phyllis Boring finds additional literary prototypes for Carmen: the mother figures in Fernando Arrabal's novels and plays; Princesa Gaetani in Valle Inclán's *Sonata de primavera*; Estanislaa in Juan Goytisolo's *Duelo en Paraíso*, and the mother in Franciso Ayala's "Himeneo" (81-83).

16. According to the anthropologist Sherry Ortner, "In virtually every culture [woman's] permissible sexual activities are more closely circumscribed than man's, she is offered a much smaller range of role choices, and she is afforded direct access to a far more limited range of its social institutions. Further, she is almost universally socialized to have a narrower and generally more conservative set of attitudes and views than man, and the limited social contexts of her adult life reinforce this situation. This socially engendered conservatism and traditionalism of woman's thinking is another—perhaps the worst, certainly the most insidious—mode of social restriction and would clearly be related to her traditional function of producing well-socialized members of the group" (85).

17. A number of critics have testified as to the authenticity of the language in Delibes's novels. Studies that analyze or describe this language include: Manual Alvar, "Lengua y habla en las novelas de Miguel Delibes"; Agnes Gullón, *La novela experimental de Miguel Delibes*; Alberto Gil, "Experimentos lingüísticos de Miguel Delibes"; and Antonio H. Martínez, "Los códigos de la ironía en *Cinco horas con Mario* de Miguel Delibes." Also see Alfonso Rey, *La originalidad novelística de Delibes*, pp. 188-89, 198-200.

18. Carmen Martín Gaite in *Usos amorosos de la postguerra española* evokes the education, environment and cultural expectations of women during the postwar period. Also see Yaw Agawu-Kakraba's discussion of Carmen's voicing of Francoist discourse.

19. See Brad Epps's analysis of Isabel's desire in "The Politics of Ventriloquism: Cava, Revolution and Sexual Discourse in *Conde Julián*."

20. The *Sección Femenina* of the Spanish Falange instructed women precisely along these lines. Geraldine Scanlon cites a tract published in 1955: "La mujer nueva no tenía que ser ni la 'mujer modernista,' que empieza por negar su feminidad, evitar la maternidad, ser 'buena amiga' del marido, y acaba por ser un simpático compañero [sic] del varón, comprometiendo la propia virilidad de él, ni tampoco la 'buena señora' intratable como madre, tormento como esposa y soporífera como compañera. Sería una 'mujer de su tiempo,' feliz en la maternidad, educando a sus hijos, demostrando un interés femenino por los asuntos de su marido y proporcionándole un refugio tranquilo contra los azares de la vida pública" (324).

21. Delibes later regretted having made Carmen such a caricature: "Para mí el error fue acumular tantos defectos sobre una misma persona. En España hay muchas Menchus o muchos Menchus que no se reconocen como tales por la sencilla razón de que tienen a su niña en la Universidad, ¿verdad?, o porque fuman un pitillo después de las comidas o por cualquier otra menudencia. Si yo no hubiera concentrado tantos defectos, si la caricatura hubiera sido más piadosa, quizá la fuerza aleccionadora del libro hubiera sido mayor" (*Conversaciones* 77).

22. By symbol, Peirce meant symbolic activity in a very broad sense, comprising words, concepts, emblems—all "signals agreed upon" (168). As to the problematics of the term Peirce remarked: "The word *Symbol* has so many meanings that it would be an injury to the language to add a new one. I do not think that the signification I attach to it, that of a conventional sign, or one depending upon habit (acquired or inborn), is so much a new meaning as a return to the original meaning" (167).

23. Obviously, I am not abiding by the distinction (made in nineteenth-century aesthetics) between allegory and symbol. For discussions of the Romantic origins of this distinction, as well as its tenability, see Paul de Man, "The Rhetoric of Temporality" and Craig Owens, "The Allegorical Impulse."

24. To this list could also be added the fictionalized Isabel in Juan Goytisolo's *Reivindicación del conde don Julián*, as well as in Carmen Martín-Gaite's *El cuarto de atrás*.

25. Interestingly, *El español y los siete pecados capitales* by Fernando Díaz-Plaja was published in 1966, the same year as *Cinco horas con Mario*. The Spanish intellectual tradition of such self-criticism can be traced back (at least) to Larra, continuing through nineteenth-century liberalism and the Generation of '98.

26. Drawing from Heidegger's notion of "idle talk," Teresa Boucher discusses Carmen's "language of inauthenticity" in "The Widow's Peak / The Widow Speaks."

27. Various critics place greater emphasis on Carmen's status as *verdugo* or as *víctima*. Gonzalo Sobejano argues most eloquently for the *verdugo* interpretation, whereas Alfonso Rey and Fernando Morán stress her victimization. Matías Montes Huidoro goes so far as to consider Carmen Sotillo as "uno de los personajes femeninos más maltratados por la crítica hispánica contemporánea" (67). Isaac Montero discusses the complexity of Carmen's dual status as *víctima* and *verdugo* and how it places her in "Limbo."

28. Granted, as critics have pointed out, this tendency to polarize is softened by a measure of ambiguity. The novel avoids depicting Mario "all good" and Carmen as "all bad." But I would argue that it does present Mario as "primarily good" and Carmen as "primarily bad," and that readers are still compelled to polarize them. For discussions of ambiguity in the novel see: Vicente Cabrera and Luís González-del-Valle, *Novela española contemporánea: Cela, Delibes, Romero, y Hernández*; and Arnold Verhoeven, "La muerte de Mario, ¿infarto o suicidio? La ambigüedad intencionada de Delibes."

29. I am suggesting a line of questioning similar to Foucault's formulation of tasks in "The Order of Discourse": We must "on the basis of discourse itself, its appearance and its regularity, go towards its external conditions of possiblity, towards what gives rise to the aleatory series of these events, and fixes its limits" (67).

30. For an interesting example of how an art historian works with the concept of index, refer to Richard Shiff, "On Criticism Handling History."

31. See Geraldine Scanlon, *La polémica feminista en la España contemporánea (1868-1974)* for a description of the restrictions imposed upon women during the Franco regime, pp. 321-356.

32. Phyllis Zatlin Boring argues that Delibes's novel, *El príncipe destronado* (1973) "represents a reversal, even an apology for the author's previously unfavorable treatment of the Spanish mother, particularly the formidable Carmen (Menchu) of *Cinco horas con Mario*" (79).

33. Yaw Agawu-Kakraba also discusses the implications and effects of using a female character to portray a political system that excluded women. See her article, "Miguel Delibes and the Politics of Two Women."

34. Kristeva in *The Powers of Horror* associates rituals of defilement with the incest taboo and argues that they all converge on the maternal: "The abject confronts us... within our personal archeology, with our earliest attempts to release the hold of *maternal* entity.... It is a violent clumsy breaking away, with the

constant risk of falling back under the sway of a power as securing as it is stifling" (13). For a useful summary of Kristeva's theory of abjection, see: Elizabeth Grosz, *Sexual Subversions*, pp. 71-78.

35. I am reminded of a poem by Neruda, written during the Civil War, in which he performs a similar ritual of defilment to expunge Spain of the loathsomeness of tradition:

> En las noches de España, por los viejos jardines
> la tradición, llena de mocos muertos,
> chorreando pus y peste se paseaba
> con una cola en bruma, fantasmal y fantástica,
> vestida de asma y huecos levitones sangrientos
> y su rostro de ojos profundos detenidos
> eran verdes babosas comiendo tumba,
> y su boca sin muelas mordía cada noche
> la espiga sin nacer, el mineral secreto,
> y pasaba con su corona de cardos verdes
> sembrando vagos huesos de difunto y puñales. (*Obras Completas* 274)

Another poem associating Spain with the abject is Antonio Machado's "¡Soria fría, Soria pura!" with its images of decay: "murallas roídas," "casas denegridas," and "sórdidas callejas" (*Campos de Castilla* 73-74).

36. The sociologist Amando de Miguel in *Desde la España predemocrática*, comments on the glaring absence of women in Franco's government and bureaucracy (as of 1975). As a point of departure he cites the (ungrammatical) reaction of a "publicly progressive" politician to rumors that his wife "anda metida en política": "Me haría gracia—si no me entristeciese—que alguien pueda suponer que mi mujer piensa en política" (82). According to Miguel, "Ninguno de los 114 ministros que ha tenido Franco ha sido mujer, y se pueden contar con los dedos de la mano las que han llegado a nivel de director general o equivalente. Si nos molestáramos en repasar el fichero actual de altos cargos de la Administración Pública (desde ministros a jefes de sección), veríamos que de unos 9,000 cargos no llegan a 300 los que corresponden al sexo femenino, y de ellas una buena proporción se ocupan de tareas secretariales o afines" (82).

37. I am indebted to Brad Epp's analysis of ventriloquism in Goytisolo's *Reivindicación del conde don Julián*. Additional studies of ventriloquism in narrative include: Patricia Joplin, "The Voice of the Shuttle is Ours"; Elizabeth Harvey, *Ventriloquized Voices: Feminist Theory and English Renaissance Texts*; Patrick O'Donnell, *Figuring Voice in Narrative*; and Elizabeth Rosner, "Silencing the Ventriloquist: The Book of Secrets."

38. In his interview with Pilar Concejo, Delibes discusses his stage version of the novel. Alan Sommerstein, in his introduction to Aristophanes's plays, describes the false phalli worn by comic actors in ancient Greece, pp. 29-31.

39. See Eric Lott's study, *Love and Theft: Blackface Minstrelsy and the American Working Class*. For African-American minstrel performers to wear blackface was common practice. Lott notes that this practice also allowed performers to "work against the grain"; for "it was possible for a black man in blackface, without a great deal of effort, to offer credible imitations of white men imitating him" (113).

40. Showalter here refers to "muted group theory," which, according to Mary Crawford and Roger Chaffin, was developed by anthropologists "to describe situations in which groups of people exist in asymmetrical power relationships (e.g., blacks and whites; colonizer and the colonized). The theory proposes that language and the norms for its use are controlled by the dominant group. Members of the muted group are disadvantaged in articulating their experience since the language they must use is derived largely from the perceptions of the dominant group. To some extent, the perceptions of the muted group are unstable in the idiom of the dominant group. In order to be heard, muted group members must learn the dominant idiom and attempt to articulate within it, even though this attempt will inevitably lead to some loss of meaning. The experiences 'lost in the translation' to the dominant idiom remain unvoiced, and perhaps unthought, even within the muted group" (21). For further explanation of muted group theory see: Elaine Schowalter, "Feminist Criticism in the Wilderness"; Mary Crawford and Roger Chaffin, "The Reader's Construction of Meaning: Cognitive Research on Gender and Comprehension"; Shirley Ardener, Ed., *Perceiving Women*; and Cheris Kramarae, *Women and Men Speaking*. For a critical discussion of problems with the theory see Deborah Cameron, *Feminism and Linguistic Theory*, pp. 140-46.

41. As Foucault points out: "It would of course be absurd to deny the existence of the individual who writes and invents. But I believe that—at least since a certain epoch—the individual who sets out to write a text on the horizon of which a possible eouvre is prowling, takes upon himself the function of the author: what he writes and what he does not write, what he sketches out, even by way of provisional drafts, as an outline of the oeuvre, and what he lets fall by way of commonplace remarks—this whole play of differences is prescribed by the author-function as he receives it from his epoch, or as he modifies it in his turn" ("Order" 59).

42. Yaw Agawu-Kakraba discusses Carmen's paradoxical silencing by this text: "Although the novel outwardly projects Carmen's monologic internal discourse, she is simultaneously, and why not, strategically figured as a constitutive absence" ("Miguel Delibes and the Politics of Two Women" 68).

43. According to Umberto Eco, in the Peircian typology of signs "every sign appears as a bundle of different categories of signs.... Nevertheless the classification was still possible for, according to Peirce, the different trichotomies characterized the signs from different points of view and signs were not only precise grammatical units but also phrases, entire texts, books. Thus the partial success of the Peircian endeavor (along with his almost complete failure) tells us

that if one wants to draw a typology of signs one must, first of all, renounce the straight identification of a sign with a 'grammatical' unit, therefore extending the definition of sign to every kind of sign-function" (302n).

IV. LACKING CHARACTER:
LOURDES ORTIZ'S *LUZ DE LA MEMORIA*

> The nature of the character in a novel cannot be presented any better than is done in this statement, which says that the "meaning" of his life is revealed only in his death. But the reader of a novel actually does look for human beings from whom he derives the "meaning of life." Therefore he must, no matter what, know in advance that he will share their experience of death: if need be their figurative death—the end of the novel—but preferably their actual one. How do the characters make him understand that death is already waiting for them—a very definite death and at a very definite place? That is the question which feeds the reader's consuming interest in the events of the novel. (Walter Benjamin, "The Storyteller" 100-01)

A Failure of Character

Un estallido, esa masa sanguinolenta, quizá las tripas debajo, apenas ocultas; así de fácil. Apretar el gatillo y ahí está evidente la muerte en esa cosa roja que yace ahora en el suelo —"¡Mi perro! ¡Estás loco, mi perro!" —, el guau, guau que ni siquiera pudo balbucir, callado ahora, petrificado en esa sangre que se pone oscura, que mancha las baldosas, que se extiende, que sube por las paredes, que va a tragarte; la muerte tan simple . . . el perro destripado, sanguinolento y ella a tu lado ahora y tú todavía con la pistola en la mano, callado allí, esperando, y los gritos: "Esto no puede ser. Estás loco. Has querido

matarme. Eres un sádico, un puerco, sucio sádico.
¡Pobrecillo!" (7).

This startling opening passage of *Luz de la memoria* immediately posits the enigmas of the narrative.[1] Who is this character? Is he deranged? Why did he shoot the dog? What is his relationship to the dog's owner? And was he indeed trying to kill her? As in any narrative text, such initial questions arouse in readers a desire for explanation—in Roland Barthes' words, "a passion for sense" (qtd. in Brooks 37). Readers who desire to make sense of this dense, disorderly narrative will assume the task of constructing an intelligible psychological portrait of a seemingly deranged protagonist, while simultaneously plotting a biographical trajectory that logically explains his irrational behavior.

Based on his behavior in the opening scenes, readers will refer to models from already-read texts and register Enrique as a familiar type— the alienated misfit with a fragmented psyche—so common to modern psychological and existential novels. Immediately after shooting the dog, Enrique is committed to a psychiatric hospital in a highly agitated state. In a montage of shifting, fragmentary scenes, he narrates his immediate experiences in the hospital interspersed with scenes from his past and quotations from novels, histories, movies, and comic strips. At the end of the first chapter Enrique faces the psychiatrist but cannot or will not speak—a silence he will maintain through the greater part of the novel. The doctor hands him a file containing reports submitted by his parents and estranged wife. He informs Enrique that his therapy will entail reading the reports and writing his reactions. Readers, in turn, will surmise that Enrique's disjointed narration must be part of that very dossier.

As readers then, we occupy the psychoanalyst's chair. Our task is to read and analyze the reports submitted by family members along with Enrique's own garbled writings. As we sort through the miscellaneous data, we must balance, compare, and judge the testimony of others with Enrique's often contradictory memories, for each of them represents only a partial and self-interested view. In submitting their accounts of events, the wife, mother and father are most concerned with absolving themselves of responsibility for Enrique's problems. Enrique's own memories are also suspect, given his derangement and extreme malleability; clearly, he is in no condition to organize and interpret his own past with any authority. In his confused narrations, childhood memories merge seamlessly with fragments from movies, comic books, and histories—just as his accounts of the hospital experience merge with his memories of the prison experience. At times it is difficult or impossible to discern *who* is narrating—Enrique or an external narrator—given the constant slippage from first-, to second- and third-person narrations. The text continually sets stumbling blocks in the way of the sense-making process, thwarting readers' efforts to complete the case study.

Albeit with difficulty, the determined reader can create an adequate explanatory narrative that draws from psychological novels and the conventional wisdom of a pop-psyche age. The Enrique of this reading is a social deviant, product of an "hogar intransigente," who after a series of experiments with political movements and alternative life-styles, finally self-destructs (35). In their reports his fellow characters provide ready-made diagnoses that uphold this "failure" of character. To his father Enrique "siempre ha sido un individuo sin personalidad, timorato, apocado, en fin . . . usted me entiende, no era un muchacho normal" (50). Pilar asserts that Enrique "[c]arece de un sentido de la realidad. . . . [D]e alguna manera quiere autodestruirse" (99). Enrique will for the most part concur with these diagnoses, characterizing himself as "un fracasado," and insisting: "[N]o 'soy' nada, porque he destruido uno tras otro, sucesivamente, los papeles que he ido asumiendo" (189).

This trajectory of decline continues after Enrique regains the ability to speak and leaves the hospital, presumably cured—although significantly, neither the moment he resumes speaking nor his official cure is narrated. In the final sections of the novel, he reunites with his estranged wife, Pilar, although still under the terms of their sexually open marriage. Pilar, in turn, introduces him to *el rollo*, the counter-culture of the early nineteen-seventies, and he spends his days and nights engaged in the proverbial sex, drugs, and rock-and-roll. As Enrique grows increasingly apathetic and irresponsible, he violates even the relaxed norms of the counter-culture. The normalizing, therapeutic task, previously conducted by the psychiatrist, is now taken over by Pilar, who continually scolds him: "Te quieres destruir; no sé por qué, pero estoy convencida de que te quieres destruir. Me lo han contado; me han dicho que estás todo el día fumando, que te estás convirtiendo en un inútil, . . . en un gorrón que pretende vivir a costa de los demás" (176).

In his monologues Enrique admits that since involving himself in the counterculture, his sense of failure and futility has grown. "El rollo" proves to be merely another meaningless game, another "camino de aburrimiento" (146). Even his playful discourse *on el rollo*, his most extended speech-act in the novel, leads him to despair:

> Todo es cuestión de rollo, nuestro propio rollo. ¿Cuál de vosotros no se ha enrollado nunca? Todo lo mío ya sabéis que es enrollamiento... el enrollarse o no enrollarse, esa es la cuestión, y el que no se enrolle que tire la primera piedra y me da de pronto como depresivo y me pongo a hipear,... os juro que estoy ya harto de enrollarme,... y me da como triste, como pesado, al pensar que hay rollos bonitos y rollos molestos y que algunos rollos son más compensadores, más "enrollantes," más apetitosos y otros, en cambio, son rollos pobretones a los que se les acaba la cuerda en seguida y lloriqueo, gimo casi y todo es broma aún, pero Enrique se da cuenta lejanamente de que algo pasa, de que eso del rollo, mi propio rollo, es necesario y de que uno no hace más que buscarse nuevos rollos para seguir tirando, pero este rollo, nuestro rollo de ahora, es una mierda, es una pura mierda.... (160-62)

Having begun in a mock-academic style meant to entertain his friends, his discourse leads him to desperation. His life in *el rollo*, presumably freer, has become indistinguishable from his life inside the prison or hospital walls:

> [L]e gustaría, me gustaría tener capacidad para desear de nuevo, para salir de la apatía que se prolonga hasta el sexo y sabe que, allá en la cárcel, que allá entre las cuatro paredes blancas después, las cosas parecían suceder, seguir existiendo, uno pensaba que afuera seguía el rollo, que había cosas que se podían esperar, cosas que recuperar, cosas que ahora, ya afuera, se convierten en ese transcurrir abúlico de las horas en casa de Laura, en ese andar sin rumbo por las calles de Madrid, aceptando ya sin lucha todo lo que antes hubiera considerado como la *merde*. (162-63)

Lacking here is the conventional novelistic character with an all-consuming desire that defines and drives him. Enrique, emptied of all desire for identifiable objects, desires only to desire. Near the end, however, he will identify an object of desire, as increasingly, he looks to death's "embrace" for salvation from boredom, futility, and failure.

In the final sections of the novel Enrique and Pilar travel to Ibiza where, in a sense, he falls out of character. His primary unifying trait, passivity, no longer holds, and he becomes domineering and aggressive, quarreling with Pilar and engaging in violent sex. In an extended (and for the most part, unspoken) address to Pilar, he considers different models for suicide, among them, a woman who had jumped to her death from a nearby apartment when Enrique was a child. Near the end, still maintaining this silent dialogue with Pilar, he dwells upon his failures: "[L]as cosas, Pilarcita, no son como uno quisiera y ya sé que toda la historia es inútil, que amar así como tú y yo no sabemos amarnos, no es más que prolongar esa sensación de fracaso cotidiano, fracaso ante una realidad que no nos gusta, como diría el otro, pero también fracaso ante uno mismo" (201). Shortly afterwards, in a final (perhaps) definitive act, Enrique jumps (or falls) from a tower to his death. From killing the dog to his apparent suicide, this biographical trajectory charts a progressive decline, a progressive failure. Failing to desire, Enrique fails to cohere. Paradoxically, the "unity" of his character depends upon the repetition of failure.

But if Enrique fails as a character, his generation also fails, for the novel clearly creates a satiric portrait of a "generación jodida" (177). The scenes recalling the activities of Marxist-Leninist cells portray the sectarian polemics and schisms as ineffective game-playing—"juegos de niños" (59). And the scenes dramatizing the counter-culture depict the foolish babble of hippies under the influence. Moreover, all the characters who join Enrique in these activities reveal themselves as hypocrites, posturers, opportunists, or fools. Enrique himself, Ortiz has claimed, is a composite of characters she encountered during her own involvement in clandestine political organizations and in the counter-culture.[2] The novel situates itself in the final years of the Franco regime, and clearly, through its narrative of failure, it dramatizes the oppressiveness of the society and the frustrated rebellion of Ortiz's generation.[3]

This narrative design, then, in which Enrique's failure stands for a generation's failure, could be termed a verisimilar, or *iconic* reading, according to the terms employed in the discussion of *Cinco horas con Mario*. Readers favoring this interpretation will seek the "person-likeness" in Enrique and consider him as a psychological "case," a character who fails to self-actualize, fails to cohere. They will recognize in turn, that Enrique exemplifies a generation whose rebellion also fails to self-actualize and to cohere. This reading, the text's "narrative program," relies upon readers' cultural beliefs in the unitary self; it depends upon their desires for the interpretable character, for "plottable" events that point towards resolution and closure.[4] Ironically, this reading answers readers' desires for unity of character and of plot, but at the cost of a character's utter failure .

A Failure of Reading

The reading I have just outlined, with its thematics of failure, depends upon finding verisimilitude and logic in a disorderly and heterogeneous text. Although supportable by the evidence, it may leave a certain residue of dissatisfaction in readers' minds; for order to comply with this narrative program, readers must join the plot, or conspiracy, operating within the novelistic society—a plot that aims to define, discipline, and normalize a disruptive character; and furthermore, readers must ignore certain metafictional elements that interfere with the storyline and forestall a definitive resolution.

In opposition to the narrative program, there emerges a counternarrative, also supportable by the evidence, in which Enrique figures not as a tragic figure, lacking in character, but rather as a master gameplayer, adroit at eluding the forces of normalization. Readers favoring this counternarrative will find prototypes for Enrique, not in the failed characters of psychological and existential novels, but rather in the elusive, undefinable characters of postmodernist fiction. Within this interpretive frame, Enrique's lack of character provides him with an excessive vagueness, enabling him to evade all attempts at definitive interpretation—by his interpreters both inside and outside the fictional world. In other words, under the terms of this counternarrative, Enrique succeeds as an elusive hero, but at the cost of a failure of reading.

Within the logic of this counternarrative, the central problem facing the novelistic society is a troublesome, deviant character who must be normalized, brought back into the fold. In a multi-faceted display of power, that society exerts every means available to regain control over him. Enrique has already defied the political regime by participating in clandestine Marxist-Leninist groups, and the regime has punished him with torture and imprisonment. In addition, he has defied his society's moral regime by engaging in a sexually open marriage. Both these challenges fall well within Western traditions of rationally justifiable opposition to oppressive regimes. But the transgression that initiates the action —the killing of the dog—challenges the regime of sense. This act threatens simply because it is irrational, unpredictable, and explainable only *speculatively* in terms of displaced rage.[5] Enrique himself is aware of the effect of this act, "el gesto," upon those around him. Speaking to himself, he reflects:

> y sabes que para todos ellos lo único digno de ser comentado tras el gesto, de ser relatado, recordado en charla tras charla semidolida, semientristecida, sería el hecho de la vida, pero de una vida como posibilidad, una vida de pronto arrebatada dejando ante ellos toda una serie de interrogantes, de imágenes más o menos borradas de un ser que alguna vez—"¿te acuerdas, a él le gustaban mucho los calamares . . ." (43)

This puzzling act of transgression, killing the dog, has opened a gap in the texture of his life, spawning "toda una serie de interrogantes" as his fellow characters look to his past for answers. In doing so, they produce a diagnostic discourse that purports not only to explain his character, but also to persuade him to internalize that explanation, making it his own. The principal instrument in this disciplinary process is of course the biographical dossier—the case study—assembled by the psychiatrist with the collaboration of Enrique's family. As Enrique reads the various reports and writes his commentaries, he will thereby participate in the diagramming, sense-making process and become officially "cured."[6]

Although Enrique gives the impression of passive compliance, he resists the self-diagramming process in various ways, most obviously, by his silence. His silence thus serves both as barrier and spur to the excessive production of diagnostic discourse. Enrique relates his present muteness to the comforting silence of the womb: "esa resistencia mía para dejar el silencio, para salir de esa cómoda estadía en el seno materno, creciendo allí tan bien arropadito, y ese silencio que ahora me es devuelto es una rebelión más contra aquél que me fue arrebatado para darme una vida con una palmadita en el culo" (19). Often, however, it is not clear to Enrique whether his silence is rebellion or incapacity. At times he wants to cooperate with the good doctor; at times he opens his mouth to speak or to scream but emits no sound. He engages in a dialogue of sorts with the analyst by nodding or shaking his head in response to questions. But he does not assume power by taking a stand, refusing, or actively resisting. To do so, would be to collude with the power-mongering forces in the fictional world, to fight power with power.

In character with his passivity and malleability, Enrique does not remain completely silent. He appears to collaborate with the therapeutic program by writing notes—the stream-of-consciousness monologue— which ostensibly, would help to explain his abnormality. But Enrique's writings, while abetting the explanatory process, simultaneously subvert it. Equivocal, contradictory, and variable, his memories never achieve the cohesion and authority of a confession. Finding it impossible to rest on a single version of his life, he is caught in a web of multiple interpretations. Certain of his memories uphold the characterizations that his parents provide of his childhood, while others times contradict them. Enrique concurs with the picture of himself as an unhappy child, rejected by his parents, living in an "hogar intransigente" where mediocrity rules. But at the same time he insists on a happier interpretation: "En realidad también yo fui feliz, piensas, también mi infancia fue modélica, algodonosa, y quieres imaginarte ahora en el Retiro jugando con Eduardo y Julián a policías y ladrones y a tú-la-llevas" (42). Enrique becomes acutely aware of the fictitious nature of whatever account of his life he may create, given the inevitable mixing of heterogeneous cultural materials into his autobiography. Doubting his very capacity to remember, Enrique reflects:

> Invento, te dices, porque esa imagen construida de ti mismo, esa imagen que intentas rescatar del recuerdo— ¿recuerdo de dos años, de un año?, te preguntas—es sólo un cuadro recompuesto por ti mucho más tarde, con tantos y tantos datos recogidos, con pedazos de novelas, con informes mal digeridos de psicólogos, con estudios sobre el edipismo infantil, los celos, la agresividad en el niño, informes que durante cuatro años devoraste buscando raíces. "Me interesa un huevo la psicología" le dijiste a Ernesto (41).

Of course psychoanalytic therapy relies on such undigested, confused, "intertextual" material to reveal the "hidden truths" about the subject. From this undifferentiated material the psychoanalyst sorts, selects, and orders the significant facts in the case study—the mass of documents that captures, fixes, and defines the subject. But significantly, in Enrique's case, the undifferentiated stream-of-consciousness material is never organized and interpreted by the psychiatrist. Neither does Enrique succeed in ordering and interpreting the many images that besiege him "en una sucesión de formas inconclusas que se deslíen en la memoria, perfilando contornos" (36). The elision of this vital step in the therapeutic process raises doubts as to the substance of Enrique's "cure" and the extent of his cooperation. Certainly, from the fictional society's point of view, his subsequent abnormal behavior would suggest that his cure was a failure. But if considered an elusive, "unconstituted subject" who refuses all attempts to constitute him, Enrique succeeds in resisting the powers that seek to document his life; he manages to elude definition, classification, and normalization.

Enrique's very passivity therefore becomes a most effective mode of opposition. As Leo Bersani has argued, an excessive response to the exercise of power is sometimes the optimal means of resisting: "By appearing to obey the imperative of diagramming (and perhaps thereby constituting) the self, one may subvert the underlying strategy by responding excessively to the formal appeal of the diagramming activity itself" (5). Through most of the novel, Enrique seems to allow the doctor, his family and his friends, to freely have their way with him, to freely diagnose his illness and explain his life. It is, however, his very vagueness and lack of personality that obstruct the diagramming process, making it impossible to truly pin him down, making evident the inadequacy and fictitiousness of any explanation of his character. Enrique's lack of character could be seen as a kind of heroism in that he refuses to accept or construct a definitive "fiction" that would explain his own nature; he does not flee from what Leo Bersani calls "the frightening invisibility of our 'nature,' from that constant gliding of our desires which both sustains life and ruins the possibility of any settled understanding of life" ("The Subject of Power" 12).

Through the first half of the novel, Enrique's excessive vagueness thus effectively obstructs the interpretive efforts of his fellow characters. In the latter segments of the novel, a metafictional shift occurs that obstructs the interpretive efforts of empirical readers. Gradually, Enrique the character assumes the role of *writer*—indeed, of this very novel— thus further complicating the reading process. The first sign of a "desdoblamiento" on Enrique's part occurs when, immediately after his release from the psychiatric hospital, he makes love with his estranged wife Pilar: "[H]e hecho el amor como si estuviera escindido, como si el Enrique jodedor, amantísimo, apasionado, se viera contemplado desde las alturas por un Enrique algo cínico, que analiza con curiosidad los avances eróticos . . ." (139-40). From this point onward, Enrique will intermittently play the role of distant, cynical observer of himself as a character.

Soon after this schism comes the first explicit suggestion that Enrique, the character, is simultaneously Enrique the writer:

> Supongamos que todo me lo he inventado yo. Supongamos que Enrique no fue jamás ese pobre enfermo, embecilizado, que contempla la escena sin demasiado entusiasmo. Enrique no fue nunca ese estudiante, quizá tímido, masturbador precoz y arrepentido, que se encogía de sorpresa ante las ligas negras de la hermosa mujer desnuda; Enrique no fue tampoco ese muchacho dubitativo, amante de la justicia y deseoso de libertad que fue pasando sucesivamente por varias organizaciones clandestinas para después, tras un largo y no demasiado morboso episodio carcelero, acabar despansurrando a un perro de coquetón nombre anarquista. . . . (145)

Here Enrique layers fiction upon fiction by raising the possibility that all the disjointed biographical documents in the text-dossier—including those written by Enrique (the character) and by his family members—are mere inventions of Enrique as writer. Next, he poses the question of *how* to narrate an alternative "pasado aventurero," a problem that will continue to preoccupy him through the remainder of the text: "Enrique el mudo no sería entonces más que un pretexto de este otro personaje, ¿más real?, más aburrido, que decide plantearse cómo contar de una manera algo romántica el puñetero lío de esa vida—y de esa muerte—a la que desgraciadamente no le encuentra demasiado sentido" (145).

This preoccupation—"¿cómo contar?"—intensifies through the segments that recount Enrique's drug experiences. In the chapters centering on his "viaje" with LSD, an external narrator, presumably Enrique the writer, poses the problem: "¿Cómo narrar el ácido de Enrique? Es algo intransferible, nos diría él, algo que transcrito pierde valor; podría intentarse contar al mismo momento del transcurrir, . . . pero eso nos daría una visión parcial, deformada, en absoluto descriptiva" (165). When Enrique attempts to describe his experiences as they occur, he speaks "un lenguaje articulado en el que faltaban las conexiones lógicas" (165). The hallucinogenic experience aptly dramatizes the problematics of "cómo contar," for its chaos and intensity defy the mind's ability to impose pattern upon experience.

At the end of the novel, while in Ibiza with Pilar, Enrique proposes once more that he write a novel based on his memories, but he is stymied over how to conclude the book. Picking up a thread woven through his previous monologues, he revisits the deaths of Trotsky, Louis XVI, and Socrates, and considers them as prototypes for ending his novel (and his life). Finally, he chooses as a model the suicide of a woman who jumped from a window to the patio below his family's apartment when he was a child. After a long night of drunkenness, quarreling, and sadistic sex, Enrique insists on climbing an abandoned tower. Just at the moment when Pilar seemingly has convinced him to descend, he falls, reenacting the woman's death.

Lending ambiguity to his demise, the metanarrative theme gives rise to a series unanswerable questions. Was Enrique's death accidental, intentional, or simply self-prophesied? If a suicide, does his death signify a rebellion against the powers that rule this fictional world, or a surrender? More fundamentally, *who* dies? Enrique the writer, Enrique the character, or both? After rather absurdly embroiling ourselves in these questions, we may realize that we have been led down the garden path, and this very realization points to the central irony of the novel. By participating as readers in the interpretive enterprise to plot and define Enrique's life and character, we have unwittingly joined forces with the powers-that-be in the fictional world, with those who attempted to interpret and normalize a deviant character. A novel which at first seem committed to the writing and reading of the human personality, ultimately challenges this very legibility.

"All narrative may in essence be obituary," writes Peter Brooks, for "the retrospective knowledge that it seeks, the knowledge that comes after, stands on the far side of the end, in human terms on the far side of death" (95). Working retrospectively, "the end writes the beginning and shapes the middle"; "only the end can finally determine meaning [and] close the sentence as a signifying totality" (Brooks 22). If, for example, the ending of *Luz de la memoria* provided clear markers that Enrique's death constituted a rebellion, then readers would interpret his suicide as an ecstatic gesture by a defiant and excessive character who, refusing to submit to the norms of the fictional world, flamboyantly resigns from it. On the other hand, if the text pointed to his death as a surrender, this same abnormal character, whose life is unbearable because of his inability to conform, is driven to sacrifice himself. In both cases the final death lends "authority" to the narrative; it is a touchstone for the interpretive process, working retrospectively to satisfy readers' "passion for sense" (Brooks 37).

True to postmodern form, in *Luz de la memoria* the retrospective interpreting process is forestalled by the indeterminacy of its ending, by its dissolution into a metafictional endgame. As readers, we can neither "plot" the text satisfactorily, nor encapsulate Enrique within a stable psychological paradigm, into a "character." Of course, we can with some validity adhere to the narrative program outlined above, in which Enrique figures as an alienated misfit who self-destructs and thereby signifies the wasted potential of a "generación jodida" (177). But we cannot uphold this reading without colluding with a discredited and repellent novelistic society, and without ignoring the metafictional elements that preclude a definitive ending. So if Enrique's character proves elusive, so do our character-roles as readers. Enrique, as object of readerly pursuit, slips into the void of incomprehensibility, and as readers we may shrug and admit the failure of the sense-making project.

Death, Desire, and the Other

According to the two readings outlined thus far, narrative and counternarrative, any perceived unity of character and plot depends upon failure. Either we register Enrique as a failed character, a lost soul who ultimately resigns from the fictional society, or we consider him a master of elusiveness, a species of postmodern hero, who evades all definitive interpretations. In the latter case we must simultaneously admit the failure of the sense-making, plotting operation—in other words, our failure as readers. The first, more cohesive reading may prove unsatisfactory, given the uncomfortable complicities and single-mindedness it requires. But the second option, while frustrating readers' desires for narrative cohesion, simultaneously opens a provocative line of questioning: Does the failure of our interpretive designs on this novel give way to a different mode of desiring? Does this novel point towards an expansion of readerly desires?

Before considering these questions, let us further examine the character of narrative desire.[7] I began this chapter by restating a narrative truism: the enigma, once posed, arouses in readers a "passion for meaning"—a desire that compels us to read on and motivates our interpretive practice with the promise of truth revealed. Leo Bersani would call this narrative desire a "structured desire," by which he means "desiring impulses sublimated into emotional 'faculties' or passions and thereby providing the basis for the notion of a distinct and coherently unified personality" (*A Future for Astyanax* 5-6). Continuing, Bersani argues that "the viability of the structured self depends on an impoverishment of desire, for the desiring imagination's contacts with the world are limited by the need for preserving the intelligibility of a psychic structure" (6). It is this impoverished, structured desire, bound to belief in the unitary self, that traditional narrative arouses in its readers, and that *Luz de la memoria* ultimately refuses.

In opposition to this structured desire, Bersani posits a fragmented, disruptive desire, which "could be thought of as a disease of disconnectedness," a refusal of one part of the structure to being defined by its relations to other parts (*Future* 66). Arguably, such a fragmented, disruptive desire is activated under the terms of the reading just outlined, in which Enrique succeeds in evading all self-structuring forces. But the novel stops short of displaying that "celebratory failure of self" that Bersani finds in the "visionary" novels he analyzes (x). Indeed, the denial of readers' narrative desires by *Luz de la memoria* remains predominantly negative. The reiteration of failure—of marriage, of friendship, of political struggle, of self, and of reading—so permeates both narrative and counternarrative, that it appears to leave no suggestion of an alternative, expansive desire.

It is, however, precisely this predominant negativity that not only displays the problematics of narrative desire but also points towards an alternative. In other words, death, as the sign of absolute negativity, works thematically in this novel to expose and disrupt the complex operations of narrative desire. Earlier, in my discussion of Enrique's ambiguous death, I cited Peter Brooks' claim for an affinity between narrative and obituary (22). Brooks in turn, is drawing from Walter Benjamin who observed: "Death is the sanction of everything that the storyteller can tell. He has borrowed his authority from death" (94). Benjamin recognized that just as the "meaning" of a character's life is only revealed in his death, the meaning of a novel can only be revealed retrospectively by its ending, whether a figurative or literal death (100-01). Narrative, always sliding irrevocably towards "the end," holds out the promise of "meaning," of enigma resolved. Readers well-trained in narrative conventions and seduced by narrative desire, will desire and expect such resolutions. In other words, readers desire stasis, an end to desiring—tantamount to a desire for death.

We have seen how Enrique the character's fall from the tower, selected by Enrique the writer among other possible endings, is offered almost gratuitously, as a mockery of narrative's free-falling movement towards stasis. A closer examination of Enrique's discourse on death reveals it as a commentary on the kinship of narrative, thanatic, and erotic desires.[8] During his final hours of excess, in an extended, interior monologue, he conflates the killing of the dog with his final violent sex act, the dying Bakunin with Pilar, the novel's ending with its beginning. In doing so, however, he affirms not circularity, but a linear (narrative) necessity that impels him towards "ese momento de deseo y destrucción":

> la necesidad de que aquello, aquella mujer por lo menos, se te entregase por entero, como la muerte, como aquel perro despanzurado sobre el piso; momento que no llegaste a concretar ni siquiera a trasladar al pensamiento, pero en el cual intuías, intuyes ahora, que podías hacerlo; aquel perro como testimonio sobre el piso y el cuerpo de Pilar debajo, jadeando, confundiendo en un polvo increíble el dolor que recibía de ti con el goce, goce esperado, presentido como prolongación del placer, al interrumpir el dolor que llega a ser la antesala del mismo y se convierte a su vez en deseado. (194).

In the post-coital stasis that follows, Enrique again connects Eros and Thanatos with his narrative destiny: "[S]oy finalista, hermosa mía—estaba destinado a conducirnos a este momento junto a esta carretera, con esta paz, tras este polvo, donde ya no hay voces, ni gestos ni nada más que este estar aquí los dos sin deseos, sin aspavientos" (195). His commentary suggests that both the sex act and the narrative act—whether written or read—lead inevitably towards the destruction of desire. This "finalist" movement toward death in erotic and narrative practices must, however, be repeated; desire must be aroused and destroyed over and over again—hence the suggestion of "eternal return" in Enrique's conflation of the novel's beginning and end: "[E]s así como deseabas repetir una y mil veces el rito de la posesión-destrucción, destrucción concluida sabiamente en un orgasmo" (194).

Moreover, this obsessive "rito de posesión-destrucción" requires a submission of self to other and a loss of self in other. During the sex act, Enrique observes: "sé que precisamente en ese doblarse de ella, en esa sumisión, reside la fuente de mi deseo" (193). He imagines himself telling her: "deseaba matarte, ahora sé que la muerte es precisamente el instante álgido de la posesión, . . . te das cuenta de que en ese momento de deseo y destrucción, en el que la necesidad de dominar y poseer llegaba hasta el límite" (194). According to Enrique's masculinist logic, female submits to male just as a narrative text submits to a reader's interpretive desire—although outside of a masculinist logic, "who submits to whom," in sex as in reading, is certainly a more ambiguous and reversible relation.[9]

In a study of character in modernist and postmodernist texts, Thomas Docherty has argued that the dependence of narrative desire upon submission derives from its kinship with Eros and Thanatos:

> Theories of motivation which presuppose that desire seeks to be satisfied are condemned to a tension-reduction model of motivation, in which a desiring character seeks stasis (or self-hood) of some kind. The erotic desire, then, is for the union of the subject with another subject which at the moment of satisfaction of the desire becomes an object in the experiential perception of the desiring subject. The erotic desire is a quest for self-realization and self-aggrandizement through a subservient "other." The possession of a desired object is the aim. And the thanatic desire is that which looked for the calm of death through a kind of passive subservience of its subjectivity to an other subject, that is, assimilation and reification of the self by an other. (225-26)

Operating within a masculinist logic of gender relations, Eros and Thanatos both require a relation of dominance and subservience that is dramatized in *Luz de la memoria*. For Enrique, Eros demands that the feminine other submit to his desire; and inversely, Thanatos demands that he submit to the otherness of death. It is perhaps due in part to this inverse relation that Eros and Thanatos derive their intimate connections within the logic of gender.[10] Clearly, this novel displays the close interrelations of Enrique's erotic desire, expressed through his sadistic possession of Pilar's body, and his desire for death's embrace. Moreover, the novel's metanarrative commentary suggests that readerly desire demands a similar act of "posesión-destrucción": an imposition of meaning that ultimately destroys desire (194). In each case, what is desired is stasis, an end to desiring—which, according to Docherty, permits no *ekstasis* (226).

In developing this notion of *ekstasis*, Docherty distinguishes (perhaps too neatly) between desire and need, asserting that erotic and thanatic motivation, "leading to stasis, are pertinent to the 'needy' character and not the desiring one" (230).[11] From this point on, he will associate *desire* with *ekstasis*—"the possibility of movement beyond the present self, the possibility of Romantic transcendence of an identity or of a centered and unified self" (230). Desire, for Docherty, offers "the condition of subjectivity in place of 'character' or 'self' " (230). And whereas need is motivated by Eros and Thanatos, the motivation of desire is *Agape*, which

> is capable of going beyond the realm of one's own sense and "present self," in order not only to "see" the other "as it is in itself," but more radically to "be" that other. Fiction motivated by Eros or Thanatos inevitably places the reader in second or third person, to whom a discourse, the "authorized version," or authoritarian discourse of the author is addressed either directly or indirectly through the "meaning" of the stable (static) characters. (230)

In other words, fiction driven by Eros or Thanatos depends upon a narrative program that seduces readers by arousing their desires for stable meaning, coherent character, and unambiguous endings. Agape allows readers to transcend these structured desires, to respond to an *other* seduction, in which readers experience being as "a series of fleeting and deferred instantiations of future subjectivity" (Docherty 230).[12]

Can we find in *Luz de la memoria* any such appeal to Agapeic desire, that desire to "not only 'see' the other," but "more radically to 'be' that other"? (Docherty 230). Given the predominant negativity of this text, its seeming commitment to failure, wherein would such an affirmation of otherness reside? Enrique comes closest to expressing such a desire near the end of his hospital stay, in an act which offers the only hint of an impending cure. Still mute, Enrique writes a note to the doctor, expressing his desire to join "the others": "Quiero salir de esta celda. Quiero ver a los otros. En este manicomio hay otros y quiero estar con ellos" (113). After joining the other patients gathered in the prison patio, Enrique describes their childlike games: "Aquí todos juegan, piensas y te gustaría jugar como ellos, dejarte llevar, ver enemigos en cada esquina, jugar a policías y ladrones" (118). He compares their activities to the movements of a deranged bear that he remembers from childhood visits to the zoo: "Recuerdas al oso blanco del zoo de tu infancia que daba vueltas rítmicas, siempre iguales, en aquella ridícula jaula cilíndrica" (117). Like the bear, the patients follow a strange rhythmic routine in which their steps are regulated and controlled in accord with "leyes de la locura," which give them a strange illusion of freedom. In a further comparison he likens the bear and the patients to the people outside—ostensibly free, but really controlled by invisible laws and norms:

> [S]e mueve, según extrañas leyes propias y también fuera, piensas, también ellos fuera, aparentemente libres, aparentemente relajados, yo fuera, sin controles, se movían, nos movíamos con esa extraña sensación de libertad de los dos osos del estanque y, sin embargo, con la misma monotonía que el oso de la jaula cilíndrica, con la misma reiteración y parsimonia. (118)

Enrique has grasped that the rules, the norms of social discourse, are fundamental and apparently inescapable. This emphasis on repetition as entrapment would seem to serve the narrative program by reinforcing Enriques's sense of futility and leading him to embrace death as the only freedom. He will declare near the end, in silent address to Pilar: "Tú podrías intentar entenderlo, podrías darte cuenta de que todo es un juego, pero a veces, Pilar, los juegos se repiten y resultan tremendamente aburridos, los juegos dejan de ser apasionantes y uno se ve, como yo ahora, sentado bajo el olivo, sabiendo que todo se reduce quizá a esta elección, a esta cicuta por fin definitiva" (202). Leo Bersani would explain this tragic sense of entrapment as a consequence of the constant deferral of our structured, "impoverished" desires ("needs," for Docherty), which attach themselves first to one fetish then another without ever leading to plenitude:

> An important psychological consequence of sublimated (civilized) desire may be a suicidal melancholy. In our sublimations, our desires never die. But the endless repetition of desires suppressed by guilt and angry frustration ultimately leads to the fantasy of death as the absolute pleasure.... The repeated refusal to confess our desires gives them a kind of criminally immoral activity from which the definitive immobility of death might rescue us. (6)

While asserting that "desire is inseparable from repetition," Bersani is seeking a mode of repetition apart from repression and sublimation, outside of this dialectic of enslavement (11). He argues that the diversification of our desires depends upon finding new ways to repeat.

Indeed, Enrique's involvement *el rollo*, following his release from the hospital, initially represents an attempt to find a new game, a new way to repeat. But as we have seen, his word-play with *el rollo* leads him to the same sense of entrapment and despair. Enrique begins in a ludic vein, speaking with tongue in cheek: "Todo es cuestión de rollo, nuestro propio rollo. ¿Cuál de vosotros no se ha enrollado nunca? Todo lo mío ya sabeis que es enrollamiento" (160). But he concludes with a bald statement of futility: "Enrique se da cuenta lejanamente de que algo pasa, de que eso del rollo, mi propio rollo, es necesario y de que uno no hace más que buscarse nuevos rollos para seguir tirando, pero este rollo, nuestro rollo de ahora, es una mierda, es una pura mierda" (161).

Much earlier, I suggested that Enrique's excursus on *el rollo* reinforces the narrative program of failed character. Like the circular movements of the caged bear, *el rollo* works metaphorically to represent Enrique's entrapment in a series of meaningless games, and at the same time, it operates as a clear historical referent that supports the critique of a "generación jodida." However, if refigured in terms of a metafictional reading, *el rollo* serves as an emblem for the "involved," labyrinthine text itself; and as a corollary, *enrollamiento* aptly describes the reader's involvement in this messy and problematic text.[13] If refigured even more broadly, *el rollo* signifies the web of discourse at large, while *enrollamiento* describes the subject's entanglement in discourse, in alterity. Rather than suggesting a Sysiphean consignment to endless repetition, the reader's *enrollamiento* in this *rollo* of a text may then point towards an alternative mode of desiring.

Speaking of the power of desire to en-roll, entrap us in discourse, Ross Chambers contends that

> it is through our desires that we are "imprisoned" within a universe of ideological representation, the dominance of which functions as a principal means of social control. What and how we desire—the "desirable" in short—is socially mediated; but desirability simultaneously strengthens the grip of dominant representation of the real by making them the objects of libidinal attractions. (175)

To counter the seductive power of the ideological systems that produce our desires for structure, sense, and unitary self, Chambers suggests a strategy and tactics of "oppositional reading" that would seek the "forms of desire that arise within ideological systems, like 'noise' in systems of information, as by-products" that are not, however, fully controlled by the system" (175).[14] Reading, Chambers argues, "has the power to produce shifts in desire; and desire does not produce just 'fantasy' but reality itself" (xii). Given that desire is triangulated, mediated by discourse as other, any change in desire requires turning away from an investment in ourselves as desiring subjects, away from the designated objects of desire, and towards reading (and re-writing) the mediating substance itself. In other words a change in desire requires an *enrollamiento* in discourse, seeking freedom in the play afforded by the discursive system itself.[15]

In a telling statement, Enrique suggests that his mad ravings are the "hemlock of Socrates": "[Q]uizá mi pire constante no es sino la cicuta del viejo, pero con la esperanza aún de que al despertar todo haya cambiado" (200). Although his mad discourse is a fatal poison, it also offers hope for change "upon awakening"—suggesting that like Plato's *pharmakon*, Enrique's poison is also his cure.[16] By en-rolling himself in discourse, as immanently social, as other, Enrique dies as an individual, dispersed among multiple identities and voices. His mad, desperate discourse leads him towards death, but also towards otherness.

Returning, then, to the question of where we might find in this text an appeal to Agapeic desire, I venture that, by delving deeper into the thematics of death, we find an affirmation of otherness. We have seen how Enrique's indeterminate "death" serves as a mockery of narrative's absolute free fall towards stasis. And we have seen how his meditations on death reveal the operations of narrative desire, by depicting its affinity to both Eros and Thanatos. In the present context, Enrique's melancholic meditations on his own death, his loss of self, simultaneously serve as affirmations of plural identity. In one of his extended interior monologues while locked in his hospital cell, Enrique reflects on

> esa absoluta normalidad de la muerte, esa muerte que se volvía cotidiana y perdía su dramatismo, ese todos-somos-capaces y te diriges hacia atrás, hacia siglos y siglos de historia pasada e intentas imaginar a todos los demás, imaginarte, por ejemplo, soldado en las Termópilas, en Auschwitz, entre la enorme masa de obreros semidesnudos que arrastraban las piedras redondeadas de las pirámides y entonces la catapulta, la bala de cañón, la cuerda de arrastre que se desprende y tú allí, aplastado ahora, mancha roja ya ... (44)

He continues leaping through the centuries, identifying with *víctimas y verdugos* both anonymous and reknowned, contemplating the universality and banality of death, while at the same time admitting, "Todo esto es muy trillado" (44). As he relives the scene of the dog's death, he is in one moment the killer and in the next the dying "Bakunín": "y ves sus enormes ojos, sus ojos no quejosos, ni siquiera asustados, sino de sorpresa, los ojos de Bakunín, aplastado sobre las baldosas y se acercan hacia ti, que estás nadando en tu mancha de sangre, y sus cabezas son ahora enormes lámparas" (45).

In his next interior monologue, Enrique continues these transhistoric meditations, ever more overtly identifying with a plurality of deaths through the centuries. He begins with an affirmation of plural identity: "Yo soy éste, yo era aquél, soy éste que lee, era ese que lee, que desmenuza las palabras . . ." (55). The immediate pretext for this *desdoblamiento* is his memory of the Marxist-Leninist organization, in which he had assumed the alias "Enrique-Gonzalo-Julián." He then recalls his participation in the sectarian purges, how he expelled others and others expelled him. Amidst these memories, he introduces fragments of testimony from the Moscow show trials of 1938, when leading Bolsheviks were purged and executed by the Stalinist regime. From this point of departure, Enrique evokes the scene of a firing squad: "La muerte por fusilamiento: el hombre apoyado contra el muro, los ojos vendados" (65). Soon he is identifying himself with the victim, addressing himself as *tú*: "y ellos enfrente y tú con los ojos vendados jugando a adivinar sus rostros, a imaginar la cara satisfecha de esos hombres que hoy juegan a matarte" (65). Then, he switches roles, speaking as a soldier in the firing squad who attempts to absolve himself of responsibility: "yo sólo soy un número, un soldadito traído aquí por azar" (66). This same soldier appears next in a confessionary, speaking to a priest:

> Padre le aseguro que yo no he sido . . . sólo recibo órdenes, no soy más que un pequeño engranaje sin importancia mientras ellos deciden, aprietan el botón que nos hace levantarnos, ponernos la guerrera, cargar con el fusil, mi fusil vació, tranquilizador, apunten fuego y aquello que se despoma, que quizá sangra ahora, yo no he tenido la culpa, no soy culpable señor juez . . . (66)

Suddenly, through a metamorphosis, the soldier in the firing squad becomes Lieutenant Calley, in the act of testifying about the Me Lai massacre in Viet Nam: "[N]o soy culpable, señor juez, soy simplemente un teniente Calley más en esa inmensa serie nurembergiana de soldados . . ." (66). As this "shape-shifting" continues, Enrique again sees himself blindfolded, leaning against the *paredón*; then abruptly, he turns into the executioner, "yo Enrique-Calley"—shooting his victims in one moment, testifying in another (67). Through further metamorphoses, Enrique-Calley becomes Enrique-Mercader, and the dead dog becomes the murdered Leon Trotsky. As he evokes the murder scene, Enrique imagines himself as the assassin Ramón Mercader, wielding the icepick over Trotsky's head. He replaces the vision of "el perro despanzurrado sobre la baldosas" with the sight of "el viejo que se desploma sobre su escritorio" (69). All these death scenes fade in and fade out "con una rapidez de película lenta," leading once more to that recurring image of the neighbor woman who leapt to her death: "Allí estaba el cuerpo y allí estaba aquella mancha roja que se hacía más grande junto a la cabeza, aquella mancha color sangre de toro que brotaba y se extendía como un reguero de tinta vertida sobre el suelo gris de cemento" (69, 71). This of course is the model that Enrique will later choose for his own death, or rather, the model that Enrique, the writer, will choose for his character.

I have cited at length this pastiche of death-scenes to illustrate the striking dialogism of Enrique's interior "monologue." Here, death—that ultimate and universal sign for loss of self—serves as an opening to otherness, as a figurative "pretext" for an expression of plural identity. It affords Enrique the opportunity (still within the narrative logic) to wander, to become a textual nomad, to meld his voice into a "collective enunciation" (Chambers 129).[17] The overriding tone in this monologue is clearly melancholic, as Enrique admits his capacity to kill, as he ponders the universality and inevitability of death. But I dare say, we find in this wildly allusive pastiche an exuberant melancholy, as Enrique identifies transhistorically with one then another victim and victimizer. Both grammatically and literally, he is switching *persons*, constantly alternating his usage of *yo*, *tú*, and *él*, constantly making himself *other*. While not quite festive, his playful, melancholic writing betrays an emerging utopic desire for the solidarity denied him in the fictional society. As Ross Chambers has suggested, the literature of melancholy is "the site of the 'suicidal' gesture by which are enacted the implications of a certain 'truth': the truth that 'I am the other, since I am the other's other, the condition being only that I accept, 'suicidally,' the otherness of my own identity' " (105). Melancholic writing therefore "enacts itself as . . . the place of the disappearance of the autonomous self into a would-be harmonious enunciatory collectivity" (109).

I repeat once more the question: wherein would an alternative conception of desire be spawned by the text *Luz de la memoria*? And I suggest that it emerges precisely in Enrique's "death-writing," in this melancholic, discursive pastiche. Whereas the narrative program depends upon a failure of character, and whereas the metanarrative leads to a failure of reading, the social, dialogic character of Enrique's death-writing affirms a desire for plural, mobile subjectivity. This affirmation of collectivity resides in the multiple juxtapositions of Enrique's life and death with the lives and deaths of others—Trotsky, Louis XVI, Socrates, Lieutenant Calley, *et al*. It resides in the constant slippage among subject pronouns and aliases. It resides also in the metafictional game-playing that allows Enrique, as writer, to slip out of the narrative noose. In sum, an alternative mode of nomadic, liberatory desire is suggested by Enrique's very *discurrir*. His mad discourse and ultimate free fall into a void of incomprehensibility, exemplify Ross Chambers' notion of discourse as textual stream: "an art of 'running' that is not synonymous with flight," but rather "an art of *always* being running, as is the stream—an art of permanent elusiveness" (54).

NOTES

1. *Luz de la memoria* (1976) is Lourdes Ortiz's first of six novels: *Picadura mortal* (1979), *En días como estos* (1981), *Urraca* (1982), *Arcángeles* (1986), *Antes de la batalla* (1992), and *Fuente de la vida* (1995). In addition, she has published a monograph, *Comunicación crítica*, two collections of short stories and several works for theater. For a comprehensive, book-length study of her fiction, see the dissertation by Lynn A. McGovern-Waite, "Telling (Her Story: The Novels of Lourdes Ortiz." Also see Robert Spires' overview: "Lourdes Ortiz: Mapping the Course of Postfrancoist Fiction." Of all her works, *Urraca* has attracted the most critical attention; thus far, few studies of *Luz de la memoria* have been published. McGovern-Waite includes a useful chapter on this novel in her dissertation. And several studies of Spanish women writers include brief discussions of *Luz de la memoria*, among them, essays by Biruté Ciplijauskaité, Janet Pérez, and Ricardo Landeira. For interviews with Lourdes Ortiz, see: Lynn McGovern-Waite, Gregorio Morales Villena, and Phoebe Porter.
2. Refer to Phoebe Porter's interview with Lourdes Ortiz.
3. Lynn McGovern-Waite emphasizes this social and generational critique in her chapter on *Luz de la memoria*.
4. I am indebted here to Ross Chambers' distinction between the "narrative function" and "textual function," as elaborated in *Room for Maneuver*. The narrative function has "ideological affinity with autonomized subjects and centralized power" and "tends to position the reader so as to encourage maximum identification with the (textually produced) narratee. It is a limitation of 'readerly' freedom. . . . [T]his 'narrative function' is subject to erosion and subversion by a

less controlled and controlling 'textual' function" that subverts "notions such as those of the autonomous subject or the discursive 'transmission' of information that the 'narrative function' enacts" (13).

5. Conceivably, the dog's name, Bakunín—after the father of anarchism— could suggest a symbolic reading.

6. Throughout this section, I rely on Michel Foucault's concept of disciplinary power as outlined in *Discipline and Punish* and in *Power/Knowledge*. Leo Bersani's Foucauldian approach in "The Subject of Power" also informs my thinking. See the first chapter of this study for a discussion of discipline at work in realism.

7. In recent years a vast discourse on desire has emerged in literary criticism and theory. To discuss and evaluate all the various conceptions of desire goes well beyond the scope of this study. Such an endeavor would be worthwhile, but a labor of Hercules, given the proliferation of this discourse and the term's capacity to attract the most diverse definitions. The most useful attempt to examine the term's evolution within the philosophical tradition is provided by Judith Butler in *Subjects of Desire*. Eugene Goodheart, in *Desire and its Discontents*, offers a harshly critical survey of the recent discourse on desire. But Goodheart fails to adequately consider the most important theorists of desire to emerge, Gilles Deleuze and Félix Guattari, who develop their concept of productive, social, and expansive desire in *Anti-Oedipus* and in *A Thousand Plateaus*. For my discussion of how desire operates in narrative, I found the following studies quite useful: Peter Brooks, *Reading for the Plot*; Leo Bersani, *A Future for Astyanax*; Thomas Docherty, *Reading (Absent) Character*; and René Girard, *Deceit, Desire, and the Novel*.

8. Freud elaborates on Eros and Thanatos in *Beyond the Pleasure Principle* and in *Civilization and its Discontents*.

9. To associate the text-reader (or author-reader) relation with the sex act is not uncommon in literary tradition. G. Douglas Atkins cites Jonathan Swift's characterization of the author-reader relation in terms of sexual mastery in *A Tale of a Tub* (see Atkins, pp. 114-16). Darko Suvin recalls a passage in Brecht's *Life of Galileo* that equates sex with reading and the book with a prostitute: "Oh, irresistible sight of a book, that hallowed commodity. The mouth waters, the curses are drowned. The great Babylonian whore, the murderous beast, the scarlet woman opens her thighs and everything is different" (97). And in in *Rayuela* Cortazar calls the submissive reader a "lector-hembra."

10. The common denominator between erotic and thanatic desire is of course, the dissolution of self. As Georges Bataille points out, "In the process of dissolution, the male partner has generally an active role, while the female partner is passive. The passive, female side is essentially the one that is dissolved as a separate entity. But for the male partner the dissolution of the passive partner means one thing only: it is paving the way for a fusion where both are mingled, attaining at length the same degree of dissolution" (*Erotism* 17).

11. This distinction between *desire* and *need* is a means of conveniently disposing with the immense confusion that persists around definitions of desire. Other theorists and philosophers have sought to draw similar lines, albeit at different points, between desire and need. Such delimitations may have a "situational" validity that aids a given theorist in his particular project, but one must still grapple with the unmanageable semantic field of this messy term desire; one must still navigate its shifting definitional parameters within a vast discourse. Such messy and mobile terms may indeed serve some mysterious but vital function in discourse. Acting as "blotters" that cover huge gaps in conceptual understanding, they are capable of absorbing a multiplicity of meanings, inquiries, and speculations.

12. Docherty's notion of the appeal of Agapeic desire approximates Ross Chambers' concept of a "textual seduction." The textual function seduces readers "away from the subject position produced in the text as that of the narratee—the position of power—towards that of interpretive subject, a position that manifests the dependency of identity on otherness" (17). It thus points readers towards an *other* meaning, towards an "other self," whose identity is produced only as a function of its other, the text.

13. Once more, I am indebted to Ross Chambers' analysis of a similarly "involved" text by Hubert Aquin.

14. Here Chambers is drawing from Michel Serres' concept of noise, as that which "seems to disturb the system but without which it would not work" (Chambers 7). In information theory, noise "is parasitic—it is the element of disturbance that scrambles the messages and makes them 'other' " (222). See also William Paulson, *The Noise of Culture*.

15. Refer to René Girard's seminal study, *Deceit, Desire, and the Novel*, for a discussion of the triangular character of desire.

16. See Jacques Derrida's essay, "Plato's Pharmacy" in *Disseminations*.

17. Ross Chambers employs these terms in his discussion of suicidal writings by Gérard de Nerval and Hubert Aquin. See Chapter Three, "The Suicide Tactic: Writing in the Language of the Other" in *Room for Maneuver*.

CONCLUSION.
BEYOND CHARACTER: TOWARDS A UTOPIAN REFERENCE POINT

Through the centuries character has designated an imprinted, classifiable pattern of traits pertaining to a specific personality type. As such, character is one of our oldest "inherited ideas," and its operations depend upon a vast body of inherited cultural knowledge. In order for Torquemada to function as a coherent and "realistic" character, he must conform (more or less) to a set of cultural stereotypes about usurers. Even the irony permeating his character can only be an inherited idea, dependent upon a reader's ability to recognize a parodic exaggeration of norms and conventions. The vanguardist novella, "Andrómeda," provides a much more radical subversion of the paradigms of character; for by dramatizing how we read women (in literature and in life) by "clothing" them in layers of heterogeneous, inherited ideas, it demonstrates the impossibility of Woman as a cohesive cultural "character." In contrast, *Cinco horas con Mario*, despite its "new-narrative" veneer, depends absolutely upon the patrimonial notion of character. Carmen "works" as a character by virtue of authorial (and cultural) presumptions: that readers will interpret her in terms of prevalent social stereotypes about Spanish women, that they will join in the construction of an abject feminine other, and they will participate in an age-old social ritual of blame and expulsion. Perhaps *Luz de la memoria* goes farthest in challenging the cultural beliefs that support the inherited idea of character. Indeed, this text suggests the radical possibility of the death of character as we know it, for Enrique's demise provides the opening for an exuberant affirmation of plural identity.

Would it be possible to entirely "do away" with character, to erase those too-rigid models, paradigms, and structures engraved in our consciousness, and to replace character with a fluid, plural subjectivity?[1] It is difficult to imagine how we could read fictional and worldly beings without referring to an "ideology of the person" (Barthes, *S/Z* 191). We might, however, conceivably loosen the categorical strictures of that ideology, rendering character a more provisional and contingent phenomenon. And arguably, a more fluid conception of subjectivity is already operational. Our interpretations of ourselves and others (in literature and in life) have conventionally depended upon fixed notions of identity, based upon proper names, meaningful behavior, and definable traits. But alongside this *nominal* subjectivity, a quite subversive *pronominal* subjectivity has continued to operate, in a sense belying the notion of fixed identity: for regardless of their classification as particular types or as *others*, all beings are entitled to use the pronoun *I*.[2] This subject pronoun serves, then, as an already operational model for an "undifferentiated difference," for a mobile, interchangeable, and egalitarian subjectivity that implicitly admits, "I am the other." For this reason Barthes describes the shifter as a "utopia" (in his own shifting utopian text):

> [As] I speak . . . I insert into my discourse certain leaks of interlocution (is this not, in fact, what always happens when we utilize that shifter *par excellence*, the pronoun I?). Which leads him to imagine shifters (let us call shifters, by extension, all operators of uncertainty formed *at the level of language itself* . . .) as so many social subversions, conceded by language but opposed by society, which fears such leaks of subjectivity and always stops them by insisting on reducing the operator's duplicity. . . . Can we even imagine the freedom and, so to speak, the erotic fluidity of a collectivity which would speak only in pronouns and shifters, each person never saying anything but *I, tomorrow, over there,* without referring to anything legal whatsoever, and in which the *vagueness of difference* (the only fashion of respecting its subtlety, its infinite repercussion) would be language's most precious value? (*Roland Barthes* 165-66)[3]

No doubt, it would be impossible, at least in the proximate future, to banish character and to replace it with an "erotic fluidity of a collectivity" that speaks only in pronouns and shifters. As a governing concept, character operates all around us—in the social practices of everyday life and in the on-going manufacture of identity and otherness. Most of the texts we encounter, whether canonical or popular, depend for their legibility upon unitary models of character. But although utopias are by definition unattainable, there is no reason to discount their usefulness. Perhaps, by keeping in mind a utopian reference point, we might read and write more self-consciously, freely, and provisionally. When reading traditional texts that rely upon fixed models of identity, we might read contrapuntally and duplicitously: obeying the text's cultural logic to the minimum degree necessary for intelligibility, while at the same time reading expansively, affirming the multiplicity and dissonance of meaning, and becoming less "receptive" of received knowledge. And in reading those radical texts that enact a mobile and pronominal subjectivity, we might discover new possibilities for thought, invention, and being.

NOTES

1. Leo Bersani discusses the question of the future viability of character in the final chapter of *A Future for Astyanax*. Thomas Docherty provides a similar argument in *Reading (Absent) Character*. Both critics focus on modernist and postmodernist works that celebrate a disseminated self.
2. This holds true at least in all Indo-European languages. Refer to Emile Benveniste, *Problems in General Linguistics*, for a discussion of the uniquely mobile sign *I*, pp. 205-30.
3. Throughout the autobiographical text *Roland Barthes*, the author employs the first and third-person pronouns interchangeably to refer to himself.

WORKS CONSULTED

Agawu-Kakraba, Yaw. *Demythification in the Fiction of Miguel Delibes*. New York: Peter Lang, 1996.

——. "Miguel Delibes and the Politics of Two Women: *Cinco horas con Mario* and *Señora de rojo sobre Fondo gris*." *Hispanófila* 117 (1996): 63-77.

Alfieri, J.J. "The Double Image of Avarice in Galdós' Novels." *Hispania* 46 (1963): 722-29.

Alvar, Manuel. *El mundo novelesco de Miguel Delibes*. Madrid: Gredos, 1987.

Anderson, Warren. Introduction. Theophrastus xi-xx.

Apel, Karl-Otto. *Charles S. Peirce: From Pragmatism to Pragmaticism*. Trans. John Michael Drois. Amherst: U of Massachusetts P, 1981.

Ardener, Shirley, ed. *Perceiving Women*. New York: Wiley, 1975.

Aristotle. *Poetics*. Trans. Richard Janko. Indianapolis: Hackett, 1987.

Atkins, G. Douglas. *Reading Deconstruction. Deconstructive Reading*. Lexington: U of Kentucky P, 1983.

Auerbach, Erich. *Mimesis: The Representation of Reality in Western Literature*. Trans. Willard R. Trask. Princeton: Princeton UP, 1953.

Ayala, Francisco. "Pérez Galdós: Sobre el realismo en la literatura." *Los ensayos: Teoría y crítica literaria*. Madrid: Aguilar, 1971. 958-90.

Bakhtin, M.M. *The Dialogic Imagination: Four Essays*. Trans. Caryl Emerson and Michael Holquist. Ed. Michael Holquist. Austin: U of Texas P, 1981.

Bal, Mieke and Norman Bryson. "Semiotics and Art History." *The Art Bulletin* 73.2 (1991): 174-208.

Baldick, Chris. *The Concise Oxford Dictionary of Literary Terms*. Oxford: Oxford UP, 1990.

Balzac, Honoré de. Introduction. 1842. *The Works of Honoré de Balzac*. N. trans. 36 vols. New York: McKinlay, Stone and MacKenzie, 1915. I: 1-14.

Barthes, Roland. "From Work to Text." *The Rustle of Language*. Trans. Richard Howard. New York: Hill and Wang, 1986. 56-64.

——. *The Pleasure of the Text*. Trans. Richard Miller. New York: Hill and Wang. 1975.

——. "The Reality Effect." *French Literary Theory Today*. Ed. Tzvetan Todorov. Trans. R. Carter. Cambridge: Cambridge UP, 1982. 11-17.

——. *Roland Barthes*. Trans. Richard Howard. New York: Noonday, 1977.

——. *S/Z*. Trans. Richard Miller. New York: Noonday, 1974.

——. "Textual Analysis of a Tale of Poe." *On Signs*. Ed. Marshall Blonsky. Baltimore: Johns Hopkins UP, 1985. 84-97.

Bataille, Georges. *Erotism: Death and Sensuality*. San Francisco: City Lights, 1986.

——. *Visions of Excess: Selected Writings, 1927-1939*. Trans. Allan Stoekl. Theory and History of Literature 14. Minneapolis: U of Minnesota P, 1985.

Bäuml, B.J. Zeidner. "The Mundane Demon: The Bourgeois Grotesque in Galdós' *Torquemada en la hoguera*." *Symposium* 24.2 (1970): 158-65.
Becker, George J. *Realism in Modern Literature*. New York: Frederick Ungar, 1980.
Bell, Linda A., Ed. *Visions of Women (Being a Fascinating Anthology with Analysis of Philosophers' Views of Women from Ancient to Modern Times)*. Clifton, New Jersey: Humana, 1983.
Bem, Sandra Lipsitz. "Gender Schema Theory: A Cognitive Account of Sex Typing." *Psychological Review* 88.4 (1981): 354-64.
Benjamin, Walter. "The Story Teller." *Illuminations*. Ed. Hannah Arendt. New York: Schocken, 1969. 83-109.
_____. *The Origin of German Tragic Drama*. Trans. John Osborne. London: Verso, 1977.
Benstock, Shari, Ed. *Feminist Issues in Literary Scholarship*. Bloomington: Indiana UP, 1987.
_____. *Textualizing the Feminine*. Norman: U of Oklahoma P, 1991.
Benveniste, Emile. *Problems in General Linguistics*. Trans. Mary Elizabeth Meek. Coral Gables, Florida: U of Miami P, 1971.
Berger, John. *Ways of Seeing*. London: BBC and Penguin, 1972.
Bernstein, J.S. *Benjamín Jarnés*. New York: Twayne, 1972.
Bersani, Leo. *A Future for Astyanax: Character and Desire in Literature*. Boston: Little, Brown, 1976.
_____. "The Subject of Power." *Diacritics* 7 (1977): 2-21.
Bieder, Maryellen. "Woman and the Twentieth-Century Spanish Literary Canon: The Lady Vanishes." *Anales de la literatura española contemporánea* 17.3 (1992): 301-24.
Blanco Villalba, Carmen. "El narrador de *Torquemada en la hoguera* de Benito Pérez Galdós." *Revista canadiense de estudios hispánicos*. 18.2 (1994): 151-70.
Bly, Peter A. *Vision and the Visual Arts in Galdós: A Study of the Novels and Newspaper Articles*. Liverpool: Francis Cairns, 1986.
Bordons, Teresa and Susan Kirkpatrick. "Chacel's Teresa and Ortega's Canon." *Anales de la literatura española contemporánea* 17.3 (1992): 283-99.
Boring, Phyllis Zatlin. "Delibes' Two Views of the Spanish Mother." *Hispanófila* 63 (1978): 79-87.
Botrel, Jean-François. "La novela por entregas; unidad de creación y de consumo." *Creación y público en la literatura española*. Eds. J.F. Botrel and S. Salaün. Madrid: Castalia, 1974. 111-55.
Boucher, Teresa. "The Widow's Peak / The Widow Speaks: Carmen's Idle Talk in Miguel Delibes's *Cinco horas con Mario*." *Cincinnati Romance Review* 15 (1996): 50-56.
Boudreau, H.L. "*Cinco horas con Mario* and the Dynamics of Irony." *Anales de la novela de posguerra* 2 (1977): 7-17.
Boyle, Nicholas and Martin Swales, eds. *Realism in European Literature*. Cambridge: Cambridge UP, 1986.

Bradley, A.C. *Shakespearean Tragedy*. 1904. Greenwich, Conn: Fawcett, n.d.

Brooks, Peter. *Reading for the Plot: Design and Intention in Narrative*. New York: Alfred A. Knopf, 1984.

Brownlow, Jeanne P. "Epochal Allegory in Galdós's *Torquemada*: The Ur-text and the Episteme." *PMLA* 108.2 (1993): 294-307.

La Bruyère, Jean de. *Characters*. Trans. Jean Stewart. Harmondsworth, Eng.: Penguin, 1970.

Bryson, Norman, Michael Ann Holly, and Keith Moxey, eds. *Visual Theory: Painting and Interpretation*. London: Harper-Collins, 1991.

Burunat, Silvia. "Miguel Delibes y el feminismo." *Letras de Deusto* 14.30 (1984): 67-83.

──────. *El monólogo interior como forma narrativa en la novela española (1940-1975)*. Madrid: Porrúa Turanzas, 1980.

Bustos-Deuso, María Luisa. *La mujer en la narrativa de Delibes*. Valladolid: Universidad de Valladolid, 1990.

Butler, Judith P. *Subjects of Desire: Hegelian Reflections in Twentieth-Century France*. New York: Columbia UP, 1987.

Cabrera, Vicente and Luis González del Valle. *Novela española contemporánea: Cela, Delibes, Romero, y Hernandez*. Madrid: Sociedad General Española de Librería, 1978.

Camayd Freixas, Erik. "El monólogo literario y 'la novela de la posguerra': Miguel Delibes y Camilo José Cela." *Plaza: Revista de literatura* 11 (1986): 34-42.

Cameron, Deborah. *Feminism and Linguistic Theory*. 2nd ed. New York: St. Martins, 1992.

Capmany, María Aurèlia y Carmen Alcalde. *El feminismo ibérico*. Barcelona: Oikos-tau, 1970.

Caws, Mary Ann. "Ladies Shot and Painted: Female Embodiment in Surrealist Art." Suleiman 262-87.

──────, Rodolf Kuenzli, and Gwen Raaberg, eds. *Surrealism and Women*. Cambridge, Mass.: MIT, 1991.

Chacel, Rosa. "Esquemas de los problemas prácticos y actuales del amor." *Revista de Occidente* 31 (1931): 129-80.

Chambers, Ross. *Room for Maneuver: Reading the Oppositional in Narrative*. Chicago: U of Chicago P, 1991.

Charnon-Deutsch, Lou. *Gender and Representation: Women in Spanish Realist Fiction*. Philadelphia: John Benjamins, 1990.

Chatman, Seymour. *Story and Discourse: Narrative Structure in Fiction and Film*. Ithaca: Cornell UP, 1978.

Ciplijauskaité, Biruté. *La novela femenina contemporánea (1970-1985): Hacia una tipología de la primera persona*. Barcelona: Anthropos, 1988.

Cixous, Hélène. "The Character of Character." *New Literary History* 5 (1974): 383-402.

Clark, Kenneth. *The Nude: A Study in Ideal Form*. Pantheon, 1956.

Cohan, Steven. "Figures Behond the Text: A Theory of Readable Character in the Novel." *Why the Novel Matters: A Postmodern Perplex*. Eds. Mark Spilka and Caroline McCracken Flesher. Bloomington: Indiana UP, 1990. 113-36.

_____ and Linda M. Shires. *Telling Stories: A Theoretical Analysis of Narrative Fiction*. London: Routledge, 1988.

Correa, Gustavo. *Realidad, ficción y símbolo en las novelas de Pérez Galdós: Ensayo de estética realista*. Madrid: Gredos, 1977.

Cowan, Bainard. "Walter Benjamin's Theory of Allegory." *New German Critique* 22 (1981): 109-22.

Coward, Rosalind and John Ellis. *Language and Materialism: Developments in Semiology and Theory of the Subject*. London: Routledge and Kegan Paul, 1977.

Crawford, Mary and Roger Chaffin. "The Reader's Construction of Meaning: Cognitive Research on Gender and Comprehension." Flynn 3-30.

Cuevas García, Cristobal, and Enrique Baena. *Miguel Delibes. El escritor, la obra, y el lector*. Actas del V Congreso de Literatura Española Contemporánea, Universidad de Málaga, 12-15 de noviembre de 1991. Barcelona: Anthropos, 1992.

Culler, Jonathan. *On Deconstruction: Theory and Criticism after Structuralism*. Ithaca: Cornell UP, 1982.

Davis, Lennard. *Resisting Novels: Ideology and Fiction*. London: Methuen, 1987.

de Certeau, Michel. *Heterologies: Discourse on the Other*. Trans. Brian Massumi. Theory and History of Literature 17. Minneapolis: U of Minnesota P, 1986.

de Lauretis, Teresa. *Alice Doesn't: Feminism, Semiotics, Cinema*. Bloomington: Indiana UP, 1984.

_____. *Technologies of Gender*. Bloomington: Indiana UP, 1987.

Deleuze, Gilles, and Félix Guattari. *Anti-Oedipus: Capitalism and Schizophrenia*. Trans. Robert Hurley, Mark Seem, and Helen R. Lane. Minneapolis: U of Minnesota P, 1983.

_____. *A Thousand Plateaus: Capitalism and Schizophrenia*. Trans. Brian Massumi. Minneapolis: U of Minnesota P, 1983.

Delgado, Luisa Elena. " 'El interés del relato': Estrategias narrativas en la serie de *Torquemada*." *Anales galdosianos* 25 (1990): 58-67.

Delibes, Miguel. *Cinco horas con Mario*. Barcelona: Destino, 1966.

_____. Entrevista. *Conversaciones con Miguel Delibes*. By César Alonso de los Ríos. Madrid: Magisterio Español, 1993.

_____. Entrevista. "Dialogando con Miguel Delibes." By Paco Piedra. *Ventanal* 8 (1984): 13-51.

_____. Entrevista. "Miguel Delibes: Realismo y Utopia." By Pilar Concejo. *Hispanic Journal* 2.1 (1980): 101-07.

de Man, Paul. *Allegories of Reading*. New Haven: Yale UP, 1979.

_____. "The Rhetoric of Temporality." *Interpretation: Theory and Practice*. Ed. Charles S. Singleton. Baltimore: Johns Hopkins UP, 1969. 173-209.

Demetz, Peter. "Balzac and the Zoologists: A Concept of Type." *The Disciplines of Criticism: Essays in Literary Theory, Interpretation, and History*. Eds. Peter Demetz, Thomas Greene, and Lowry Nelson, Jr. New Haven: Yale Up, 1968. 397-418.

Derrida, Jacques. "Plato's Pharmacy." *Dissemination*. Trans. Barbara Johnson. Chicago: U of Chicago P, 1981. 61-171.

_____. *Spurs: Nietzche's Styles*. Trans. Barbara Harlow. Chicago: U of Chicago P, 1979.

Díaz-Plaja, Fernando. *El español y los siete pecados capitales*. Madrid: Alianza, 1966.

Docherty, Thomas. *Reading (Absent) Character: Towards a Theory of Characterization in Fiction*. Oxford: Clarendon, 1983.

Donahue, Darcy. "Mujer y hombre en Ortega." *Ortega y Gasset Centennial*. Proc. of an International Symposium at the University of New Mexico. 1-5 nov. 1983. Madrid: José Porrúa-Turanzas, 1985: 133-38.

Donoso, Anton and Harold C. Raley. *José Ortega y Gasset: A Bibliography of Secondary Sources*. Bowling Green, Ohio: Bowling Green State U, 1986.

Eco, Umberto. *A Theory of Semiotics*. Bloomington: Indiana UP, 1979.

Engler, Kay. *The Structure of Realism: The Novelas Contemporáneas of Benito Perez Galdós*. North Carolina Studies in the Romance Languages and Literatures 184. Chapel Hill: U of North Carolina P, 1977.

Eoff, Sherman. *The Novels of Pérez Galdós: The Concept of Life as Dynamic Process*. Washington University Studies 1. Saint Louis: Washington U, 1954.

Epps, Brad. "The Politics of Ventriloquism: Cava, Revolution and Sexual Discourse in *Conde Julian*." *MLN* 107 (1992): 274-97.

Fagoada, Concha. *La voz y el voto de las mujeres: El sufragismo en España, 1877-1931*. Barcelona: Icaria, 1985.

Felman, Shoshana. "Rereading Femininity." *Yale French Studies. Feminist Readings: French Texts / American Contexts* 62 (1981): 19-44.

Fernández-Cifuentes, Luis. "Entre Gobseck y Torquemada." *Anales galdosianos* 17 (1982): 71-84.

_____. "Fenomenología de la vanguardia: El caso de la novela." *Anales de literatura española* 9 (1993): 45-59.

Ferrara, Fernando. "Theory and Model for the Structural Analysis of Fiction." *New Literary History*. 5.2 (1974): 245-68.

Ferreras, Juan Ignacio. *La novela española en el siglo XIX (hasta 1868)*. Madrid: Taurus, 1987.

_____. *La novela por entregas, 1840-1900*. Madrid: Taurus, 1972.

_____. *Los orígenes de la novela decimónica (1800-1830)*. Madrid: Taurus, 1973.

Fetterley, Judith. *The Resisting Reader: A Feminist Approach to American Fiction*. Bloomington: Indiana UP, 1978.

Fineman, Joel. "The Structure of Allegorical Desire." Greenblatt 26-60.

Fletcher, Angus. *Allegory: The Theory of a Symbolic Mode.* Ithaca: Cornell UP, 1964.

Flynn, Elizabeth, and Patrocinio P. Schweickart, eds. *Gender and Reading: Essays on Readers, Texts, and Contexts.* Baltimore: Johns Hopkins UP, 1986.

Forster, E.M. *Aspects of the Novel.* 1927. New York: Harcourt, Brace, Jovanovich, 1955.

Foucault, Michel. *Discipline and Punish: The Birth of the Prison.* Trans. Alan Sheridan. New York: Random House, 1979.

──────. "The Order of Discourse." Trans. Ian McLeod. *Untying the Text: A Post-Structuralist Reader.* Ed. Robert Young. Boston: Routledge, 1981. 48-78.

──────. *Power / Knowledge: Selected Interviews and Other Writings, 1972-1977.* Trans. Colin Gordon, Leo Marshall, John Mepham, Kate Soper. Ed. Colin Gordon. New York: Pantheon, 1972.

Frank, Waldo. "La mujer norteamericana." *Revista de Occidente* 67 (1929): 70-82.

Franco, Francisco. *Discursos y mensajes del Jefe de Estado, 1968-1970.* Madrid: Dirección General de Información, Publicaciones Españolas, 1971.

Freadman, Richard. *Eliot, James, and the Fictional Self.* Houndsmills, Eng.: 1986.

Freud, Sigmund. *Beyond the Pleasure Principle.* Trans., Ed. James Strachey. New York, Norton, 1961.

──────. *Civilization and Its Discontents.* Trans., Ed. James Strachey. New York: Norton, 1961.

Frye, Northrup. *Anatomy of Criticism.* Princeton: Princeton UP, 1957.

Fuentes, Victor. *Benjamín Jarnés: Bio-grafía y metaficción.* Zaragoza: Institución Fernando el Católico, 1989.

──────. "Jarnés: Metaficción y discurso estético-erótico." *Jornadas jarnesianas: Ponencias y comunicaciones.* Zaragoza: Insitutución Fernando el Católico, 1989. 65-76.

──────. "La dimensión estético-erótico y la novelística de Jarnés." *La novela lírica.* Ed. Darío Villanueva. Tomo 2. Madrid: Taurus, 1983: 240-52. 2 tomos.

Furst, Lilian R. *All is True: The Claims and Strategies of Realist Fiction.* Durham: Duke UP, 1995.

Fuss, Diana. "Fashion and the Homospectatorial Look." *Critical Inquiry* 18 (1992): 713-35.

García Morente, Manuel. "El espíritu filosófico y la feminidad." *Revista de Occidente* 69 (1929): 289-306.

García Sarriá, F. "El plano alegórico de *Torquemada en la hoguera*." *Anales galdosianos* 15 (1980): 103-111.

Gauthier, Xavier. *Surréalisme et sexualité.* Paris: Gallimard, 1971.

Gil, Alberto. "Experimentos lingüísticos de Miguel Delibes." *Crítica semiológica de textos literarios hispánicos. Las Actas del Congreso Internacional sobre semiótica e hispanismo celebrado en Madrid en los días del 20 al 25 de junio de 1983.* 2 tomos. Ed. Miguel Angel Garrido Gallardo. Madrid: Consejo Superior de Investigaciones Científicas, 1986. 2: 631-41.

Gilman, Stephen. "Cuando Galdós habla con sus personajes." *Actas del Segundo Congreso Internacional de Estudios Galdosianos*. Las Palmas de Gran Canaria. 1978. 2 vols. Madrid: Editora Nacional, 1979. I: 128-34.

———. *Galdós and the Art of the European Novel, 1867-1887*. Princeton: Princeton UP, 1981.

Girard, René. *Deceit, Desire, and the Novel: Self and Other in Literary Structure*. Trans. Yvonne Freccero. Baltimore: Johns Hopkins UP, 1965.

Gold, Hazel. "Galdós and Lamennais: *Torquemada en la hoguera* or the Prophet Deposed." *Revistas canadiense de estudios hispánicos* 13.1 (1988): 29-48.

———. *The Reframing of Realism: Galdós and the Discourses of the Nineteenth-Century Spanish Novel*. Durham: Duke UP, 1993

Gómez de la Serna, Ramón. *Automoribundia (1888-1948)*. Buenos Aires: Editorial Sudamericana, 1948.

González, Anabel, Amalia López, Ana Mendoza and Isabel Urueña. *Los orígenes del feminismo en España*. Madrid: Zero, 1980.

González, Bernardo Antonio. *Parábolas de identidad: Realidad interior y estrategia narrativa en tres novelistas de posguerra*. Potomac, Md.: Scripta Humanista, 1985.

Goodheart, Eugene. *Desire and Its Discontents*. New York: Columbia UP, 1991.

Gracia García, Jordi. *La pasión fría: Lirismo e ironía en la novela de Benjamín Jarnés*. Zaragoza: Institución Fernando el Católico, 1988.

Gray, Rockwell. *The Imperative of Modernity: An Intellectual Biography of José Ortega y Gassett*. Berkeley: U of California P, 1989.

Greenblatt, Stephen, ed. *Allegory and Representation*. Selected Papers from the English Institute, 1979-80. New Series 5. Baltimore: Johns Hopkins UP, 1981.

Greimas, A.J. *On Meaning: Selected Writings in Semiotic Theory*. Trans. Paul J. Perron and Frank H. Collins. Minneapolis: U of Minnesota P, 1987.

Grosz, Elizabeth. *Sexual Subversions: Three French Feminists (Julia Kristeva, Luce Irigaray, Michèle le Doeuff)*. Sydney: Allen and Unwer, 1989.

Gullón, Agnes. *La novela experimental de Miguel Delibes*. Madrid: Taurus, 1980.

Gullón, Germán. *La novela como acto imaginativo*. Madrid: Taurus, 1983.

———. *La novela del XIX: Estudio sobre su evolución formal*. Amsterdam: Rodopi, 1990.

Gullón, Ricardo. *Galdós: Novelista moderno*. Madrid: Taurus, 1960.

———. *La novela lírica*. Madrid: Cátedra, 1984.

———. *Psicologías del autor y lógicas del personaje*. Madrid: Taurus, 1979.

Guzmán, Flora. "La mujer en la mirada de Ortega y Gasset." *Cuadernos hispanomericanos* 403-05 (1984): 179-89.

Hartman, Geoffrey. *The Fate of Reading and Other Essays*. Chicago: U of Chicago P, 1975.

Harvey, Elizabeth D. *Ventriloquized Voices: Feminist Theory and English Renaissance Texts*. London: Routledge, 1992.

Harvey, W.J. *Character and the Novel*. Ithaca: Cornell UP, 1965.

Hayles, N. Katherine. *The Cosmic Web: Scientific Field Models and Literary Strategies in the Twentieth Century*. Ithaca: Cornell UP, 1984.

Heath, Steven. "Realism, Modernism, and 'Language-consciousness.'" Boyle and Swales 103-22.

Heilbrun, Carolyn. *Toward a Recognition of Androgyny*. 1964. New York: Alfred A. Knopf, 1973.

Hershberger, Robert P. "Filming the Woman in Benjamin Jarnés's *El convidado de papel*." *Letras peninsulares* 7.1 (1994): 193-208.

Herzberger, David K. "Split Referentiality and the Making of Character in Recent Spanish Metafiction." *MLN* (1988): 419-35.

Hochman, Baruch. *Characters in Literature*. Ithaca: Cornell UP, 1985.

Honig, Edwin. *Dark Conceit: The Making of Allegory*. New York: Oxford UP, 1966.

Horace (Quintus Horatius Glaccus). *The Complete Works of Horace*. Trans. Charles E. Passage. New York: Frederick Ungar, 1983.

Ilie, Paul. "Benjamín Jarnés : Aspects of the Dehumanized Novel." *PMLA* 76.3 (1961): 247-53.

Irigaray, Luce. *Speculum of the Other Woman*. Trans. Gillian C. Gill. Ithaca: Cornell UP, 1985.

―――. *This Sex Which Is Not One*. Trans. Catherine Porter. Ithaca: Cornell UP, 1985.

Iser, Wolfgang. *The Act of Reading*. N. trans. Baltimore: John Hopkins UP, 1978.

―――. "Interaction between Text and Reader." *The Reader in the Text: Essays on Audience and Interpretation*. Eds. Susan R. Suleiman and Inge Crosman. Princeton: Princeton UP, 1980. 106-19.

Jarnés, Benjamín. "Andrómeda." *Revista de Occidente* 38 (1926): 137-67.

―――. *El convidado de papel*. Zaragoza: Nueva Biblioteca de Autores Aragoneses, 1979.

―――. "Musas de Francia." *Revista de Occidente* 76 (1929): 139-42).

―――. *La novia del viento*. Mexico City: Nueva Cultura, 1940.

―――. *El profesor inútil*. Madrid: Revista de Occidente, 1926.

Jelinski, Jack B. "Mario as Biblical Analogue in Miguel Delibes' *Cinco horas con Mario*." *College Language Association Journal* 38.4 (1995): 480-89.

Jerez Farrán, Carlos. "Las bodas de doña Carnal y don Cuaresma en *Cinco horas con Mario*." *Neophilologus* 74 (1990): 225-39.

Johnson, Roberta. *Crossfire: Philosophy and the Novel in Spain, 1900-1934*. Lexington: U of Kentucky P, 1993.

Joplin, Patricia Klindienst. "The Voice of the Shuttle is Ours." *Stanford Literature Review* 1-2 (1984): 25-53.

Jordanova, Ludmilla. *Sexual Visions: Images of Gender in Science and Medicine between the Eighteenth and Twentieth Centuries*. Madison: U of Wisconsin P, 1989.

Jornadas Jarnesianas: Ponencias y comunicaciones. Zaragoza: Institución Fernando el Católico, 1989.

Jung, Carl. "La mujer en Europa." *Revista de Occidente* 76 (1929): 1-32.

Juvenalis, Decimus Junius. *The Satires of Juvenal*. Trans. Rolfe Humphries. Bloomington: Indiana UP, 1958.
Kelch, Jan. *Peter Paul Rubens: Kritischer Katalog der Gemälde im Besitz der Gemäldegalerie Berlin*. Berlin: Dahlem, 1978.
Knight, G. Wilson. *The Wheel of Fire*. London: Methuen, 1965.
Knights, L.C. "How Many Children had Lady Macbeth?" *Explorations*. London: Chatto and Windus, 1951. 1-40.
Kramarae, Cheris. *Women and Men Speaking: Frameworks for Analysis*. Rowley, Mass.: Newbury, 1981.
Krauss, Rosaline and Jane Livingston. *L'Amor Fou: Photography and Surrealism*. New York: Corcoran Gallery of Art, Abbeville Press, 1985.
Kristeva, Julia. "Julia Kristeva." Trans. Marilyn A. August. *New French Feminisms: An Anthology*. Eds. Elaine Marks and Isabelle de Courtivron. Amherst: U of Massachusetts P, 1980. 137-41.
_____. *Powers of Horror: An Essay on Abjection*. Trans. Leon S. Roudiez. New York: Columbia UP, 1982.
Kronik, John W. "Galdós and the Grotesque." *Anales galdosianos, anejo*. Symposium, Department of Spanish and Portuguese, University of Southern California. 1-3 abril, 1976. Madrid: Catedra: 1978. 39-54.
_____. "La retórica del realismo: Galdós y Clarín." Lisourgues 47-57.
Lacan, Jacques. *Feminine Sexuality: Jacques Lacan and the école freudienne*. Eds. Mitchell, Juliet and Jacqueline Rose. London: Macmillan, 1982.
Landeira, Ricardo, and Luis T. González-del-Valle. Eds. *Nuevos y novísimos: Algunas perspectivas críticas sobre la narrativa española desde la década de los 60*. Boulder, Colorado: Society of Spanish and Spanish-American Studies, 1987.
Ley, Charles David. "Galdós comparado con Balzac y Dickens, como novelista nacional." *Actas del Primer Congreso Internacional de Estudios Galdosianos*. Las Palmas de Gran Canaria. 1973. Madrid: Editora Nacional, 1977. 291-95.
Lisorgues, Ivan, ed. *Realismo y naturalismo en España en la segunda mitad del siglo XIX*. Barcelona: Anthropos, 1988.
Lodge, David. *The Modes of Modern Writing: Metaphor, Metonymy, and the Typology of Modern Literature*. Ithaca: Cornell UP, 1977.
_____. *Small World*. London: Secker and Warburg, 1984.
López, Ignacio Javier. *Realismo y ficción: La desheredada de Galdós y La novela de su tiempo*. Barcelona: Promociones y Publicaciones Universitarias, 1989.
López-Campillo, Evelyne. *La Revista de Occidente y la Formación de minorías (1923-1936)*. Madrid: Taurus, 1972.
López Martinez, Luis. *La novelística de Miguel Delibes*. Murcia: U de Murcia, 1973.
Lowe, Jennifer. "Narrator and Reader in *Torquemada en la hoguera*: Some Further Considerations." *Anales galdosianos* 18 (1983): 89-95.

Lukács, Georg. *Studies in European Realism: A Sociological Survey of the Writings of Balzac, Stendhal, Zola, Tolstoy, Gorki and Others.* London: Merlin Press, 1972.
MacGuigan, Maryellen. "Is Woman a Question?" *International Philosophical Quarterly* 13.4 (1973): 485-505.
McGovern, Lynn A. Interview. "Lourdes Ortiz: Novela, prensa, política, etcétera." *Ojacano* 9 (1994): 46-57.
_____. "Telling (Her) Story: The Novels of Lourdes Ortiz." Dissertation. University of Virginia, 1992.
Machado, Antonio. *Campos de Castilla.* Madrid: Cátedra, 1984.
Macklin, J.J. "B. Pérez Galdós: *Fortunata y Jacinta* (1886-87)." Williams 179-203.
Mailloux, Steven. *Rhetorical Power.* Ithaca: Cornell UP, 1989.
Marañon, Gregorio. "Notas para la biología de Don Juan." *Revista de Occidente* 7 (1924): 15-53.
_____. "Nuevas ideas sobre el problema de la intersexualidad y sobre la cronología de los sexos." *Revista de Occidente* 66 (1928): 258-93.
Martin, Wallace. *Recent Theories of Narrative.* Ithaca: Cornell UP, 1986.
Martín Gaite, Carmen. *Usos amorosos de la postguerra española.* Barcelona: Anagrama, 1987.
Martínez, Antonio H. "Los códigos de la ironía en *Cinco horas con Mario* de Miguel Delibes." *Confluencia* 7.2 (1992): 29-35.
Martínez Latre, María Pilar. *La novela intelectual de Benjamín Jarnés.* Zaragoza: Institución Fernando El Católico, 1979.
Medina, Jeremy T. *Spanish Realism: The Theory and Practice of a Concept.* Potomac, Md.: José Porrúa Turanzas, 1979.
Miguel, Amando de. *Desde la España predemocrática.* Madrid: Paulinas, 1976.
Miller, D.A. *The Novel and the Police.* Berkeley: U of California P, 1988.
Miller, J. Hillis. *Ariadne's Thread: Story Lines.* New Haven: Yale UP, 1992.
Mitchell, W.J.T. *Iconology: Image, Text, Ideology.* Chicago: U of Chicago P, 1986.
_____, ed. *The Language of Images.* 1974. Chicago: U of Chicago P, 1980.
Molinaro, Nina L. "Confessions of Guilt and Power in *Cinco horas con Mario.*" *Letras peninsulares* 7.3 (1995): 599-612.
Montero, Isaac. "El lenguaje del Limbo." *Revista de Occidente.* 2a época. 21.61 (1968): 101-17.
Montes Huidoro, Matías. "Cinco horas con Carmen." *Kaninas* 4.2 (1986): 67-80.
Morales, Gregorio Villena. "Entrevista con Lourdes Ortiz." *Insula* 479 (1986): 1, 10.
Morán, Fernando. *Novela y semidesarrollo (Una interpretación de la novela hispanoamericano y española).* Madrid: Taurus, 1971.
Mount, A.J. "H. de Balzac: *Lost Illusions* (1837-43)." Williams 17-39.
Mulvey, Laura. *Visual and Other Pleasures.* Bloomington: Indiana UP, 1989.
Munich, Adrienne Auslander. *Andromeda's Chains: Gender and Interpretation in Victorian Literature and Art.* New York: Columbia UP, 1989.
Neruda, Pablo. *Obras completas.* 3a ed. Buenos Aires: Losada, 1967.

Nora, Eugenio G. de. *La novela española contemporánea* II.1 2 vols. Madrid: Gredos, 1962.

O'Donnell, Patrick. *Figuring Voice in Narrative*. Iowa City: U of Iowa P, 1992.

Ortega y Gasset, José. *La dehumanización del arte e otros ensayos de estética*. 2nd ed. Madrid: Revista de Occidente, 1976.

―――――. "Para una caracterología." *Revista de Occidente* 41 (1926): 241-53.

―――――. "La poesía de Ana de Noailles." *Revista de Occidente* 1 (1923): 29-41.

―――――. "Propósitos." *Revista de Occidente* 1 (1923): 1-3.

Ortiz, Lourdes. *Luz de la memoria*. Madrid: Akal, 1976.

Ortner, Sherry B. "Is Female to Male as Nature Is to Culture?" *Woman, Culture, and Society*. Eds. Michelle Zimbalist Rosaldo and Louise Lamphere. Stanford: Stanford UP, 1974. 67-87.

Owens, Craig. "The Allegorical Impulse: Toward a Theory of Postmodernism." Wallis 203-35.

Pasto-Crosby, Lisa. "Unconventional Character Introduction in the Torquemada Series." *Romance Languages Annual* 1 (1989): 577-82.

Pauk, Edgar. *Miguel Delibes: Desarrollo de un escritor (1947-1974)*. Madrid: Gredos, 1975.

Paulson, William R. *The Noise of Culture: Literary Texts in a World of Information*. Ithaca: Cornell UP, 1988.

Pedraza, Pilar. *La bella, enigma y pesadilla (Esfinge, Medusa, Pantera . . .)*. Barcelona: Tusquets, 1991.

Peirce, Charles Sanders. *Collected Papers of Charles Sanders Peirce*. Eds. Charles Hartshorne and Paul Weiss. Vol. 2. Cambridge, Mass.: Harvard UP, 1960. 8 vols.

Pérez, Janet. *Contemporary Women Writers of Spain*. Boston: Twayne, 1988.

Pérez Firmat, Gustavo. *Idle Fictions: The Hispanic Vanguard Novel, 1926-1934*. Durham, N.C.: Duke UP, 1982.

Pérez Galdós, Benito. *Ensayos de crítica literaria*. Ed. Laureano Bonet. Barcelona: Península, 1990.

―――――. *Fortunata y Jacinta (Dos historias de casadas)*. 1886-87. México, D.F.: 1983.

―――――. *Torquemada en la hoguera, Torquemada en la cruz, Torquemada en el purgatorio, Torquemada y San Pedro*. 1889-95. Madrid: Alianza, 1967.

Petruso, Thomas F. *Life Made Real: Characterization in the Novel Since Proust and Joyce*. Ann Arbor: U of Michigan P, 1991.

Phelan, James. *Reading People, Reading Plots: Character, Progression, and the Interpretation of Narrative*. Chicago: U of Chicago P, 1989.

Pino, José Manuel. del Pino. *Montajes y fragmentos: una aproximación a la narrativa española de vanguardia*. Amsterdam: Rodopi, 1995.

Pointon, Marcia. *Naked Authority: The Body in Western Painting, 1830-1908*. Cambridge: Cambridge UP, 1990.

Porter, Phoebe. Entrevista. "Conversación con Lourdes Ortiz." *Letras femeninas* 16. 1-2 (1990): 139-44.

Price, Martin. *Forms of Life: Character and the Moral Imagination in the Novel.* New Haven: Yale UP, 1983.

Quilligan, Maureen. *The Language of Allegory: Defining the Genre.* Ithaca: Cornell UP, 1979.

Radulian, Dimitri. "Torquemada, un usurero atípico." *Actas del Cuarto Congreso Internacional de Estudios Galdosianos, 1990.* Las Palmas de Gran Canaria: Cabildo Insular, 1993. 497-501.

Ragland-Sullivan, Ellie. "The Sexual Masquerade: A Lacanian Theory of Sexual Difference." *Lacan and the Subject of Language.* Eds. Ellie Ragland-Sullivan and Mark Bracher. New York: Routledge, 1991: 49-79.

Rey, Alfonso. *La originalidad novelística de Delibes.* Santiago de Compostela: U de Santiago de Compostela, 1975.

Rimmon-Kenan, Shlomith. *Narrative Fiction: Contemporary Poetics.* London: Methuen, 1983.

Rodríguez, Jesús. *El sentimiento del miedo en la obra de Miguel Delibes.* Madrid: Pliegos, 1979.

Roh, Franz, "Realismo mágico." *Revista de Occidente* 48 (1927): 274-301.

Romero Tobar, Leonardo. *La novela popular española del siglo XIX.* Barcelona: Ariel, 1976.

Rorty, Richard. *Philosophy and the Mirror of Nature.* Princeton: Princeton UP, 1979.

Rose, Jacqueline. Introduction. Lacan 17-57.

Rosner, Elizabeth. "Silencing the Ventriloquist: The Book of Secrets." *World Literature Written in English* 31.1 (1991): 80-86.

Scanlon, Geraldine M. *La polémica feminista en la España contemporánea (1868-74).* Madrid: Siglo Veintinuno, 1976.

Schiebinger, Londa. "Feminine Icons: The Face of Early Modern Science." *Critical Inquiry* 14 (1988): 661-91.

Schraibman, José. "Torquemada y la Inquisición." *Actas del Cuarto Congreso Internacional de Estudios Galdosianos, 1990.* Las Palmas de Gran Canaria: Cabildo Insular, 1993. 531-540.

Schyfter, Sara E. *The Jew in the Novels of Benito Pérez Galdós.* London: Tamesis, 1978.

Seltzer, Mark. *Henry James and the Art of Power.* Ithaca: Cornell UP, 1984.

Sherzer, William M. "Narrative Play and Social Context in *Torquemada en la hoguera*." *Anales galdosianos* 23 (1988): 67-72.

Shiff, Richard. "On Criticism Handling History." *History of the Human Sciences* 2.1 (1989): 63-87.

Shirley, Paula W. "The Narrator/Reader Relationship in *Torquemada*, or How to Read a Galdosian Novel." *Anales galdosianos* 20 (1985): 77-87.

Shoemaker, William H. *The Novelistic Art of Galdós.* 3 vols. Valencia: Albatros, 1980.

Showalter, Elaine. "Feminist Criticism in the Wilderness." *Writing and Sexual Difference.* Ed. Elizabeth Abel. Chicago: U of Chicago P, 1982. 9-35.

Silverman, Kaja. *The Subject of Semiotics.* New York: Oxford UP, 1983.

Simmel, Georg. "Lo masculino y lo femenino: Para una psicología de los sexos." *Revista de Occidente* 5 (1923): 218-36 / 6 (1923): 336-63.

──────. "Cultura femenina." *Revista de Occidente* 21 (1925): 273-301/23 (1925): 170-99.

Smeed, J.W. *The Theophrastan 'Character': The History of a Literary Genre.* Oxford: Oxford UP, 1985.

Sobejano, Gonzalo. *Novela española de nuestro tiempo (en busca del pueblo perdido).* 2a ed. Madrid: Prensa Española, 1975.

Sobejano-Morán, Antonio. " 'Dramatis personae' y manipulación narrativa en *Cinco horas con Mario* y *La Cólera de Aquiles.*" *Crítica hispánica* 16.2 (1994): 387-93.

Sommerstein, Alan H. Introduction. *Lysistrata, The Acharnians, The Clouds.* By Aristophanes. Harmondsworth, Eng.: Penguin, 1973. 9-38.

Soria Olmedo, Andrés. *Vanguardismo y crítica literaria en España.* Madrid: Istmo, 1988.

Spires, Robert C. *Beyond the Metafictional Mode: Directions in the Modern Spanish Novel.* Lexington: UP of Kentucky, 1984.

──────. "Lourdes Ortiz: Mapping the Course of Postfrancoist Fiction." *Women Writers of Contemporary Spain.* Ed. Joan L. Brown. Newark: U of Delaware Press, 1991.

──────. *Transparent Simulacra: Spanish Fiction, 1902-1926.* Columbia: U of Missouri P, 1988.

Spivak, Gayatri Chakravorty. "Displacement and the Discourse of Woman." *Displacement, Derrida and After.* Ed. Mark Krupnich. Bloomington: Indiana UP, 1983. 169-95.

──────. "Finding Feminist Readings: Dante-Yeats." *Social Text* 3 (1980): 73-87.

Steinberg, Leo. *The Sexuality of Christ in Renaissance Art and in Modern Oblivion.* New York: Pantheon-October, 1983.

Steiner, Wendy. *The Colors of Rhetoric: Problems in the Relation Between Modern Literature and Painting.* Chicago: U of Chicago P, 1982.

──────, ed. *Image and Code.* Ann Arbor: U of Michagan P, 1981.

Stern, J.P. *On Realism.* London: Routledge and Kegan Paul, 1973.

Suarez, P. Manuel. "Torquemada y Gobseck." *Actas del Segundo Congreso Internacional de Estudios Galdosianos.* Las Palmas de Gran Canaria. 1978. 2 vols. Salamanca: Gráficas Cervantes, 1980. II: 369-82.

Suleiman, Susan Rubin, Ed. *The Female Body in Western Culture: Contemporary Perspectives.* Cambridge: Harvard UP, 1985.

──────. *Subversive Intent: Gender, Politics and the Avant-Garde.* Cambridge: Harvard UP, 1990.

Suvin, Darko. "The Cognitive Commodity: Fictional Discourse as Novelty and Circulation." *Mosaic: A Journal for the Interdisciplinary Study of Literature* 19.2 (1986): 85-99.

Theophrastus. *Theophrastus: The Character Sketches.* Trans. Warren D. Anderson. Kent: Kent State UP, 1970.
Todorov, Tzvetan. *The Poetics of Prose.* Trans. Richard Howard. Ithaca: Cornell UP, 1977.
Tsuchiya, Akiko. *Images of the Sign: Semiotic Consciousness in the Novels of Benito Pérez Galdós.* Columbia: U of Missouri P, 1990.
Ullman, Pierre I. "The Exordium of Torquemada en la hoguera." *Modern Language Notes* 80 (1965): 258-60.
_____. "Torquemada, ¿San Eloy o Dagoberto?" *Anales Galdosianos* 13 (1978): 49-58.
Urey, Diane F. *Galdós and the Irony of Language.* Cambridge: Cambridge UP, 1982.
Valbuena Briones, Angel. "Un diálogo de imágenes bíblicas en la narrativa de Delibes." *Studies in Honor of Donald W. Bleznick.* Eds. Delia V. Galván, Anita K. Stoll, and Philippa Brown Yin. Newark, Delaware: Juan de la Cuesta, 1995.
Vela, Fernando. "El arte al cubo." *Revista de Occidente* 46 (1927): 79-86.
Verhoeven, Arnold. "La muerte de Mario, ¿infarto o suicidio? La ambigüedad intencionada de Delibes." *Neophilologus* 70 (1987): 61-74.
Villanueva, Dario, Ed. *La novela lírica.* 2 tomos. Madrid: Taurus, 1983. Tomo 2.
_____. *Teorías del realismo literario.* Madrid: Espasa-Calpe, 1992.
Wallis, Bryan. *Art After Modernism: Rethinking Representation.* Boston: New Museum of Contemporary Art, 1984.
Warner, Marina. *Monument and Maidens: The Allegory of the Female Form.* London: Weidenfeld and Nicolson, 1985.
Watt, Ian. *The Rise of the Novel: Studies in Defoe, Richardson, and Fielding.* Berkeley: U of California P, 1957.
Wellek, René. "The Concept of Realism in Literary Scholarship." *Concepts of Criticism.* Ed. Stephen G. Nichols, Jr. New Haven: Yale UP, 1963. 222-55.
Williams, D.A., ed. *The Monster in the Mirror: Studies in Nineteenth-Century Realism.* Oxford: Oxford UP, 1978.
Winner, Anthony. *Characters in the Twilight: Hardy, Zola, and Chekhov.* Charlottesville: UP of Virginia, 1981.
Woodbridge, Hensley C. *Benito Pérez Galdós: A Selective Annotated Bibliography.* Metuchen, N.J.: Scarecrow, 1975.
_____. *Benito Pérez Galdós: An Annotated Bibliography for 1975-1980.* Unpublished. Carbondale, Ill.: Dept. of Foreign Languages and Literatures, Southern Illinois University, 1981.
Zuleta, Emila de. *Arte y vida en la obra de Benjamín Jarnés.* Madrid: Gredos, 1977.